B53 048 667

D0541377

ROTHERHAM LIBRARY & INFORMATION SERVICE

RIGi

13 MAY 2013
19 MAY 2014

29 SEP 2015
- 8 FEB 2016

MALTBY

DINNINGTON

21 JUN 2018

20 MAY 2014

26 JUL 2016

- 7 AUG 2018

13.3.19

09 JUN 2014
WATH
10|14

12 SEP 2010
17 SEP 2016

14 JUN 2019
- 7 OCT 2020

21 NOV 2014

31 AUG 2017

15 MAY 2013

- 9 NOV 2017

30 NOV 2017

This book must be returned by the date specified at the time of issue
the DATE DUE FOR RETURN.
The loan may be extended (personally, by post, telephone or onli
a further period if the book is not required by another reader, by
the above number / author / title.

Enquiries: 01709 336774

www.rotherham.gov.uk/libr

Luck and a Lancaster

Harry Yates, DFC

Airlife
England

This edition published in 2001 by
Airlife Publishing, an imprint of
The Crowood Press Ltd
Ramsbury, Marlborough
Wiltshire SN8 2HR

www.crowood.com

This impression 2013

© Harry Yates 1999

All rights reserved. No part of this publication may be reproduced or
transmitted in any form or by any means, electronic or mechanical,
including photocopy, recording, or any information storage and retrieval
system, without permission in writing from the publishers.

British Library Cataloguing-in-Publication Data
A catalogue record for this book is available from the British Library.

ISBN 978 1 84037 291 5

Printed in Great Britain by CPI Antony Rowe, Chippenham, Wiltshire

Dedication

Dedicated to the memory of Inia Maaka, great of stature and of heart, and held in great affection by all who flew and served with him. It was Mac who suggested that I write this book, and it was in no small measure as thanks to Mac for his lifelong friendship that I wrote it. But the task proved to be a long one. To my great regret, it was uncompleted at the time of his death at home in Napier, New Zealand on 16 January 1996.

Acknowledgements

For their memories, photographs, advice and encouragement, for their contributions great and small, I offer my gratitude to the following:

John Aitken, DFC
Barry and Sue Aldridge
John Barton, RAF Bomber Command Assn, New Zealand
Gwenda Birnie
Geoff Fallowfield
S/Ldr P.N. Kirby, HQ New Zealand Defence Force
June Maaka
Ron Mayhill, DFC
Bill Otway
Bob Rodgers, DFM, DFC
Randal Springer, 75 Squadron Association
Ken Wootten
and my wife, Eileen, and all the members of my family

ROTHERHAM LIBRARY SERVICE	
B53048667	
Bertrams	11/04/2013
AN	£11.99
SWI	940.5449

CONTENTS

1 If I only had Wings   9

2 An Apple for the Teacher   19

3 Stormy Weather   31

4 Graduate and Don   44

5 The Kiwis, the Callow, the Cleric &
      the Ladykiller   62

6 French for Beginners   78

7 P-Peter   100

8 *Deutschland, Deutschland* . . .   115

9 But God Disposes   134

10 Rio Rita   147

11 Cologne and Back   167

12 Again the Jinx   182

13 All over by Christmas?   202

14 N-Nan   226

    Epilogue   241

    Site Plan of Mepal Airfield   248

    Index   250

CHAPTER ONE

IF I ONLY HAD WINGS

I remember it still, almost as though it was yesterday. The day was hot, indeed gloriously so. We stood in our flying gear on the concrete of the dispersal pan, seven of us gazing up to that familiar shape, the purposeful nose rounded in Perspex by the bomb aimer's window, the front turret with its Brownings and the angular canopy beyond. No one spoke. No one needed to. We all felt the same, quiet pride.

The date was 18 August 1944, two weeks and five raids since we had reported for duty with 75 Squadron. The object of our attention, of our unbounded admiration, was a Lancaster B1 newly arrived from the Maintenance Unit. Aside from factory test pilots and the ATA girl who had brought it here, not a soul in the world had known the thrill of flying it. I was to be the first. Before any aircraft was taken onto an operational squadron it was subjected to an acceptance test. That we were now to fly. And then this beautiful machine would be allocated, amazingly, to us.

As yet only the squadron markings, the famous AA, graced each side of the fuselage, red against the black, metal skin. The identification letter had to wait until, on our return, we could pass the aircraft fit for service. A letter was not a matter of indifference to aircrew. The boys voiced several inventive if somewhat indelicate preferences as we climbed aboard. But Archie, the newest man in the crew, would have none of it. Turning to me he said, 'I don't give a damn which letter they give us, skipper . . . so long as it isn't P-Peter.'

I knew he meant it. He was on board a Lancaster P-Peter on the night of the infamous Nuremberg raid of 30 March 1944. It was Bomber Command's blackest night of the war. Ninety-six aircraft failed to return, twelve more crashed in England. Many things went awry during the operation, the worst an unforecast tailwind of atrocious strength. It carried the main force far ahead of the Pathfinders. They were left with no option but to wait and circle under a brilliant moon. For forty-seven minutes there was not a single marker to be seen, but many a night-fighter. All told, the enemy put up two hundred of them.

Archie's P-Peter was mauled in several running battles. He witnessed the suffering of friends and crewmates. The survivors got the bombs away but couldn't fly their crippled kite home against the wind. They were forced south. By the grace of God they made it to North Africa and landed wheels-up on a broad, sandy beach.

Archie struggled doggedly on to Gibraltar. By the time he set foot on English soil again three months had elapsed. Being indefatigable he sought an immediate return to operations. Being a New Zealander he requested a posting to 75. He was in the pool on the day we arrived only six strong (the seventh having quit us the night before). We were all rookies but Archie was a veteran of fifteen raids. To him we must have looked only marginally preferable to a series of different or scratch crews. To us he was a man of proven experience and resolve, a priceless asset.

Archie rarely mentioned the Nuremberg raid, but then air-crew tended to look forward, not back. It left its mark, though. No coincidental link went unnoticed. Some filled him with foreboding and real fear. He sincerely believed his presence on board another P-Peter would open the path to hell. He had walked it once and survived. Only a fool would willingly go that way a second time, and Archie was no fool.

As usual I flew the air test at under 10,000 ft so the boys could work without oxygen. We completed our checks and pronounced the aircraft battle-worthy. Her handling seemed markedly more responsive and accurate than the ageing kites I usually flew. I couldn't resist a corkscrew (standard drill for evading an enemy fighter), then another, then one more. Our new charge, though nameless, did not disappoint.

As calm returned to us, a vivid and totally unexpected sense of home came upon me together with a great need to see my family one more time. I suppose this was natural enough. The Battle Order for the night would probably include us, and who knew what that would portend? And if the answer was nothing this time, we would still have all of two dozen ops of our tour to go.

But there was one other reason why home, that singular place of the heart, should spring to mind. At the end of my last leave I had made a promise to my father: when an opportunity presented itself I would return, but above the rooftops on a flying visit. Now I had a chance to make good on that promise.

I asked Bill for a course to Stony Stratford, my home town. We eased down to 200 ft. A mile north of Wolverton station we flew over the LMS railway line and the fields I had walked so often as a kid. The Ouse sparkled briefly below. We all but clipped the tall trees in whose shadows lay shoals of silvery roach and bream, the catching of which once occupied my every childish thought. Ahead stood a row of little houses, the sixth from the top my parents'. I pulled the Lancaster around in a wide circle and ran in over the rooftops, scattering cows in the surrounding fields.

Our arrival interrupted lunch. As we came around again my father appeared in the garden, extravagantly thrashing the air with a white cloth. At a circumspect distance my mother and sister, Joan, waved and gesticulated with equal vigour. I made a third low-level pass to return their waves. And then it was done. I climbed away to 2,000 ft for two steep turns and a farewell waggle of the wings.

So we took our leave for Mepal, my second home now and home for all of us in 75. We entered the circuit and received permission to land from Control. With the undercarriage down and locked I turned across wind, then again to straighten up on the runway ahead. And with flaps down and Tubby calling out the airspeed, we sailed over the airfield boundary and touched down.

As we clambered down the aircraft steps at dispersal a bowser pulled-up.

'How many gallons?' I asked the driver.

'Two thousand', he replied.

That meant no soft trip to occupied France, Holland or Belgium but, almost certainly, a penetration deep into the Third Reich. We made straight for B Flight office. Our names were indeed on the Battle Order, with twenty-four other crews. Briefing was not until 1800 hrs. There was time for an unhurried lunch and, for the boys, an hour or two relaxing in the sunshine.

For me relaxation was not on the agenda. I was still fired up from the air test and the sight of my family in the garden of our home. My mind was racing. It seemed an improbable slice of luck for a crew like us, virtual rookies, to be given a permanent aircraft. Usually that honour was reserved for the experienced crews, the gen men, on the station. It was pool kites for the rest of us.

I just had to have another look at my Lancaster, and grabbed my bicycle. As I pedalled towards her I saw a figure in overalls stroking red paint onto the starboard side. He was executing a letter P. I was utterly aghast. As it was, the dangers and demands of our night's work would be daunting enough. But to take Archie to Germany in a Lancaster P-Peter was the final straw. I determined there and then to keep the news from him for as long as possible. I would tell the others to get him on board the aircraft even if they had to pick him up by the scruff of the neck and throw him in.

I cycled away wondering if Fate would deal us a double blow tonight and send us to Nuremberg. I glanced at my watch. The time was still only three o'clock. We would have to sweat it out for a few hours yet before we were told.

I was seventeen years old at the outbreak of war and worked as a junior clerk in the offices of a printing company. They paid me the handsome sum of thirty-two shillings and sixpence per week. After paying my dear old mother for food and board I was left with seven shillings for clothing, cigarettes and a weekly visit to the picture palace with my best girl. Destitution usually arrived by Wednesday of each week.

My education had been as basic as it could be. But in the thirties a basic education was a good education. I'd had a very happy childhood and left school three months after my fourteenth birthday with strictly limited ambitions. My birthplace was my father's and my grandfather's. No one thought of leaving for wider horizons. Stony was a quiet town of three thousand souls. I felt that I knew every one of them and they all knew me.

Like many lads my passion was soccer. I played as a kick-and-run right winger for Wolverton Town. Once, an Everton talent spotter came to watch us. It might have been the doorway to my dreams but nothing came of it. Still, I had the consolation of a few medals and a miniature silver cup for my dressing table. And, in any case, the war soon came to overshadow all things.

On the evening of 14 May 1940, as the BEF's fate unfolded in Northern France, Anthony Eden made a broadcast in which he announced the formation of the Local Defence Volunteer Force (later called the Home Guard). Next morning I cycled to the Police Station in the town square and signed-up with my fellow patriots.

Now invasion was on everybody's lips. Signposts were ripped out and place names obliterated. In the meadows by the river and in all the big fields stout posts were driven into the ground to snare enemy planes and gliders. If not these unwelcome guests then hordes of fearsomely armed parachutists were expected, or Fifth Columnists bent on sabotage. In preparation and perfect innocence we drilled with broom handles or mounted patrols and lookouts armed with a pair of binoculars. Our only recourse, should a silhouette cross the moon or someone mutter '*Gott in Himmel*' in the darkness, was to run like hell to HQ. Stopping a bullet for King and country was firmly against orders.

The highpoint – probably the only point – of our patrols was the bacon and egg breakfast served at four a.m. in the town garage. If everything else had an air of unreality about it, this at least hit the stomach with a satisfyingly real thump.

But change was afoot. We were told that a consignment of Canadian Ross rifles was being sent. Two weeks later it arrived though the accompanying ammunition did not fit.

'Don't worry, chaps. Jerry will never know', explained Charlie Green, the pork butcher who had appointed himself our Company Commander.

Luckily, his theory was never put to the test. When the correct ammunition finally arrived a major dilemma confronted our leader. We were thirty in number but there were only six rifles. After much deliberation we were summoned to the public bar at the Crown to hear the wisdom of Solomon. Standing on the bar Charlie announced a rifle shooting contest in the field behind the pub on the following Saturday afternoon. The best six shots would each be given a rifle to keep safely and in good working order, and to carry whenever on duty.

Saturday arrived and we all assembled to be given six rounds each. To my delight, when the firing ceased and the points were totted up, I was placed second. Charlie handed me my hardware but no ammo. This would be kept strictly under lock and key for issue only in dire emergency. As he so rightly said, 'If we gave you the bullets you'd only waste them on rabbits.'

I could hardly get home quick enough to show off my prize. My Dad, in his duties as an air raid warden, had been put in charge of a mere stirrup pump which he kept in the shed at the bottom of the garden. But what was that compared to a Ross . . . and one of only six in the town? The house was empty. I stood the rifle in the hall and rehearsed my words. But the moment the front door opened and my mother walked in, triumph turned to dismay.

'What's *that* thing doing here?' she demanded.

'I won it in the contest, Mum. Now I can keep it and . . .'

'Oh no, you don't,' she cried, 'I won't have a gun in *my* house. I mean it. You get on that bike of yours and take it back to Charlie Green now.'

She was incensed that an adult had blithely handed her boy a gun.

I could see it was useless to argue. Utterly crestfallen, I did as I was told and explained my situation sheepishly to Charlie. But for a butcher he was a compassionate chap, and after that I was always given charge of the patrol binoculars.

Despite the privations of rationing and blackout, my remembrance of this time is of days of idyllic simplicity and peacefulness. The glorious summer of 1940 is vivid in my memory. With my father's help I built a hen house. My grandfather presented me with a strutting cockerel whose life with fifteen hens must have been idyllic, too. Corn was scarce so I fed them potato mash. Most days yielded a dozen eggs to supplement our rations and earn me some sorely needed pocket money. The family ate well, my father's allotment providing fine vegetables both for us and for our relatives in the town. Catching game fell to me and my faithful collie, Bob. Together we walked the fields to check my rabbit snares or went fishing for perch with redworms or a live minnow. If lucky I brought home two or three fat perch or even a small pike which mother used to soak overnight in salted water, 'to take out the muddy taste', she always said. And if the fish weren't biting I gave it up and swam with my dog in the cool, reedy river.

Evenings found some of the men not yet called to arms taking guard with a cricket bat on the 'rec'. As the shadows grew long and the skies red so we retired to the companionship of the pub. A pint cost threepence and sometimes a good few were sunk.

The well-worn cherry and batting pads and the cold, frothy ale had a certain, timeless appeal. But I was never a great cricketer, much less a carouser. That summer, the first call on my affections belonged to a dark-eyed girl named, as I well recall, Bess. Nothing on earth was sweeter to me than to idle with her across the fields to Cosgrove or haunted Passenham, hand in hand in the balm of evening. But not even this token of life's ineffable beauty could divert a young man's attention from the drama of war and, in particular, the drama enacted daily over southern England.

The Battle of Britain must have been the most glamorous recruitment campaign ever. Thousands of young men from all walks of life were inspired by the daily exploits of Fighter Command. A popular show song of the time said it all: *If I Only Had Wings.* Every pilot flying a Hurricane or a Spitfire was fêted. Some became household names, even idols. How could anyone but be stirred by the exploits of Ginger Lacey or the tin-legged Douglas Bader, Stanford Tuck with his swashbuckling moustache or Sailor Malan with his heroic demeanour and film-star looks?

For me there was also an infinitely more humble and personal example to follow. This was my oldest and closest pal, Cyril Downing, with whom I had shared a classroom in infants' school and played football as a youth. He was a few months senior to me and at the beginning of 1940 he volunteered. In what seemed like no time at all he was posted to 42 Squadron of Coastal Command stationed at Lossiemouth. He began flying operationally as an air gunner on Beaufort twin-engine torpedo bombers.

On leave Cyril would visit our house and recount hair-raising scraps with the German naval squadrons docked at Kiel, Bremerhaven and Wilhelmshaven. How I envied him. The last time I saw Cyril, then a Flight Sergeant proudly wearing his air gunner's wings, was in October, 1940. I told him that I, too, had volunteered for flying duties. A few days later his aircraft went missing in an attack on a cruiser off Cuxhaven. Cyril had left a deep and abiding impression on me. It was as if the cold waves had closed over my own brother that day.

Even so, my desire to fly was unchecked. I awaited the RAF's reply with mounting trepidation and worried in case my limited schooling would count against me. Could it be that, in reality, becoming one of these pilot types required a university education or even an old school tie? Was it the preserve of sons of the well-to-do? But this, as I was to discover, was far from true. Terrible thing though it was, the war brought opportunity. The great British class system counted for surprisingly little. I saw nothing of it in all my RAF days.

So it was that one morning the longed-for official envelope rattled through our letterbox. I was requested to report to RAF Cardington for an interview and assessment.

Cyril had, of course, told me all about his day there. It began with a stringent medical examination. In one curious exercise he had to blow a mercury bubble up inside a tube and sustain it for sixty seconds. This was probably some check on the physical response to oxygen deprivation. But, naturally, Cyril knew nothing of that and saw only a large trapdoor to one of the less glamorous services.

With the advantage of Cyril's hindsight I decided on a crash training programme. I practised holding my breath until my head was splitting. I practised in the street, on the bus, even one Sunday in the choir when I punctuated the Lord's Prayer with an almighty exhalation. The Rev'd Steer's beady eye searched for a sign in each angelic countenance. But my hour of judgement was postponed, at least until the RAF medical orderly asked me to blow. The mercury bubble shot up for ninety triumphant seconds. I thought I should be given command of a squadron.

Oral and written tests were the next obstacles to surmount. Finally in late afternoon, I faced a formidable selection panel of five very senior RAF officers of which the lowest rank was Group Captain. All wore the coveted pilot's wings above rows of ribbons. One by one they plied me with questions but, no doubt well aware of an eighteen-year-old's extreme nervousness, always with a kindly, approachable manner. I was elated on leaving Cardington and felt sure that, simple country lad or no, I would be given my chance.

Back on Home Guard duty in Stony I awaited my fate. Three months had passed since the Battle of Britain had been won. The *Luftwaffe* retreated from flights over southern England by day and began to bomb our cities by night, inaugurating the Blitz on London on 7 September. The air war had entered a new phase.

The fear of invasion hung on. More rifles and uniforms were bestowed upon the Home Guard – and even ammunition. Wild rabbit appeared on Stony dinner tables and, mysteriously, at the back of Charlie's shop. Still my mother remained adamant. I was not allowed to bring a rifle into the house. In truth, the idea that Hitler might launch his stormtroopers against North Bucks was wearing a bit thin. I passed my hours of lookout duty perched on the town reservoir, binoculars scanning not the starry heavens but the hedgerows in search of courting couples.

Again one morning an official envelope dropped on to the doormat. I tore it open and read, '. . . pleased to inform you that you have been selected for training as a pilot/air gunner. You will receive call-up papers shortly.'

I let out a whoop of pure joy and danced into my parents' arms, waving the letter above my head. There was still the little matter of avoiding an air gunner's career, of course. For that I had to prove my suitability as a pilot. I vowed that I would, or break my neck in the process.

On 5 May 1941 I embraced my parents and left the family home to report to RAF Stratford-on-Avon. There, two weeks of unremitting square bashing was meted out to budding aircrew as an introduction to military life. Footsore, I finished my stint and transferred to No.10 Initial Training Wing, Scarborough, for a make-or-break course. Now the serious work began. Early morning PT on the seafront reduced us all to jelly. But this was light relief compared to the intensity of ground studies.

The syllabus initiated us into the mysteries of airmanship; theory of flight; armaments; aero-engines; navigation; astronomy, meteorology; instruments; map reading; photography; RAF law and aircraft recognition – all in just six weeks. This demanded a Herculean effort, even from the more academic among us. Looking again at my notebooks after all these years I am astonished at the technical content and variety of facts which we absorbed. To do so we studied all day and late into the evening. There was barely a moment for relaxation, and Scarborough's publicans certainly weren't on first name terms with many of us.

For all that, much of the syllabus was of little practical benefit. Parts of it had no connection to flying whatever. For example, in the dusty corners of RAF law we studied the abstruse restrictions placed upon civilians trading with airmen. Any such trade was at the civvies' risk. No airman could be arrested or compelled to appear before the courts for any debt below £30.

Some of the boys thought it was safe to ignore such pedantry. No examiner, they argued, could seriously expect to determine our suitability as pilots with questions about trade or debt. Others suspected that the more eccentric the subject, the more inevitable was its appearance on the exam paper. Bereft of such subtle reasoning I just learned all I could, and fortunately so because the second opinion proved the more accurate.

Having scraped together a bare minimum of exam passes I was entitled to display the white flash of a Leading Aircraftsman on my forage cap. The pay increased modestly, too. But to me these were trifles. All along I had been driven by a single and once seemingly impossible ambition. But now I knew. I would sit at the controls of an aircraft in a matter of only days.

At the beginning of July I reported to the de Havilland School of Flying at Hatfield, officially titled No.1 Elementary Flying Training School. In those days the airfield was simply a large, green expanse. There were no runways. On the perimeter were the brick-built administration quarters. The office of the Chief Flying Instructor, Squadron Leader Pedley, was located in the centre to afford him an uninterrupted view across the field. Each new intake was mustered before this somewhat formidable man and treated to a pithy address, much mimicked afterwards by the barrack's wags but never disregarded.

'Gentlemen,' he bristled, 'I hope you appreciate how privileged you are to be here. We are going to give you the opportunity to bend one of His Majesty's aeroplanes.' And off he went, explaining

17

in unmistakable terms how very unfortunate such an outcome would be.

> 'No doubt you think accidents are just damned dangerous. But to me they are the result of sloppy work. They are costly. They are disruptive. They are far too frequent. For reasons beyond my control I can't make 'em a hanging offence. But I can impose the maximum sentence within my power. That means the end of the course for the guilty party, and the end of his career as a pilot. Will you all reflect on that?'

We could hardly do otherwise.

Two mornings later, with that welcome still ringing in my ears, I awoke to my red letter day. A small party of rookies, myself included, was driven around the perimeter to a flight tent surrounded by half-a-dozen Tiger Moths. I was introduced to my instructor, Pilot Officer Eastwood. My first impression was of a clean-cut slight figure (for some reason all the instructors were flyweights). He was reserved, indeed rather formal and not at all the buccaneering spirit that the press accounts had led me to expect of these flying types. But he had an alert eye that was already sizing me up and a quiet authority that engendered my youthful respect.

After a lengthy and nervous wait I was called out to the aircraft. I climbed into the rear seat of Tiger Moth N6848 and stared at the sparse interior. The engine fired, roughly at first, then settled into a rhythmic crackle. Because of its noise P/O Eastwood had to communicate by talking into a length of rubber hose and by hand signals. I watched dumbly as he began by demonstrating the effect of the controls. Then he taxied downwind, turned crosswind and stopped, completing the standard drill prior to take off.

That done and without further ceremony, he turned into the wind. The Aldis light flashed green and he opened the throttle. The wash from the propeller hit my face. The grass under and around us was flattened to the soil. Slowly, we gathered speed. Contact with the uneven turf modulated from bumpy to jarring and then, before I even realised it, we were free and airborne.

I remember the novelty of looking down as we cleared the airfield boundary, then across to the widening horizon and up again into a lightly clouded sky. This is it, I told myself. This is what all the dreams and all the waiting had been for. The ground receded below and with it, I suppose, the small world of my boyhood. This was the start of a new and exhilarating life, albeit tempered by the wartime service values of duty, discipline and, if necessary, self-sacrifice.

CHAPTER TWO

AN APPLE FOR THE TEACHER

I had emerged from all the RAF's sober interviews, lectures and examinations still wedded to a romantic notion of flying. Spitfires roaring away in defence of the realm, tearing into a marauding foe above the English Channel – that was the thing.

Yet far from an anti-climax, actual flying was a revelation. It may have been prosaic stuff in a pedestrian little biplane. But the rasping note of the engine, the blast of air and that exultant sense of space and freedom produced a reality quite beyond the power of my imagination to foretell.

At the same time, whereas the heroism and glamour of being a fighter pilot had lured me to the cockpit, the hunger to fly for its own sake quickly took over. I gained a more level-headed appreciation of my place in the order of things. Just to learn what was required of me day by day at Hatfield would be heroism enough for now.

In that first thirty-five minutes of instruction P/O Eastwood demonstrated the most basic precepts: ground procedure, straight and level flying, climbing, gliding and some gentle turns. Thereafter we generally flew twice each day. I learned to take off into wind, fly a circuit and, in theory at least, make a glide approach landing.

Like most trainees I found height deceptive to judge. Usually I came over the boundary far too high and correcting madly. But that only served to push down the nose and raise airspeed. When the approach was straightened out my airborne see-saw just refused to touch down. It floated on and on until, driven by sheer desperation, my instructor seized his controls and lifted us clear. Around we went again, circuit after circuit, with the same result until, gradually, I found Mother Earth with a little more assurance.

Of the sixty trainees on my course one or two experienced no such difficulty. They were the natural flyers who by some God-given gift could conjure whatever they pleased out of a Tiger Moth. Of the four categories under which our flying ability was assessed these chaps were Exceptional. They had 'fighter pilot' written all over them.

Not so the many more stragglers on the course who bore the emotional burden of a Below Average assessment. As their circuits multiplied and flying hours mounted, so did the tension.

At Hatfield time and tension were inextricable. From the moment we were first called to the aircraft a clock started ticking. It was the clock that ticked away our entitlement to flying instruction. It ran with each visit to the cockpit but for little more than ten hours in all. If a trainee had not soloed by then he was on the way to gunnery or bombing school.

Apart from The Comet, the airfield local, the only escape from this pressure, the only relief from learning how to land, was learning how to spin. For safety reasons this manoeuvre was a prerequisite for solo flying. The drill was to climb to 3,000 ft and, with the engine idling, pull the joystick hard into the stomach. The nose came up steeply until the aircraft stood on its tail. This was the brief, still moment when, it was said, the attentive trainee might hear the wind whistling *Nearer My God To Thee* through the wing struts. With or without the Aeolian accompaniment it was only a second or two until a wing dropped. Now he had to act fast, applying hard rudder before a stall and sending the aircraft spinning earthwards.

The real purpose of the exercise followed. To counteract the spin, opposite rudder was applied whilst easing the stick forward. This stabilised the aircraft in a simple dive. Next controls were centralised, then gentle back pressure applied. This eased the aircraft into a graceful, upward curve. If done correctly all the height was recovered and at 3,000 ft the sequence could be repeated.

Up to this point I had taken P/O Eastwood to be a scrupulously correct, even starchy individual. But to his spinning instruction he added some riotously chuck-about aerobatics. I marvelled at them and at my instructor. He was flying for his own enjoyment, though, and strictly off the teaching manual. No doubt he also needed an escape, not from pressure, perhaps, but from the numbing boredom of endless circuits and bumps.

On the morning of 14 July P/O Eastwood handed me over to his fellow instructor, F/Lt Connor. I completed two take offs and landings. Whilst I was taxying downwind for a third, F/Lt Connor asked me to stop. To my complete surprise he jumped down to the ground.

'It's all yours,' he shouted, 'Make a circuit and landing. If the approach doesn't pan out or someone gets in the way, on with the juice and go around again. Do that as often as you want but finish with a daisy cutter. Off you go. Good luck.'

He sauntered towards the centre of the field, leaving me to stare at his back. Turning to the seat where his back had been, I never felt more nervous or alone. I kept my mind off it by bursting into song as soon as I was airborne – as I recall, a wholehearted rendition of *Amour, Amour* and my one and only public appearance as a tenor.

All too soon the boundary and the moment of reckoning came around. I took a deep breath and, to my huge relief, popped a tolerably smooth landing. It was no daisy cutter but F/Lt Connor nodded his approval just the same.

Up to then I had logged eight hours and fifteen minutes of instruction. Now the ten-hour clock was behind me. The pressure and the rivalry could be left to others. It was only necessary to keep improving and to complete the course without mishap.

Over the ensuing days the numbers flying solo burgeoned. Activity on the airfield became concentrated on perfecting take offs and landings and one or two more advanced manoeuvres. As training intensified so the accident rate rose. Under instruction there were always mature and skilled hands to lift the aircraft to safety. But instructors were in the air less and less, and flying solo was an unforgiving business. The toll in broken bones was low, but not so in broken Tigers.

One morning P/O Eastwood asked me to fly an hour's solo. All the instructors had been summoned to a meeting at the Chief Flying Instructor's office. Not for the first time the subject was the unacceptable accident rate. Squadron Leader Pedley opened the discussion in his inimitable style while, outside, I turned my aircraft into the wind and began building up to take-off speed.

As the airspeed indicator registered sixty-five mph something went profoundly wrong. The nose did not ease upward into the air. Instead, my Tiger underwent the metamorphosis into a high-speed plough. Huge clods of turf flew over my head, followed by chunks of wooden airscrew. There was a hideous crescendo and everything shuddered to a halt. The whole airfield was momentarily stilled. In this strange calm I tried to come to terms with my situation. The nose of the aircraft was buried in the soil. The wing assembly had all but disintegrated. The tail was pointing accusingly skyward. I was half out of the cockpit, having been restrained by my straps, thank God. My pride was badly bruised, but nothing else.

Everything burst upon me at once. People ran from out of

nowhere, screaming at me to get the hell out of it. I took a moment to realise why and another to find that I couldn't release my buckle. The fire tender bounced across the field, its bells echoed by the ambulance not far behind. The whole world was awash with chaos and cacophony, and all because of a hapless, one-time printer's clerk and failed pilot. And misery upon misery, the whole show was taking place slap-bang in front of the Chief Flying Instructor's office window.

'Well, your timing was immaculate', was P/O Eastwood's verdict, delivered with a levity I found inexplicable. But, in fact, my spot of gardening was a source of secret amusement to all the instructors. I had committed the unpardonable crime of cutting short S/Ldr Pedley in full cry. The poor man had stormed over to his window, outraged at my temerity, and bellowed, 'Look! Do you see what I bloody well mean?'

That afternoon an escort marched me solemnly to S/Ldr Pedley's office. I was the condemned man on his final procession to the Lord High Executioner. Everything said I had flown for the last time. As I entered the room he stood facing the window, a small and upright figure with his hands behind his back. He spun around and I gave him my most martial salute.

'Were you injured?' he asked first and in an emollient, even kindly voice which surprised me. When I replied, 'No, sir', he smiled, of all things. I could almost feel him asking himself, 'What the hell am I going to do with this chap?' But what he said was, 'You understand the regrettable position in which you place me?'

Then he spoke with no hint of regret, setting forth this position with the most brutal clarity. His tone had hardened. Any hope of clemency lingering in my breast was extinguished. S/Ldr Pedley became the personification of swift and terrible justice. Of course, he had been through this all before. He must have felt immense frustration at his pupils' unchanging fecklessness. We feared him as a man given to anger or, at least, as one adroit in giving the impression of it. Now I saw that it was the former, unfortunately. His composure began to crack. He became visibly exercised and, finally, he let fly.

'Have you the slightest idea what your stupidity will cost the RAF?', he demanded. 'Do you think Tiger Moths grow on bloody trees?' He paced up and down, firing unanswerable questions at me. 'How can we do our work here with idiots like you reducing every aircraft to matchwood? What kind of airman doesn't know the damned difference between up and down?' and so on.

I desperately wanted to defend myself with some questions of my own. Had anyone thought to examine the wreckage, especially the controls and the undercarriage? Had the last engineer to work on the aircraft been questioned? But in my heart I knew that being of such lowly station all blame would attach to me. There was nothing to be done but withstand the barrage in silence and to attention, and await the *coup de grâce*.

I waited, but it did not come.

Striving manfully for some restraint, S/Ldr Pedley said, 'I've spoken to your instructor who thinks you might make a pilot. That's saved you this time. But one more mistake and, by God, I'll reduce you to the lowest form of life in the RAF.'

His fist hit the desk and I was dismissed. Shell-shocked by this development I sought out P/O Eastwood to express my profound gratitude. 'Any accident that you walk away from is a bloody good bit of instruction', he said and slapped me on the back.

I had not escaped official censure, however. S/Ldr Pedley autographed my logbook which reads, 'Headquarters No. 50 Group (T) endorsement: Error of judgement taking off. I.I. Pedley, S/Ldr. July 22nd, 1941.' That was the only endorsement of my flying career. One was more than enough, particularly when I could not quite bring myself to accept that justice was done.

Young men in uniform cannot be permitted the luxury of youthful rebellion. But young they still are and will be impulsive, if that is their way, or headstrong and sometimes foolhardy. At the age of nineteen I was probably all three. In any event only forty-eight hours after my reprieve by S/Ldr Pedley I hatched a strictly illicit flightplan that might have finished me off.

On 24 July I flew my first cross-country solo, Hatfield–Halton–Henlow–Hatfield. The flying time was sixty-five minutes and it immediately set me thinking. My home at Stony Stratford was only thirty-four miles north-west of the airfield. I needed no map to find it, just good visibility. My parents would be cockahoop at their son's aeroplane over the roof. Half of the town would know about it by evening. My father would be stood his ale at The Case Is Altered, his local in Wolverton Road, for a week at least.

The more I thought it over, the more irresistible and foolproof the idea seemed. On the following Saturday the sun shone from a sky of china blue. Visibility was almost unlimited. I only needed to be allocated an hour's solo, and I was.

Once airborne I quickly sighted the expanse of glasshouses which lay between the airfield and St Albans. The A5, the old Roman

Watling Street, pointed a straight track north. I took up station wide on the port side, passing Dunstable and Fenny Stratford. Ahead, unmissable on the northern boundary of dear old Stony, rose the grassy embankment of the reservoir where I had spent so many hours on Home Guard duty.

To starboard was our familiar cul-de-sac of little, semi-detached houses, bordered on three sides by pasture. At all of 2,000 ft I banked the Tiger as steeply as I dare, lining up the port wing on the chimney pots of our house. On the second pass and the third no one appeared below. But by the fourth the back garden, which was recognisable, contained two tiny, agitated figures, which were not. What wouldn't I have given then to loop the loop or, better still, to execute a slow roll? But my flying skills were embryonic. The steep turn was my limit, especially as I was employing one hand to wave wildly to the figures below or to punch the air in exultation.

It all lasted only a couple of minutes. Then I engineered a tentative wobble of the wings and made off to the south. Thirty minutes later I touched down at Hatfield, glowing with satisfaction.

P/O Eastwood greeted me with a cheery 'Good trip?' 'Great', I shot back, but not another word. Had those few moments of bravado become known to S/Ldr Pedley my career piloting anything more entertaining than a mop and bucket would have been over. But now I felt as I had as a boy, having braved the local farmer's ire to scrump Coxes from his orchard. The evidence of my trespass had been eaten. And very enjoyable it had been, too.

By six o'clock every evening the day's training activity on the airfield came to a close. The Tiger Moths were pegged-down and put to bed. Then the evening stillness was lost to the lovely roar of high-powered aero-engines. The doors of the great hangar at the far end of the airfield were pushed slowly back. Out of the shadows rolled a streamlined, twin-engined aircraft with the most beautiful proportions, reminiscent of the legendary de Havilland Comet. This was the prototype of the Mosquito and for an hour almost every evening it was flown by the chief test pilot, Geoffrey de Havilland.

For the humble trainees these were moments of wonder, chiefly at the sheer beauty and power of the thing. As it sped across the field the noise was thunderous. I swear the ground trembled beneath our feet. And to see it return over the boundary, engines spluttering on idle as only the Merlin could, was an inspiration to any pilot.

I imagine each of us also wondered if one day he and this fabulous machine, both in our way graduates of Hatfield, might be reunited in anger against the enemy. Certainly, I did. When my operational flying career finally began all of three years later this was still my most cherished ambition.

Meanwhile, by virtue of our presence we were party to the prototype's flight schedule. This sort of information was highly-restricted. To permit such free access to it by sixty awestruck but by no means dumbstruck trainees seemed hardly credible to me. Not that careless talk could have cost much. Within minutes of touching down, the object of our desire was secreted away again behind the locked and guarded hangar doors.

Back in the less inspiring surroundings of my cockpit I continued my education. P/O Eastwood introduced me next to low flying, which I loved from the first. At 100 ft over open fields the sense of speed, always blunted at altitude, was restored in full. Even the Tiger's sedate maximum of around ninety mph produced an exhilarating ride.

Of course, thrill-seeking only exacerbated some already very real dangers, and these the School addressed with rigid regulation. Under no circumstance were we allowed to low fly without an instructor, the only exercise where this applied. An area to the west was selected for its lack of population and topographical surprises, and low flying was permitted nowhere else. Not much more than a few fields across, access to it was granted to only one aircraft at a time. Always and in everything, the watchword was caution.

The cautionary factor also conditioned my introduction to the next staging post of powered flight: aerobatics. These comprised looping the loop, rolling off the top of the loop, and the slow roll that was so beloved of victorious fighter pilots on their return to base.

'Tomorrow we loop the loop', my instructor promised. But at ten o'clock the next morning he was missing from the flight tent. In his place, in person, was the Chief Flying Instructor. No explanation was offered, although one suggested itself as soon as we reached 3,000 ft.

Squadron Leader Pedley unleashed some truly bewildering combinations of loops, spins and rolls. His skill was of a different order to P/O Eastwood's. Each element was so cleanly and decisively executed that even at the extremes of the action, so to speak, he was unhurried. The rapidity and precision of movement seemed impossibly at odds with what I knew of a Tiger's handling. But more to the point, whereas P/O Eastwood's style had a free-wheeling, knockabout quality to it and invited the passenger to be entertained, S/Ldr Pedley's had no such object. This was a demonstration of disciplined technique and sang-froid, the very opposite of flying for the hell of it. Fly with caution, it said, until you can fly like this. It also said quite clearly, 'You're being watched, my lad'.

The Chief Flying Instructor did not usually initiate trainees into aerobatics. It wasn't done for fun. Maybe the pile-up had marked me out for this treatment. Maybe I had expressed too much enthusiasm for low flying, or flying in general? Whichever it was, from now on I would volunteer as little as possible about anything, and contemplate no more runs over the rooftops of Stony Stratford. The apple scrumper in me would have to go.

No one could deny that S/Ldr Pedley's caution had its purpose. Over-confidence had brought about the premature death of many more experienced flyers than me. One such was Cobber Kane, the great New Zealand fighter pilot. His exploits and victories in France before the *Wehrmacht* overran the country caught the imagination of the entire British public. His deeds were reported by the press almost daily. He was the leading fighter pilot in the RAF, credited with over twenty enemy aircraft, a truly phenomenal feat at that early stage of the war. And yet he could not resist the temptation to beat up the airfield, and failed to pull out of a hedge-high manoeuvre at great speed. He had been due to fly back to England that very afternoon on well-earned leave. But he had to put on a final show, and tragically final it proved.

One flying hour later I began my aerobatics instruction under P/O Eastwood. We flew north over the railway line which he liked to utilise for centring the loop. From 3,000 ft he dived straight for the tracks at full throttle. At maximum velocity he pulled back the stick and we soared up into the vertical. In the upside-down position at the top of the loop, with the ground now above us, I could see the tracks still dead centre. He closed the throttle, plummeting the aircraft earthward again. At the bottom he pulled out to resume normal flight and there below, running perfectly parallel to us, were the tracks again.

My attempts to emulate this miracle were fair enough. Two mornings later P/O Eastwood awarded me an hour's solo practice. I flew ten miles north over the same tracks, took aim and dived. Straight and level after the loop I was surprised to find my silent, steel tutors bang in line. The next loop had the same, satisfying result. So did the next. Forty minutes later I was lost in a revelry of looping enemy fighters disintegrating under my fire or, in a vain bid to shake me off, smashing onto the tracks below. When, at last, I couldn't ignore the time any longer I turned reluctantly south into the midday sunlight.

Ten minutes later the airfield had not come into view. I recognised nothing. A square search examining every landmark for familiarity yielded no clue. Over and again I asked myself what was going on. I had only flown out over the line and flown back again. It was illogical, impossible, but I was lost.

I could already hear myself bewailing life's injustice to an implacable S/Ldr Pedley. But even this thought presupposed a more or less happy landing. In reality, however, the needle of my fuel gauge was flirting with the red zone. I had no air-to-ground radio, no map and no parachute. I was severed from all that was familiar and known, above a landscape I could not explain. I was, frankly, beginning to panic. In the event the inescapable and increasingly pressing need to force-land took over my thoughts and drove me on. I abandoned the landmarks and fell to studying the rolling patchwork of fields.

Before going solo every Hatfield trainee was familiarised with 'agricultural work'. Gliding over the hedge at 20 ft and throttling back for a positive set down took about sixty yards. Stopping the aircraft used another sixty or seventy. But the fields where we practised were specifically chosen because they were flat, firm, grassy and blessed with a clear approach. In real life, of course, things just ain't like that.

The larger fields bristled with anti-glider posts. Of the rest, many were heavy with arable crops. I didn't fancy threshing my way through waist-high wheat, and then a ploughed surface might not have allowed the wheels to run. Grassland it had to be. I held a steady course, examining every green field possible. I let pass those with grazing livestock. A friesian could do a lot of damage to a little wooden kite. Of the remaining fields, most would probably do *in extremis*. But none was the proverbial piece of cake that I really needed. There were rolling hills, trees, banks and ditches, and tight corners where only a broad rectangle would do. It was easier to vacillate than to decide. Even so, I reckoned there was only ten minutes flying time left. I couldn't risk the tank running dry. If something uncomplicated didn't come along PDQ, I'd take the first available patch of green and damn the consequences.

A minute or so later I sighted a hazy, geometrical scar on the land. Barely able to contain my anticipation I flew straight for it. I made out a concrete runway, in fact a pair of them foreshortened by my angle of approach. At that moment it was the most beautiful sight in the world to me.

I could have wept with relief as I entered the airfield circuit at

1,000 ft. But my sense of deliverance was premature. Out of nowhere on the downwind leg a twin-engined Havoc, the night-fighter known as The Black Widow, slewed past from starboard with shocking violence and cut in dead ahead of me. Its slipstream snatched up my Tiger and left me powerless in the throes of a slow-motion flip. For several seconds I hung on grimly with no idea what to do. Then the turbulence subsided and order prevailed over chaos.

A training aircraft was not to be expected in this airspace, it was true. But the pilot must have seen me from some distance. Was it carelessness or some kind of joke? Either way, it was an unduly hostile welcome for a harmless biplane and a trainee whose nerves were already frayed bare.

On the crosswind leg I saw my tormentor turning off the runway. Justice demanded that I buzzed him back. But my fuel might not have stretched to another circuit. And, besides, trainees had to know their place. Such a gesture would have had disciplinary consequences, destroying my flying career for ever – assuming that I still had a flying career.

Wary of more jokers behind I hurried the final approach. There followed the inevitable long float but finally the wheels hit the runway. I was down and running on smooth concrete. No stout post nor spreading oak had claimed me, no hedge full of hawthorn, nettles and briar. Best of all, there need be no thorny telephone call to S/Ldr Pedley.

The perimeter seemed interminable. But it gave me time to recover my composure. I had to find out where I was and how to get back to Hatfield. And I had to beg petrol for the flight. This was deeply humiliating but there was no way out of it. I pulled up in front of the control tower. Not even here was the airfield name displayed. I mounted the steps with my stomach in my boots. A push of the door, and several faces turned to scrutinise me.

'Please,' I announced in supplication. 'I'm afraid I'm lost. Can you tell me where I am?'

An officer inquired casually where I was from. To my reply he said, 'Oh, you're only twenty-five miles south. You can follow the railway line practically the whole way there.' A railway line, I thought. It would have to be a railway line.

They gave me petrol, and for the first time I set off down a concrete strip. My Tiger accelerated effortlessly and slipped into the air at half distance.

Fifteen minutes later P/O Eastwood met me at dispersal with a breezy, 'How did it go?' He didn't demand to know why I was late or where I had been. He didn't realise I was late at all. Hardly believing my luck I just said, 'Yes, great, thanks', and kept it at that. The apple scrumper in me was ecstatic.

In the five decades since, I have forgotten the name of the airfield but not the helpfulness of the personnel, with the exception of the Havoc pilot, of course. They could have blown the whistle on me with a single-paragraphed letter. But my travails above the quiet farms and villages, winding lanes and copses of Home Counties' England remained a secret.

With the aid of the wallmap at Hatfield I discovered the cause of it all. I had chosen to centre my loops downline of the only rail junction for miles. There were *two* south-bound lines below me. How frequently I switched tracks in the process of shooting down all those Messerschmitts one can only speculate. But Fate certainly sent me the wrong way on the final loop.

After this experience I was more kindly disposed to the ground syllabus, which ran throughout the course, and even to the dark and claustrophobic torture of the Link Trainer.

This formidable piece of apparatus was the ancestor of today's flight simulator. I never met a pilot then or later, under training or fully qualified, who relished his thirty minutes in the cockpit.

We were introduced to it in the fourth week, though to little purpose, I think. Its *raison d'être* was to accustom us to flying in darkness without the benefit of a clear horizon. But all real flying at Hatfield was restricted to good, daylight visibility. Night flying as such was for the future. Even so, use of the Link Trainer was intensive. Each trainee was allotted twelve sessions of thirty minutes duration, shoehorned into ten already busy days.

The apparatus was housed in a small, windowless room. To look at, it was just a box with wings. The victim, for that was what it felt like, climbed into the box and a hood was closed over his head. Darkness reigned, save for the luminous glow of the instrument panel. The controls were the same as a Tiger, and all the normal sensations of flight were there from the moment the pilot switched on.

He was linked to his instructor electronically, hence the name. Sitting at a desk outside the room the instructor had dual instrumentation recording height, airspeed, compass reading, track and altitude. An electrical device which moved like a crab over a celluloid map marked the course steered by the pilot. As often as not, this would have been a disaster course. The Link Trainer was far more difficult and sensitive to control than an aeroplane. It was a real pig to fly, added to which was the claustrophobia and, in August, the heat of the cockpit. When the lesson was finally over and the hood thrown back I, for one, always scrambled out drenched in sweat and feeling a hopeless failure.

Our elementary flying course was drawing to a close. Of the original intake more than half had fallen by the wayside. The survivors still had the most difficult task ahead of them, that of the Chief Flying Instructor's test. This involved a half-hour flight during which the trainee was asked to execute every manoeuvre in the flying manual. Thirty long minutes under the critical eye of S/Ldr Pedley was perfectly sufficient to make a complete ass of oneself. My mind kept returning to the endorsement, and S/Ldr Pedley's parting shot, '. . . one more mistake and, by God, I'll reduce you to the lowest form of life in the RAF'. It could have been a promise . . . it *sounded* like a promise. I had to deny him any grounds whatsoever for making it good.

In the air S/Ldr Pedley issued his commands down the rubber hose like a parade sergeant. We rattled off every manoeuvre. Nothing went wrong and the minutes ticked by. An adequate landing finished off a test that, whilst gruelling, was essentially uneventful – and that was what mattered.

Walking away from the aircraft, I couldn't resist asking somewhat smugly, 'How did I do, Sir?' S/Ldr Pedley was poring over his clipboard, probably and quite justifiably in search of the means to cut me down to size. But he gave it up. 'I suppose', he said grudgingly, 'you might be worth persevering with.'

And so my name was posted on the notice board for transfer to Service Flying Training School, the next step in the long march to war.

On 14 August I said farewell to the instructors I had come to admire, and to P/O Eastwood who showed me special kindness. It had been an exhilarating, dangerous, fantastic experience. Of my fifty hours and thirty-five minutes flying, nearly half (the risky half) was solo. I had survived my own mischief and misadventure, an 'error of judgement taking-off', The Black Widow, even S/Ldr Pedley.

And this was but the beginning.

CHAPTER THREE

STORMY WEATHER

It was four o'clock and not yet dawn. Restless and unable to sleep, I decided to go up on deck for some air. The night was very still. Stars shone by the thousand in the heavens above. The sea was almost flat calm. Wavelets lapped gently against the bow and this, together with the monotonous drumming of the engines below, was the only sound in the night.

I had expected to see the black horizons of the North Atlantic. Instead at no great distance ahead was the light of civilisation and peace. I leant on the ship's rail and gazed at a ball of fire. After two dreary years of blackout the sight of neutral Iceland was completely spellbinding. The humble port of Reykjavik seemed to be lit up like Broadway. The waterfront shimmered with fingers of reflected light. A normal life, quietly unabashed and indomitable, still shone out in this corner of the world.

I was in a party of trainee pilots bound for Halifax, Nova Scotia, under the Empire Air Training Scheme. Before me were eleven weeks of intensive training on, alas, twin-engines. I knew now that mine would not be a Spitfire war. After the Battle of Britain, *Luftwaffe* fighters were mostly restricted to occupied Europe. Then Operation *Barbarossa*, Hitler's invasion of Russia, demanded a massive transfer of aircraft to the East. Fighter Command reacted tentatively at first, with sweeps over the occupied countries. But life was inevitably quieter and losses reduced. Pilot recruitment was cut back accordingly.

On the other hand Bomber Command losses were escalating all the time. Ominously, the durable Wellington, the Whitley – a sort of aerial bloodhound that flew nose down –, the ill-starred Manchester, the pitiful Hampden and the worse Blenheim were all twin-engined. But, then, so was the little Beaufighter that flew with some speed and infinitely more brio in defence of our cities during the Blitz. Everything was still to play for.

We had two days to pass in Reykjavik before our troopship, the

31

SS *California*, would arrive to bear us to the west. The RAF kept us occupied ashore with a regime of early morning runs, physical jerks and team games. In reality, of course, the objective was to keep us out of the town and out of trouble. In the mornings we bathed and shaved in the hot springs. Of the rest of Iceland we saw little. But unless you were keen on cod or prawns there was little to see. I thought it was a forlorn and inhospitable place, cold, windy and not a tree in sight. Life appeared no less spartan than at home, and certainly not as advertised by the luminous glory of Reykjavik by night.

It was left to the Royal Navy to provide the high point of our short stay. A German U-boat was brought into port under escort. It had been caught cold on the surface by a Coastal Command Hudson on routine patrol. When challenged, its Captain had chosen to surrender rather than risk being depth-charged. Such a capitulation was uncharacteristic and probably against orders. Perhaps his batteries were too depleted to dive again or one of his diesels was scattered in pieces about the engine room. Perhaps his wife at home in Hamburg had made him a father, and he wanted to live. Whatever the reason, it was an ignominious way for the German naval élite to quit the fight.

I went to the dock just in case the crew were led ashore. Foreigners never visited the parochial world of my boyhood and this would have been my first sight of the enemy. That was a vain hope, of course. They were in a Royal Navy brig and heading for a life on British soil, and doubtless one no less full of physical exercise and team games than our own just now.

Their U-boat looked formidable, though. It was a scowling thing, not large, a monument to stealth in charcoal-grey steel. The ease of its capture did not reassure me. We all knew there were plenty more out there just like it.

I was among the last to board the *California*. The few officers among us were ushered to small cabins. We lesser mortals were herded deep below decks and given hammocks. It was over-crowded, unhygienic and I dreaded to contemplate what else once we hit the Atlantic swell.

South-east of Iceland the *California* joined a convoy of nearly eighty ships protected by a heavy escort of destroyers and minesweepers. The guiding principle, of course, was safety in numbers, and its implementation was frenetic. The fighting ships steamed past us full ahead one way and then the other, haranguing their charges from a distance by siren and at close quarters by megaphone. The objective was to maintain the numbered order, the form and, most of all, the speed of the convoy. The latter was never more than stately. One could readily imagine that a thousand yards astern of the rest was an ancient, rusty tub, her engines giving all and still not making ten knots and her equally ancient captain cussedly ungrateful for the Royal Navy's encouragement. But his rate of knots was ours. And the slower he steamed, the higher the risk and anxiety for the rest of us.

At this time the U-boat menace had reached its peak. They hunted in packs, their presence reinforced by several German battleships marauding the sea lanes. Losses of merchant ships, their cargoes and crews bordered on the catastrophic. The life of a merchant seaman was even more dangerous than that of aircrew. God knows, they were brave men.

I lay in my hammock on the first night out from Reykjavik. Around me was a heaving mass of humanity. My mind went back to the U-boat that had been shepherded into port and to her sister vessels that had not. They were still waiting out there with intent as cold as death, only hopeful that we or others like us might sail into their grasp.

I tried to picture the utter chaos following upon a hit from a torpedo: the sleepers flung from their hammocks by the shock of the blast, the flailing arms and legs, the violent struggle for the doorway, the screams and curses as water crashed in to engulf even those clinging to the steel rails and treads of the deck ladder . . . No, my hammock would not be slept in this night or any other on the voyage.

I took up my blanket and bedded down in a quiet but chill gangway. All over the ship others had the same idea. But as it turned out the cautious slept fitfully if at all while the rest swung sweetly to and fro in their hammocks, undisturbed through each of the four nights at sea.

The last forty minutes of our journey took us through the nets and minefields to Halifax. At anchor lay scores of merchant ships, flying all the flags of the free world. On disembarkation we were warned to take care in stepping off the gangplank. After a few days at sea the physical compensations required just to walk in a straight line became habitual. On dry land they were a liability, inviting the quayside to come up and hit you in the face. It stayed beneath my feet, anyway. But then, I never got to grips with the damned swell.

About four hundred trainee pilots sailed on the *California*. Some went on to Pensacola in the USA. The rest, myself included, journeyed by rail across Canada to one of seven RAF training airfields. The newest of these was No. 36 Service Flying Training School at Penhold, Alberta, in the heart of the Prairies. Sixty-seven of us arrived there on the morning of 27 September 1941.

The airfield was new, indeed still a building site. We were Course No. 1. To judge from the bustling construction activity we might have turned up sooner than planned. The twin concrete runways were finished, though: one for take off; one for landing. And waiting for us were about twenty brand-new Airspeed Oxfords.

The hectic pace of activity also extended to our induction. That same morning we were assembled in a hangar and warmly welcomed by the Chief Flying Instructor, Squadron Leader Dale. We were allocated to one of three flights and given a lengthy run down on the sequence of instruction. In the mess after lunch our instructors were introduced. Mine was an experienced RAF career pilot, Flight Sergeant Henn, and for the first time I shook hands with a veteran of the Battle of Britain.

On 29 September I was given my first instruction in twin-engined flight. Once we were airborne F/Sgt Henn invited me to handle the controls. I flew straight and level then tried a few gentle turns. I liked the feel of the Oxford very much. It lacked the raw simplicity and fun of an open cockpit, of course. But that type of flying belonged to another era. Here was a real aircraft of its time, a piece of complex, aeronautical engineering. Naturally, after the Tiger Moth it was heavy to handle. But the compensation was massive additional power.

'No frills about it really,' explained F/Sgt Henn, 'but you have to be careful. Push it too far and it gets temperamental.' I omitted to reply that I was still incapable of pushing an aircraft at all, never mind too far.

F/Sgt Henn was not typical of his rank. He was the scion of a wealthy, old Kentish family. In the inter-war years his father had held some prominent public post. The boy had received a first-rate education and, surely, every door was open to him. But the appeal of flight proved stronger. He joined the RAF well before the war. Now in his early thirties he still enjoyed every moment of his flying. At Penhold he could pass on his knowledge and his enthusiasm. By nature open, uncomplicated and completely free of presumption, he was well equipped for the job.

Evidently, his operational experience had been eventful. Facial tissue damage, the result of burns, gave testimony to that. It was not something a pupil could ask about, but one day the subject came up. We were talking casually about Penhold and what may lay ahead for me after the course.

'You can go anywhere from here', he said, since twin-engined aircraft were flown in all three operational RAF Commands. My lodestar had always been a single-seater fighter, and I said so. He smiled wryly. 'Well, it's not all victory rolls and toasts in the mess', he replied. And he told me how, in his Hurricane a year earlier, he had been shot-up by an enemy fighter. Fire took hold. In seconds it was a conflagration. He couldn't move fast enough to escape the flames. But escape he did, landing in a field in his home county. That was the last time he flew operationally.

Typical of the man though such honesty was, it didn't reconcile me to losing my chance in a Hurricane or Spitfire. The only anti-dote to that now was work.

After six hours of dual instruction F/Sgt Henn cleared me to fly solo. I built up the hours, revelling in the aircraft and in the great sweep of the prairies below me. We were wholly fortunate to be training in this vast and peaceful land, so far from the daily tribu-lations of home. It was a wise man who decided that young pilots would do well to learn their skills here, and no doubt equally so at the SFTS airfields in America and those in Rhodesia and South Africa.

Penhold was roughly midway between Calgary and Edmonton. The nearest town was Red Deer, about ten miles away and named after the Red Deer River which flowed lazily through it. The snow-capped Rocky Mountains rising over a hundred miles away were the only variation on the horizon. To all other points of the compass the prairies ranged without end.

This was a wonderful landscape for night-flying, and after six hours' daytime solo I was given my first taste of it. In a way it was almost cheating, and not a bit like the Link Trainer. The moon was bright and full. The Rockies were clearly discernible from ground level. F/Sgt Henn performed a night take off. No sooner were we airborne than the golden glow of Red Deer courted the eye. On landing, he asked me to take over. Four circuits and bumps later he climbed out of the aircraft and waved me off down the runway. That night I flew solo for forty-five minutes, a truly memorable ex-perience and another significant milestone on the road to my wings.

After thirty-five hours' dual and solo flight I was cleared to prac-tise cross-country flying with another trainee. My partner was a solid and hard-headed Ulsterman named John Ward, also a pupil of F/Sgt Henn. On our first exercise he took the controls, leaving me

35

the short straw of map reading. Actually, it was quite straight-forward. But I was pleased to switch seats for our next exercise.

As the days and weeks passed so the weather deteriorated. By the beginning of November the temperature was falling fast. Snow flurries were frequent. There was no more night-flying unless conditions were right. But in the daylight hours the weather was more or less ignored. We flew at every opportunity, not least because Course No. 1 had to end by the arrival of the next intake of trainees in mid-December.

One cold, grey day John was at the controls and I navigating on a four-legged, cross-country flight. Snow had been falling in varying degrees for most of the trip. This was nothing new and didn't concern us. But about thirty minutes from base on the final leg we flew into a veritable blizzard. Quite swiftly, the terrain below disappeared. Forward visibility was reduced to zero. We were enveloped in a white cloak of driven snow.

We held course and, in something of a state of shock, debated the options. Gaining height and baling out was unthinkable. Neither of us was willing to return to Penhold with our Oxford strewn across the prairies. The only alternative was a forced landing, preferably at or near the airfield.

At its height the storm tossed us about like a child's kite. John struggled doggedly at the controls, ceaselessly correcting pitch and course. We were aiming for the town of Red Deer. If we could pick up the river there we might be able to follow it to within five miles of the airfield.

We reached a point where Red Deer should, theoretically, be below us. John descended to 500 ft and initiated a square search. We strained to make out something, anything, through the whiteness. Then a snake of slate-grey river appeared, just for an instant and not long enough to give us much encouragement. We had to lose all the speed we could. John applied twenty-five degrees of flaps and reduced stalling speed further by lowering the undercart. Then the river was there below us again. This time we confounded the mush and kept it in sight. Almost immediately, we were over the roofs of Red Deer.

'There's a recreation ground somewhere down there,' said John, 'What do you think?'

I knew it to be on the eastern boundary of the town, a decent size and flat, of course – a bird in the hand, as they say. By comparison, flying on in search of the airfield was an uncertain prospect at best. Anyway, we hadn't much petrol. I nodded in assent.

We circled the town cautiously, looking sideways as much as ahead for a positional check on our next and final approach. We overflew the 'strip', then we were ready to set down. As if he had been doing it all his life, John came around again and thumped the Oxford on to the snowy surface. We drew to an abrupt halt. We were safe and our aircraft was undamaged.

We sat tight and talked little. Two hours passed and at last so, too, did the storm. Residents of Red Deer began to arrive, curious to see what the wind had blown in. We jumped down for a stretch of the legs and a cigarette, only to find that we were minor celebrities. It was as if no one had seen an aeroplane before. The children were insatiably interested. We lifted them inside and let them take turns in our seats. Someone took our picture.

But we knew that at Penhold brows would be deeply furrowed by our non-arrival. We had to get on our way. John built up the rpm and let the Oxford run diagonally across the field. We lifted off at about one hundred and fifty yards, and looked back to the upturned faces and waving arms of the townsfolk.

Remembering those times, I sometimes wonder whether a Canadian not many years younger than I might still gaze at a faded image in the family album and tell his great-grandchildren, 'That's me when I was a kid, and those were the crazy English guys who landed on our sports field.'

Crazy or not, we were treated like prodigal sons on our return to base, particularly by F/Sgt Henn. He had given us up for dead, and never expected to see our Oxford come flying home. Chief Flying Instructors, however, seemed to have a duty to be heavy-handed, and S/Ldr Dale complied to the letter. We were arraigned before him the next day. He carped and gibbered through the motions of a severe reprimand, concluding with a school-masterly, 'Don't let it happen again!'

Until now, the course had been free of mishap. So if Penhold was his first command he'd probably not taken a trainee to task before. It occurred to me that I might be the only one in the room with direct experience of these matters. Maybe John felt the heat. But I had been roasted by S/Ldr Pedley and was only too pleased to escape a repetition of that.

A few days later I travelled by bus to Red Deer. I was muffled up in my greatcoat against the biting cold but, soft Englishman that I was, felt frozen to the marrow. I came across the same recreation ground. It was early evening, and the field was strung with coloured lights. The locals had sluiced in water from the river and allowed nature to create an immense skating rink. Dozens of couples, arm in arm, glided and twirled past me, their faces lit up with pleasure. It was a sight to behold. I left thanking Providence that John and I had arrived in our Oxford above a field covered only by snow.

My trip to Red Deer was for the purpose of buying an American flying jacket made of leather with a sheepskin lining. An enterprising local man had seen a commercial opportunity when the RAF arrived at Penhold, and I was his first customer. The vendor extracted a high price. But the jacket was worth it and something for any pilot, never mind a trainee, to covet.

Generally, expeditions beyond the airfield boundary were rare. We were granted little leisure time. Station life was enjoyable but strenuous. We were subjected to a hard gym regimen under first-class instruction. On the soccer pitch the trainees and ground staff fought out some needle matches. Any surviving high spirits or surplus energy was respectively suppressed or expended by a vigorous, daily drill on the parade ground.

I was never fitter or stronger than in those three months. Yet like most of my colleagues I also put on weight as never before, at least a stone. Not just unrationed but seemingly limitless meats, poultry, fish, eggs, fruit and candy made the canteen a glutton's paradise. We ate like kings.

Occasionally, postal gifts arrived from home. The parson's sister, Miss Steer, sent me woollen gloves, a scarf and a jumper, all knitted by her own hand. I might have been flattered by their heroic dimensions, had I thought that was how she remembered me. But I suspect that heroism played no part in it. Like her brother, Miss Steer never married. The epitome of English spinsterhood, she clearly had but the vaguest acquaintance with the male physique. The scarf was endless and the jumper extended to my knees. Still, it was a kind gesture, and nice to know that the genteel but always patriotic ladies of the parish were doing their bit to bash Jerry.

The RAF built a cinema on the airfield for entertainment and diversion. But the bonhomie and banter of the mess was much the greater source of fun. Bonds of friendship developed between all twelve inhabitants of our billet. John Ward was one. Maurice Kitson, a fine pilot, was another. A pair of Londoners, Lawrie Lawrence and Rob Robson (their real Christian names were never used) had first met as a result of one dating the other's sister. They volunteered together and remained inseparable all the way to that wooden hut in Alberta.

How well I remember Lawrie. He was a delightful chap, full of life and wit. My old logbook still bears his mark. On the front cover he wrote 'Pilot Officer' before my name. This jape flowed from our rivalry for one of only five or six commissions to be awarded at the end of the course. Everyone else who won his wings would become a Sergeant Pilot. Notwithstanding my mediocrity in Ground Studies, I had some hopes of an officer's rank. Several of my friends had me down for one. Only Lawrie, however, took it upon himself to make the point in writing. As it turned out, the commission eluded me. I can't say that Lawrie tempted Fate. As is the way with such things, Fate needed no tempting.

Six days after our forced landing in Red Deer, John and I were cleared for another four-legged, cross-country flight. It was my turn at the controls. We took off in great spirits and in fine weather. Cloud cover was well above our altitude of 5,000 ft and visibility was good. So it remained until we turned on to our third leg. Without warning, our forward visibility began to deteriorate rapidly. This time snow was not the cause. We had flown into a violent prairie dust storm.

The instructing staff had warned us about such storms. But we never really expected to see one. Three specific though not uncommon meteorological conditions were needed to generate the phenomenon: a drought or a dry spell lengthy enough to render bare earth friable; hurricane-force winds; and zero precipitation. Once established they propelled their dust load to tremendous heights and over wide areas. To experienced flyers they were a dreaded danger. To a pair of acolytes encountering such extremes for the first time they were a likely sentence of death.

Visibility was no better than in the snow storm. I peered upward for the sun but saw only shadowy whorls and streams of dust. We were immersed in a sea of the stuff. For a while we didn't appreciate the portent of it. Still so buoyed up by the Red Deer escapade, we could see no bar to a similar resolution now. We railed at our evil luck, the wind, the stone-cold certainty that no one would swallow our story a second time.

'You don't know any playing fields around here?' John joked. But the laughter died away. Our conversation became more sombre and realistic. This time we were not on the final leg close to home. We were not flying over known terrain. There was no possibility of our navigating blind back to Red Deer, Penhold or anywhere else. Our best, our *only* hope was that we get lucky and fly out of the storm.

I initiated a square search procedure, as had John so successfully over the Red Deer River. Now, though, it was to no avail.

Whichever direction we flew, the same, swirling mass of brown particles filled the air below us. John gave up his attempts to navigate and declared his maps redundant. For half-an-hour we flew on instruments alone. We were comprehensively lost. There was nothing to be gained from going on until the remaining petrol was used up. I didn't ask John what he thought we should do next. I knew what he was thinking. The possibility of a bale-out didn't even arise. I lowered the undercart and flaps. We were going down.

The descent was as slow and shallow as I could manage. But the dust only thickened to a dense, featureless bank. I pressed on psychologically, at least, beyond the point of no return.

At an altimeter reading of 300 ft there was still nothing to see but dust. Our altimeter was, of course, set for Penhold and had no currency elsewhere. Terra Firma could be at any point below us. I forsook the artificial horizon and searched beyond the nose of the aircraft with every ounce of my concentration. John called out the notional altitude to give the speed of our descent. We passed 150 ft . . . 100 ft . . . 50 ft, and still only dust. At zero I was quite terrified and had to fight the temptation to pull out and climb back to safety, however temporary. My heart was pounding, my arms felt weak. Suddenly the swirling mass in front of us solidified. The ground was there and coming up with awful finality. There was one second, no more, in which to slam shut the throttles and wrench the column into the pit of my stomach.

Our wheels embraced the hard ground in the most unexpected and gentle caress. I had given everything up to luck and come out of it with the sweetest landing I'd ever made. We rolled to a standstill in visibility of a few yards. With a massive sigh of relief I switched off the engines. John was silent, his face turned away. For several seconds he didn't acknowledge me, didn't move at all. Finally, he looked across. I saw that his eyes were filled and realised that he had not expected to be alive at that moment.

We scrambled out to check the aircraft. It seemed all right. The storm was still raging. There was no point in one or both of us setting off to find help. We could so easily have lost our bearings. Anyway, we hadn't a clue which way to walk. We smoked a cigarette and waited for the wind to drop. After fifteen minutes we heard the low note of an engine. It grew louder and out of the dust emerged a jeep driven by a farmer. Gaunt and gangling, he stared at us as if we had landed from Mars.

A two-minute drive brought us to his farmstead. At the door stood his wife, all aflutter.

'Just the two of 'em. They're alright', drawled the farmer. We climbed out of the jeep. 'Come in, come in', she said. 'Coffee's on the stove. That was a might too close, young man. Fell on my knees and prayed when you came over. Guess the Lord was merciful.'

When the wind moderated we went out to take another look at the Oxford. Evidently, our approach had brought us directly over their roof (the only one for miles). The wheels couldn't have cleared it by more than a few feet, although we saw nothing. But that was not the last discovery. The nose of the aircraft was all but over-hanging a deep drainage ditch which, again, neither John nor I had seen. Any more height and we would have dropped into it with unpredictable consequences. Any less, and the farmer's wife would have been praying with good cause. Lady Luck had crewed with us after all.

I telephoned F/Sgt Henn to report that our aircraft was parked in a field about one hundred and fifty miles from Penhold. He was not grateful for the news. I sensed a storm of a different kind gathering back at base.

Late the next morning F/Sgt Henn arrived aboard a laden petrol bowser. He'd been on the road for almost five hours and wasn't much interested in making conversation. Oblivious to us the bowser crew set about their work and pulled the aircraft away from the ditch. A flight mechanic had travelled with them. He was tightlipped, too, and immersed himself in checking over the engines and cleaning the air filters. Then he and F/Sgt Henn closed the door of the Oxford on us, turned into the wind and roared away, vectoring dust. For our sins we were left to journey back to Penhold with the bowser crew.

The stormclouds darkened further the moment we arrived. An order was lodged for us at the gate: 'Report to S/Ldr Dale's office now, and be quick about it.'

'What have you got to say for yourselves this time?' he demanded. But he didn't hear us out. What was a simple, indeed irrefutable, explanation to us – the weather – became an excuse to him, and a lame one at that. By implication, the very wind that had brought us to this pass was of our own making. Far from saving the aircraft, we endangered it. We alone bore responsibility for the whole, sorry waste of time and money.

'Not a single incident on the entire course,' he fumed, 'not one, but for you. Well, do I let the pair of you go on until someone gets killed?'

Yet he did let us go on, and without so much as an endorsement.

41

There were no more storms, no more forced landings. I went into the exam room having completed ninety-one hours and twenty minutes of flying time in Airspeed Oxfords.

On 17 December 1941 the wings ceremony was held. A little over seven months since I first donned an RAF tunic at Stratford-on-Avon, S/Ldr Dale pinned on the coveted silver wings. I had torpedoed my assessment, of course, and missed the commission. But the consequences of that could wait till later. Right then, like every new Sergeant Pilot from Penhold and all my friends from the billet, I was too happy and too proud to care.

APPENDIX TO CHAPTER 3
No. 36 Service Flying Training School,
Penhold, Alberta, Canada.

Sequence of Instruction – Twin-Engine Airspeed Oxford

1*   Air Experience
2*   Familiarity of Cockpit Layout
3*   Effect of Controls
4*   Taxying
5*   Straight and Level Flight
6*   Climbing, Gliding and Stalling
7*   Medium Turns
8*   Taking-off into Wind
9*   Power Approach and Landing
10* Gliding Approach and Landing
11* Approach Overshoot Action
12* One Engine Flying
13* One Engine Power Approach
14   First Solo
15   Flapless Landings
16* Precautionary Landing
17* Low Flying (with Instructor only)
18   Steep Turns
19   Climbing Turns
20* Forced Landings
21* Action in the event of Fire
22* Abandoning of Aircraft
23   Instrument Flying
24   Take-off under Hood
25   Taking-off and Landing out of Wind
26   Night Flying
27   Formation Flying
28   Air Navigation
29   Cross-Country Flights

* Exercises to be carried out before going solo.

CHAPTER FOUR

GRADUATE AND DON

T hroughout 1941 the losses of bomber aircrew increased steadily, reaching a new plateau in the following year. Though the number of bombers was increasing, the same rate of loss was to obtain throughout the hard days of the Battle of the Ruhr in the spring and summer of 1943 and the Battle of Berlin in the winter that followed. On average one aircraft in twenty would go missing or crash on every operation.

Many a gambler might not eschew odds of 19/1. But a tour of thirty ops (thirty-five for a while in mid-1942), followed by six months' rest and then a second tour, was another and less inviting prospect. The very numbers reveal the value Bomber Command placed upon the lives and morale of its aircrew. On one hand, you couldn't simply consign your people to oblivion. There had to be some point of stand-down from impending harm. On the other, the destruction of Germany's industrial and logistical capacity and the sapping of her war-will were prizes of such incalculable worth, almost no sacrifice would have been too great. In the event, within the broader context of Allied operations none greater was ever asked.

Out in the shipping lanes of the Atlantic the Germans were asking the same of their U-boat crews. It is a striking parallel that of all German forces only they, charged with destroying the enemy's capacity to equip, suffered a rate of loss and capture comparable to our aircrew.

Buried in all this may be some universal, military truth. But for the chap staring out into the night from his gun turret or down through his bomb sight, the view was more immediate. Life was intense, blinkered and built upon the fellowship with his crew. His imperative was to do his duty . . . and survive. That was becoming more difficult as German ground and air defences developed. Searchlight and flak battery co-ordination was improving and the number of fighters continually increased.

In turn, the RAF accelerated its offensive capacity via the four-engined Short Stirling Mark 1, first flown operationally by 7 Squadron in February, 1941. However, the dependency on twin-engined aircraft, chiefly Wellingtons, carried on into 1943. The Wellington was a slow but reliable performer. Its designer, Barnes Wallis, employed a geodetic grid in the construction of the fuselage. It could soak up enormous punishment, though the fabric skin was alarmingly combustible. In time the bomb load, ceiling and range would come to be seen as inadequate. And they were far from sophisticated machines. At first they were not even equipped with self-sealing petrol tanks. But the German public was forced to see that Britain survived as a foe. More particularly, with the coming of area bombing in the spring of 1942 it saw that real destruction could visit Hamburg, Essen or Berlin as readily as Guernica, Warsaw, Narvik, Rotterdam, London, Coventry or Southampton. German homes and industry, untouched throughout 1914–18, came under direct, nightly assault.

Boarding the troopship at Halifax for the voyage home I was grimly reconciled to a bit part in this mighty effort. Faced with events of such towering enormity one could but be philosophical. Had my two flying courses run smoothly, had I not incurred the wrath of both Chief Flying Instructors, were my assessments not just Average, perhaps then a Beaufighter might have been mine. But carrying cookies to Krupp's it would surely be now. I was in fine company, though. All my friends from Penhold expected the same. Most viewed it with equanimity. After all, we were young and optimistic. Regardless of how many bombers fell burning around us, we would survive.

We sailed in the early evening and watched the lights of the port fade slowly on the horizon. We were travelling to a land of blackout and rationing. But there were no regrets. It was our home. Our families and girlfriends were there. It was where we longed to be. Again I denied myself the comfort of a hammock for the cold steel of a gangway. Again my caution was unnecessary. The sea crossing was quiet. We docked at Greenock and travelled by sleeper to London, then to an RAF transit camp at Bournemouth. From here newly qualified pilots were directed to their next and final posting under the auspices of Training Command. But the authorities seemed unprepared for our arrival. Christmas was imminent and they didn't know what to do with us. Someone suggested the simple expedient of ten days' leave. It was a gift. We said our adieus and headed home to our families.

I couldn't know it, of course, but Christmas Eve 1941 was a portentous date for me and for so many thousands of future aircrew. A new weapon was delivered to 44 (Rhodesia) Squadron. Thus far, in the shape of the Stirling and Halifax, the four-engined bomber had not really lived up to expectations. Now the first three operational Avro Lancasters appeared on the scene and all that would quickly change.

For me, Christmas at home proved to be less of a gift than I'd thought. On Boxing Day I began to feel ill. My throat and face became painfully swollen. 'Mumps', the family doctor confirmed. 'Quite uncomfortable at your advanced age.'

'I've got to be at Bournemouth next week to get my posting.'

'Out of the question, I'm afraid. Mumps is contagious. Do you think the RAF wants an epidemic on its hands? No, you will remain in this house, young man, until I say otherwise.'

A fortnight of quarantine passed, then a month. I knocked about the house restlessly, worrying about what my pals had made of my disappearance. I didn't relish telling them on my return that I'd caught a childhood disease. But would they even be there?

After six weeks the doctor finally set me free. I reported to Bournemouth to find that Lawrie, Rob and the rest were gone. I never set eyes on any of them again, never heard their laughter or shared their sense of fun. I don't know what became of a single one, though I suppose they all found their way to Bomber Command. It was an early introduction to the severance which was commonplace in operational life.

Notwithstanding that, I have always been grateful for the doctor's caution. It lifted me out of one uncertain stream of events and into another which I was destined to survive. It gave me a second chance, and quite probably saved my life.

A few days after my return the CO sent for me. My records lay on his desk. 'Yates,' he said, 'we are posting you to No. 6 Advanced Flying School at Little Rissington, Gloucestershire. Report there tomorrow.'

He didn't see fit to furnish me with more information. I knew that 'Advanced' didn't signify anything special. Everyone was sent to one or other of these establishments. But the word sowed speculation about the type of aircraft flying there. The Beaufighter came storming back into my head. I journeyed in high anticipation. Within moments of passing through the gate, however, I saw that all the aircraft flown at Little Rissington were Airspeed Oxfords. It was to be more of the same medicine, well over a thousand hours more as it turned out.

At least flying conditions were different in dear, old Blighty. During the hours of darkness it was as though a great, black cloth had been draped across the land. Only the ubiquitous airfields escaped the pall. Beacons flashed coded identities and dimmed runway lights betrayed operational activity. In cloudless skies it presented the most stirring sight. All over the country the RAF had kindled the fire of national purpose and self-belief. Churchill's most noble words never argued more eloquently that *we* were on the offensive now and one day our victory would come.

The Americans were already here, six months or so after their declaration of war on Germany. A crash programme of USAAF airfield construction was underway. Bases were springing up all over East Anglia. The fighters were rapidly operational, joining the RAF in sweeps over France. But the Flying Fortress squadrons seemed to require an inordinate time for settling down. In the acid view of the British Serviceman, 'bedding down' might have been the more accurate term. The Yanks had all the glamour, music and money. They also had our girls though not, we believed, much respect for them. How galling, then, that at the very time the 8th Air Force was trying its luck with some fast talk and slow dancing, our bomber crews were under trial of a different sort in the skies over Germany.

Like all AFU courses, Little Rissington's was as much for holding purposes as for anything else. It was loosely structured without the usual mass intake or rigid timetable. It ended when you were ready, in my case after sixteen weeks. The content was much more technical. Its aim was to hone basic aptitude and skills ready for operational training.

For the first time I felt treated like a real pilot. During the daylight hours we practised formation flying or we frightened the life out of the sheep in the low flying area. In April, I was sent on a week's Beam Approach course at Upwood. We donned dark-tinted goggles and flew by instrument down the sodium flarepath below. This developed into practising bumps under the same conditions. But I never brought off a landing as smooth as that one in the prairie duststorm.

Missing from all this was any character assessment or tests of individual reactions under fire. I don't know what proportion of absconders were pilots. Perhaps not many. But how much better to have identified them early, rather than let them buckle on the eve of operational duty.

We were almost all bound for Bomber Command. The nature of the beast was known. For the poor devils for whom this knowledge was a dread thing, literally unbearable, there was nothing but fear and secrecy. The world showed no sympathy or understanding. To abscond was the only way out, even if that meant accusations of Lack of Moral Fibre. There must be many alive still for whom the passing years have not erased the pain of those cruel words. But better even this than that these people should get as far as the Ruhr or the main German cities. Fear there was unavoidable, death always close. No crew could afford one of their number to snap on board and plunge everything into hysteria and chaos.

Oft-times, of course, courage was not enough, nor experience and seniority. On 5 April, even as I trundled around Upwood, an illustrious pilot who embodied all these things met his end. He was Wing Commander Reginald Sawrey-Cookson, DSO, DFC, the Commanding Officer of my future squadron and the first of three COs 75 would lose during the war. He perished in his Wellington, with all his gallant crew, during a raid on the city of Cologne. He was just twenty-six.

Back at Little Rissington I was often paired with a young American named Murrell. He was an adventurer if not a mercenary. He had joined the Royal Canadian Air Force some months before Pearl Harbor. His home town was Dallas so he was quickly dubbed 'Texas'. True to the roistering image of that State he was far from the retiring sort. He lived on his adrenalin and, for the hell of it, would as soon bend the rules as not. But then, his motivation for being here wasn't duty or patriotism like the rest of us. He was looking for some action, a shoot-out. He would have given S/Ldr Pedley apoplexy, and he was the ideal man to have on board for a beat-up.

We were dispatched together on several cross-country exercises. On the first of these I had the controls and, naturally enough, made straight for Stony Stratford and my home. The time of steep turns over the chimney pots was behind me. Now, with the Oxford's added power and manoeuvrability, a beat-up was really the only honourable course.

So in we hammered from the east on full boost. We skimmed the hedged boundary of the allotments, keeping well below the height of the ancient oaks that lined it. A Stony resident was digging for victory. Texas shouted, 'Down, baby, down', but our victim needed no encouragement. He probably hadn't moved so fast for years. At the latest possible moment we pulled up and over the houses. Texas roared something about leaving paint marks on the roof and bounced up and down on his seat like a wild man. But then, he was a rodeo rider at heart.

On those occasions when Texas had the controls he never failed to mete out the full punishment. He knew how to fly. I had to sit by helpless and, for want of any other, fit response, with characteristic British reserve.

Our antics were irredeemably wilful and stupid, of course, and dangerous to others besides ourselves. Everyone had heard of cases where what began with braggery or a bit of egging-on ended in death. It took only one small misjudgement. More likely, though, was that some public-spirited citizen would note the aircraft markings and inform the authorities. The unlucky pilot could expect a court martial, and so could his navigator.

All this we understood clearly. But it made no difference. A good beat-up was so phenomenally exhilarating. To scream across the landscape at only the height of a man, with the ground reeling away under the nose of the aircraft and everything coming at you too fast to think about, to delay pulling up as the end of the run came near ... to wait, and wait ... and then astound even yourself with the audacity and precision of it all, *that* was flying. Absolutely nothing compared to it. I didn't know then how a twenty-year-old in charge of a one hundred and fifty mph machine could be expected to resist it. And I don't know now.

There were less hazardous aerial pursuits. On 30 May, I was assigned a solo height test. I pushed and persuaded my Oxford remorselessly higher, levelling off each time the old girl ran out of steam. With enough speed restored, up we went again. Finally, exhausted and teetering on a stall, she topped out at the dizzy height of 20,000 ft, well above the official ceiling.

Centuries ago, the yeoman farmers of the Cotswolds employed a peerless eye and instinct to shape the landscape. They created something of quintessential Englishness. But they never dreamt of this view of their labours. I have never forgotten it.

That very night and a good deal lower the first thousand-bomber raid was setting the old city of Cologne ablaze. The next morning the news of Operation *Millennium* filled the airwaves and every daily paper. The nation's morale scaled heights of its own. The phrase, 'a thousand-bomber raid', entered the popular vocabulary overnight. In all, Bomber Command despatched one thousand and forty-seven aircraft, including sixty-seven Lancasters that were obliged by their speed to take off much later than the rest. Number 75 Squadron, meanwhile, was still wedded to Wellingtons. But it contributed twenty-three, then its record.

However, *Millennium* was more than another maximum effort. For several weeks Sir Arthur Harris had sought to promote his area bombing policy via the publicity of such a raid. He managed it this time but only by bringing-in tired, old kites that had been pensioned-off once already to Operational Training Units. But this minor qualification was not trumpeted to an awestruck public. Nor was the record created by the forty-one losses.

Two nights later they tried again. Nine hundred and fifty-six bombers attacked Essen. It was the most they could put up, though not enough. But the same night forty-eight Blenheims made intruder sorties on German airfields. Harris didn't quibble. The second thousand-bomber raid was declared.

On 12 June 1942 I flew my final exercise from Little Rissington. I was ordered to report to the Chief Flying Instructor, Group Captain Barraclough. The end of any course was an important moment. But this one would seal my immediate fate. The Group Captain stamped my logbook, pushed it across his desk and said casually, 'You're on your way to Montrose, Yates. Flying Instructors' School.'

Instructing! I was flabbergasted. Why me, for heaven's sake? Why should I be singled-out for ten thousand circuits and bumps beside a nervous rookie? That wasn't at all what I had in mind. I argued instead for the chance to shoot the hell out of some enemy bombers. Naturally, I proposed flying a Beaufighter (rapidly achieving the status of a holy grail for me) or even the Mosquito which was now in service and just too exciting for words. Failing that, *any* operational posting was preferable if, of course, one excluded the short straw of Bomber Command.

'The decision isn't mine, I'm afraid', he said. 'It's come from higher up. I'm sorry, Montrose it is.'

Then he thought for a moment. 'I can't offer any guarantees, but . . .' He rapidly scribbled a note. 'Give this to your CO when the time comes. It's my recommendation that after twelve months as an instructor you should be given your choice of aircraft to fly operationally. Good luck. And I hope you get your night-fighter.'

Walking back to the billet I opened the logbook which read, 'Proficiency as a twin-engine pilot Above Average'. Here at last was the assessment that might have opened the door to Fighter Command, had it come earlier. But now the RAF wouldn't let me fly so much as a barrage balloon against the nightly visitation of Junkers and Heinkels.

We sat on the grass in front of the administration block, twelve in number arrayed in a half circle. A fresh breeze blew in from the North Sea a few hundred yards away. Not bluebirds but seagulls floated and wheeled above us. In shirtsleeved informality we listened to the welcoming address from Wing Commander Sewell, Chief Flying Instructor of No. 2 Flying Instructors' School, Montrose.

'. . . *the* most significant contribution,' he was saying, 'any of you will ever make to the war effort.'

I listened and tried to believe. Above us the gulls balanced on the wind, supreme aviators and the very antithesis of the tethered spirit of No. 2 Flying Instructors' School. The Wing Commander's voice droned on '. . . the effectiveness of the thousands of sorties to be flown by the men who will pass through your hands, and of the tens of thousands of tons of bullets and bombs they will discharge at the enemy, will depend . . .'.

So there it was. Others would have the satisfaction of taking up arms. My duty would be to instruct them, and be patient. The patience might be a problem. G/Cpt Barraclough's letter was already burning a hole in my pocket.

Gulls aside (and they were a damned nuisance) Montrose was a pleasing and scenic place to fly. However, the downwind leg took us a mile out over the North Sea which, rain or shine, was never calm and never looked other than cold and forbidding. It certainly concentrated minds on mechanical reliability.

Mercifully, from the point of view of getting one's feet wet, the only single-engined aircraft were perfectly reliable. These were Miles Magisters, used extensively by Training Command at that time. In the first two weeks of the course I flew this little machine five or six times each day. The fingertip sensitivity of single-engined flying was too light for my liking. I preferred the weight of the Oxford and, inevitably, No. 2 Flying Instructors' School had its quota.

My instructor was F/Lt Harding, a high-class pilot like all the Montrose flying staff. Indeed, it would be no exaggeration to say that those who instructed future instructors saw themselves as the cream of RAF pilots. Civilian test pilots probably had a higher status, but not many others.

The first requirement for any instructor was the ability to

demonstrate clean and polished flying sequences. The second was a mastery of technical detail. To these ends F/Lt Harding set us about refining our flying skills. In the process we took pains to study every last facet, every characteristic of the aircraft. The transition from pupil to teacher was slowly taking place.

But teaching had a third requirement: the right personal qualities had to be present. Natural authority was something you either had or you hadn't. But we could all aim for a quiet imposition of order and discipline in the air. We could all (or most of us) display a calm and patient temperament, and win the pupil's confidence that way. From this flowed a respectful and good working relationship. A friendly disposition towards the pupil helped, too. But discipline had to come first.

The key, according to F/Lt Harding, was to really enjoy both teaching and flying. Without this, he said, you will never be a successful instructor. He might have added that you still had to survive the hazards of the training course.

Notwithstanding the attentions of the enemy and, sometimes, your friends, trouble with, or in, aeroplanes only ever had three causes: mechanical failure; adverse flying conditions; and human error. During my time at Montrose I had a taste of all three, with varying degrees of alarm.

On 14 July I took up Airspeed Oxford No. 1951 on a solo cross-country. Approaching Newcastle on the third leg the starboard engine quit, and I had an unscheduled exercise in one-engine flying on my hands. The airfield at Wolsingham was closest, about fifteen minutes' flying time. I went faithfully, if gingerly, by the book. I trimmed the aircraft, selected fine airscrew pitch, and reduced power and speed to a minimum. At Wolsingham I took the circuit wide, turning gently towards the good engine. With forty degrees of flaps and eighty mph on the clock, Oxford No. 1951 sailed over the boundary and settled onto the grass. The book had worked, which was only as it should be.

The repair was effected the following day. I returned to Montrose at noon. Flight Lieutenant Harding met me at dispersal with a wide grin as if to say, 'Welcome to the club'. He presumed this was my first encounter with the vicissitudes of Lady Luck. I had no wish to disabuse him of this charming thought. He was happy and that suited me. It was a change to return from one of these excursions without a summons before the Chief Flying Instructor.

A week later, though, the fickle Lady was on my trail again. Montrose was prone to mist rolling in on a sea breeze. The runway could be obscured in a moment and clear again seconds later. Equally, it could take hours. Late one afternoon I returned from another solo flight with fuel pretty low. A particularly fine bank of fog was in attendance. Only a hundred yards further inland visibility was perfect but I decided not to hang around. Edzell golfcourse was close at hand. Having walked it once or twice since arriving in the area I knew it had a wealth of invitingly accessible fairways. I landed alongside a line of towering Scots pines and put paid to the lowering of handicaps for the rest of that day. Somewhat incongruous in my flying gear I strode into the clubhouse. No one seemed to mind. The staff even insisted on serving up a superb meal of bacon, eggs and tomatoes washed down with best bitter on the house.

I braced myself for trouble back at Montrose. Again, though, W/Cdr Sewell had no inclination to carpet me. His liberality was welcome but puzzling. Maybe light and reason were kept alive in this blessed corner of Scotland. Maybe the Wing Commander wasn't especially fond of golf.

Certainly, during this period I felt myself to be washed up on some insular, little island. Training Command was part of the war effort but operationally, of course, not *in the war*. At times this distinction became very pointed, as in the case of the third thousand-bomber raid on the night of 25 June 1942. Harris threw *everything* at Bremen. The main force numbered only nine hundred and sixty. But once again OTUs were drafted in. Even Coastal Command, with no experience in such matters, was invited to contribute. It was the greatest variety of bombers ever used in one raid. Losses numbered forty-eight but, tragically, twenty-three were OTU crews.

On the night of 3 August the sea mist rolled back into my life. This time I was navigating a three-hour cross-country for Sergeant Pilot John . . . well, maybe it's kinder just to record his surname as W. Our track was base to Grangemouth, then a dead-reckoning point before turning due east to Wolsingham, north-west to Macmerry, on to Leuchars and then home.

It was a clear, starlit night. Each beacon was unmissable, the Firth of Forth silvery against the surrounding black land. We turned for home at Leuchars still in excellent visibility. But at Montrose heavy mist had swirled in from the sea just far enough to threaten the airfield. One minute the flarepath shone out. The next it disappeared from view. We had too little fuel to fly elsewhere. John lowered the undercarriage and, on full flap, came in on his final approach. Forward vision over the boundary was very dubious. He began to hold off and, as he did, I knew our fate with appalling clarity. I was burning to warn him that we were too damned high, that he was trying to bring off a three-point landing fifty feet above the flarepath. But he was concentrating so hard, I bit back the words. I could only acquiesce and hang on. John was still desperately feeling for the ground when the starboard wing dropped and all hell broke loose. The impact of the wing pivoted the aircraft around. The fuselage smashed down, crushing the undercarriage. We swivelled off the flarepath showering sparks like a rogue catherine wheel. The engines carved deep fissures marking our track across the airfield and, finally, we came to rest.

By the grace of God there was no fireball. Neither were we injured, not so much as a scratch. A little shaken, though, we extricated ourselves from our poor Oxford and stood blinking at the wreckage. Everything that wasn't broken off was shattered or bent or barely recognisable.

'Oh, Christ,' sighed John as we walked back to Flight, 'that's me finished!'

The words of P/O Eastwood after my Hatfield pile-up came to mind. 'As far as I'm concerned,' I said, 'any landing that you walk away from is a bloody good landing.'

I thought John was right, though. Surely this time, with an aircraft wrecked and lives put at risk, the axe must fall. Just or no, as a party to the incident blame would attach to me also. Bomber Command was beckoning again like the Grim Reaper.

But I had not allowed for the continuing beneficence of the Wing Commander. Barely a word was said. The small matter of the aircraft was set aside. Not only I but even John escaped blame. Naturally, anyone acquainted with Montrose's mist would have sympathy for us. But even so I began to wonder if an unspoken conspiracy was at work. Instructors, qualified or not, didn't appear to be subject to the same earthly justice as the rest of the RAF. The brotherhood looked after its own! I exaggerate, but my mind was forced along these lines.

The following week S/Ldr Symondson tested each of us in his Flight. Then we were submitted to the Chief Flying Instructor's Test. It was a gruelling business. But twelve qualified instructors emerged at the end of it, and that included John W.

My posting took me back to Gloucestershire, to No. 3 Advanced Flying Unit, South Cerney, Near Cirencester. The Barraclough letter in hand, I presented myself to my new Chief Flying Instructor, S/Ldr Moody. He assigned me to A Flight as one of its six instructors. Our aircraft, of course, were Oxfords.

A terrific *esprit de corps* and a comradeship between all the instructors were immediately apparent. A soft-spoken, unassuming Canadian named Geoffrey Frayne became a good friend. He had arrived at South Cerney some weeks before me. We shared the same billet. After a few months he was given a commission. I saw what it meant to him and well remember the quiet pride with which he wrote to his parents with the news.

Instructors seldom flew together except on instrument flying exercises. But in September 1942, Geoffrey and I had three such flights, each of two hours' duration. We should have known better, but we misspent each one low-flying. The next month he took off on a solo weather test which was, of course, all too likely to depend on instruments. He was never seen again. It was as if he had just walked off the edge of the world.

To S/Ldr Moody fell the sad, hard task of writing the letter from England that Mr and Mrs Frayne would have hoped never to receive. It must have been harder still for them that no body was recovered. There would never come the time when they might stand over a headstone and say goodbye to their son.

As for me, well, the memory of those three September flights turned to bitter gall. I asked myself if the six hours properly used might have made a difference. I was troubled by the recurring thought of Geoffrey descending through cloud to find nothing but the pitiless sea and then, utterly alone and with knowledge of the approaching end, flying on until the fuel was gone. But there were other possibilities. The truth was, we simply didn't know.

Geoffrey's silent passing shocked all the instructors. There was, though, only one course open: to force it out of our minds and carry on. The pressure of work both necessitated and aided that process.

Among my pupils were several Squadron Leaders and one Wing Commander. The Air Ministry had flushed out a substantial number of senior officers who, though wearing a pilot's badge, had been deskbound for several years. They were assigned to AFUs for a refresher course prior to operational posting. On the ground one always respected their rank. But in the air they acknowledged my role as captain of the aircraft and carried out my instructions unquestioningly though not always, it must be said, unerringly.

We worked hard, flying eighty hours or more most months. It was repetitive but never the ten thousand circuits and bumps I once feared. And if boredom did threaten there was always the low-flying area. This was a carefully defined tract of land away from the populace. In the centre was a sizeable lake surrounded by woods, a desolate spot seemingly unbeknown even to lovers and fishermen. It was best approached from the east on full bore and at tree-top height. Once over the water down went the nose towards the glassy surface. On the far bank two large trees stood not far apart, like sentinels. My target was always to pull up hard between them and shiver the treetops behind.

If you had a hangover, money trouble or you were just stuck in a rut there was absolutely nothing like it to blow your cares away. It was also useful to discourage an errant trainee from overreaching his ability, just as S/Ldr Pedley had once sought to discourage me. The conviction that he was about to expire could do quite a lot for a young man's perspective on life.

There were occasions when the instructor got the treatment. I remember one night flying with my pupil at 1,500 ft and leaning forward to switch off the port magneto and, thereby, the port engine. It was a test of pupil reaction to engine failure. The right one was a power increase on the good engine to maintain height and hard opposite rudder to counteract yaw. Then the port magneto could be reactivated at leisure, bringing the engine to life again. But no. This chap dived for the switch to the *starboard* magneto, leaving us on a black night plunging earthwards with two dead engines. In that unhappy situation the instructor can be forgiven for taking matters into his own hands.

My career as a night owl actually began with a transfer to the South Cerney Night Flight. My first night's work on 27 November 1942 demonstrates the hectic nature of those times. First, I was checked out for an hour by my Flight Commander, F/Lt Graham Smith. Then I took up my 'maiden' pupil, P/O Ireland, for two landings and an overshoot before sending him solo for an hour. Pupil no. 2 was F/Lt Newbury: one overshoot and one landing then off for an hour's circuits and bumps. A quick cup of tea and a cigarette later it was the turn of no. 3, P/O Tomlin. He was sent solo after just one landing. P/O Bakewell was next, receiving an hour's instruction in precision flying. The same hour was flown with pupil no. 5, F/O Courtman-Stock. As we made our final exit from the flarepath the stars had left the night sky and dawn was breaking. That was to be the pattern for months.

Many operational pilots considered instructing to be a soft option. We thought it too arduous for that. Sometimes, though, their point of view was difficult to refute. The activities of other airmen were of more than passing interest to us, and there circulated many tales of operational close calls and derring-do. To these a non-combatant could only listen in humility and with envy or thanks, according to his innermost reason.

One such story, which was the starting point for a larger tale told some years later, was the Fallersleben raid of 17 December 1942. The target was the Opel works situated in this small Ruhr town. Just sixteen Stirlings and six Wellingtons were sent, all from 3 Group. The smallness of the force was intended to be its virtue. The vital element was surprise. The crews were briefed to fly in under the radar and climb late to their bombing height of 5,000 ft. Thus, they would arrive over the target before the defenders had a chance to react.

Of the sixteen Stirlings, five were from 75 Squadron. One was crewed by some boys on their first op. It was a tough starter so W/Cdr Vic Mitchell, DFC, a twenty-seven-year-old Scot who had assumed command of 75 a few months earlier, opted to go along with them. It was a fateful decision. The raid was not unopposed as hoped. The size of the force merely multiplied the dangers. An average loss rate for a Ruhr op would have meant one or two of the aircraft failing to return. But eight went down. Four of these were from 75, including Mitchell's Stirling. The only crew that made it back to Mildenhall (75's then base) couldn't even find the Opel works, and executed an intruder sortie on an airfield instead. In return for attacking the wasps' nest they were twice stung by night-fighters.

Mitchell himself, his crew and the crews of two of the other 75 Sqn Stirlings were all killed. The remaining Stirling crash-landed into a Dutch lake. All seven crew members survived but were quickly captured. The bomb aimer was P/O Eric Williams who would achieve fame and a Military Cross for tunnelling out of *Stalag Luft 3* and returning to England. This was the incomparable episode of the wooden horse, later described by Williams in his book of that name and immortalised in the best traditions of the British film industry.

An instructor's lot was infinitely more peaceful than that! But I was not without some experience of what issues from the barrel of a gun. My education began with a transfer in January 1943 to Lulsgate Bottom, one of South Cerney's three satellite airfields and now Bristol Airport. In those days it was anything but an airport though it could boast two concrete runways.

I was attached, again, to the Night Flight. We flew from around eight p.m. till four in the morning, seven nights a week, weather permitting. I crawled into bed as dawn broke and out again before noon, either for the half-hour bus ride to lunch in Bristol or a couple of hours of fishing on the nearby Blagdon Lake. In the late afternoon we were back in the air to pass the Oxfords serviceable for the night's work.

Air-testing one afternoon I strayed beyond Clevedon and out over the calm, forbidden waters of the Bristol Channel. The weather was fine with five-tenths cumulus cloud at 5,000 ft, wonderful conditions in which to fly. It was like a cotton-wool playground. There was a renewed sense of speed, always lacking in a clear blue sky. And to slalom between the clouds or wind lazily through them in a game of hide-and-seek with the world at large was pure joy.

It had never occurred to me that the world at large might see this as fugitive behaviour. But the point became very clear indeed when a barrage of anti-aircraft shells burst around me. I nearly jumped out of my seat, and wrenched the Oxford into clean air. But the shells kept coming. Somewhere down on the shoreline a bunch of trigger-happy incompetents really thought they had a Junkers 88 at their mercy. None of my most violent efforts shook them off until I escaped to the north and out of range.

Later that week a fellow instructor and I popped into our favourite Bristol pub for a beer. Several middle-aged businessmen were gathered in a circle at the bar. One, whom I knew to be a gunnery officer, was holding forth to his companions with great relish. They, for their part, were obviously enjoying the joke. He couldn't wait to haul another admirer into the group.

'I was just telling these chaps', he said, grabbing my arm, 'about this bloody Junkers pilot who got a kick up the backside from my boys on Monday. Flying down the Channel without a care in the world, he was. You should have seen him scuttle off when we opened up. We gave the bugger hell.'

While he led the laughter I fought against the temptation to lift him up by the lapels. 'Really?' I said, 'Good show.' I was only glad his men were such lousy shots.

As it turned out physical violence would not have been well timed. Shortly after this episode I was summoned by the CO.

'Would you like to settle your bar bills monthly in the Officers' Mess?' he asked. My face must have been a blank. He explained, 'I'm recommending you for a commission, if that's all right with you.'

I assured him that it was. Not many days later I walked stiffly out of Moss Bros in Bristol's Park Street in a brand new Pilot Officer's uniform. I don't think I ever felt more self-conscious in my life.

A colleague suggested soaking the cap in beer. The tunic required manual weathering: stretching, creasing, everything bar jumping up and down on it. I slept in the trousers. Finally, it all took on the appearance of having fought a long and hard war not only with the Germans but with the wearer.

One lunchtime in the mess I reminded S/Ldr Moody of the letter I gave him on my arrival at South Cerney. It had been on file in his office for almost eighteen months and there was still no sign of an operational posting. But it was more than a matter of lost time. I had been a dutiful servant. Hadn't I earnt the right to choose my own instrument of war as the letter recommended?

My expectations were quite specific and they were high: night-fighting in Mosquitoes or Beaufighters or, failing that, ground-strafing in Beaufighters. Flying a bomber didn't figure anywhere. Indeed, the whole point was to avoid it.

Somewhere in the labyrinthine bureaucracy of the RAF sat a man who decided the fate of lesser mortals like myself. I fondly imagined that S/Ldr Moody could successfully appeal to him on my behalf for the necessary dispensation. Whenever our paths crossed I button-holed the CO to painstakingly re-state all my arguments and preferences. No opportunity was passed up. During those few weeks the poor man probably came to hate the words, 'About my posting, sir . . .' I can see him now seated in the mess with that glazed look in his eyes as I moved in for another go.

It wasn't very fair. But a result of some kind was a certainty. An instructor whose thoughts were continually of burning Heinkels or the thunder of twin Merlins was of limited value to a teaching establishment. He was already out of the door in spirit. The rest of him wouldn't be long in following, indeed, little more than a month in my case.

'You are to report . . .', the CO announced, searching an untidy desktop for the vital piece of paper whilst I waited scarcely able to draw breath, 'to No. 11 Operational Training Unit at Westcott. That's near Aylesbury. You'll be flying Wellingtons, I'm afraid, then on to Stirlings.'

'But, sir, that's . . .'

'Yes, 92 Training Group, Bomber Command. Well, there it is. I wish you the very best of luck.'

The door closed behind me. I walked away feeling crushed and anything but lucky. The alluring dream that I had nurtured for so long, and believed with all my heart, was over. My brilliant career, the Merlins and the Heinkels, a sporting chance of survival, were all cancelled.

Moreover, my expectations were revealed in all their vanity. The Barraclough letter had been tossed aside. My training background and flying hours and all my faith in S/Ldr Moody, now so obviously misplaced, had counted for nothing . . . indeed, less than nothing. The RAF did not even value me sufficiently to send me to 5 Group (with Pathfinders, the only part of Bomber Command to command any degree of envy and respect). Number 11 OTU was a feeder for 3 Group. Their squadrons had the worst losses. Their equipment was, until recently, second division stuff. They were the last operational Group to say goodbye to the Stirling and, certainly, the last place I wanted to go.

Not since the voyage home from Canada had I been prepared for such a posting. Then, of course, it amounted to no more than informed speculation. Now it was fact. Then, I was filled with youthful, not to say naïve, optimism. Now I had no illusions.

I was given a few days of home leave and the opportunity to pause and reflect. It was early March. The fields behind the church and down to the river were sodden from floods a week or two earlier. To my collie's distaste our morning walks kept to the pavement and tarmacadam of the town.

The years of war had wrought little change there. In the winter months of 1940–41 the sirens wailed almost nightly. German bombers overflew in their hundreds *en route* to Birmingham or Coventry. Some six hundred projectiles fell in the fields and villages around and about, and there were fatalities. But the red brick buildings of Stony and adjoining Wolverton knew nothing of fire or explosion.

The one visible sign of war was the camouflaging of the old Wolverton railway works. I would have liked to give the works manager some professional advice. From the air his factory was as conspicuous as ever. The brown and green paint was a give-away and an open invitation to attack. Safer to pretend that the place still turned out harmless coaches for the LMS. In any case, it was hardly in the front line of armaments production. My mother worked there sewing canvas for the repair of salvaged airframes.

As one does, I sought out news of my old school and workmates, neighbours and pals. The forces were so committed that every family had someone fighting somewhere. Life could be shattered by a single telegram. But despite the apprehension that this caused and the general war-weariness that weighed upon everyone, people dared to *believe* now in the end of the war and prayed with greater confidence that their husbands and sons would come safe home.

The town had a long acquaintance with such emotions. There were many local men killed, wounded, missing or captured as early as May 1940. These were the Territorials of the 1st Bucks Battalion who landed in France with the BEF in January of that year. Their last stand began on 25 May at Hazebrouck to the south of Dunkirk. Under orders to hold back the German advance in the area while the evacuation proceeded, they stood fast for four long days. At the end, surrounded by enemy tanks and artillery and their ammunition expended, they made a break under cover of darkness. Of the original battalion strength of eight hundred (some of whom pulled back with the 4th Oxfordshires and 2nd Gloucestershires the same night from nearby Cassel) only ten officers and around two hundred other ranks arrived on the beach to find a berth to England. Crucial then, their action is forgotten now. But it was magnificent.

My own circle of friends were spared entanglement in that thicket. But in later years four of them were lost at sea. On leave I always tried to visit their families, to pay my respects and keep alive a few memories. They bore their loss with quiet and unfailing dignity. I was touched by them all.

I journeyed to Westcott with a new perspective. It had been fair enough to push for a night-fighter. Now I had failed and couldn't go on bewailing the fact. Like every other ordinary son of my unexceptional town I had to bow to the inevitable. Fate, Luck, Providence, call it what you like, had made this small job of piloting a bomber my duty.

I would try to do it well.

CHAPTER FIVE

THE KIWIS, THE CALLOW, THE CLERIC & THE LADYKILLER

I left South Cerney an instructor of sixteen hundred hours standing but arrived at Westcott a crewless skipper of a heavy bomber, and a trainee again.

My immediate task was to put together a crew. I walked into the Officers' Mess on my first evening and looked around. The usual types were there, the bar billiards and bridge players, the jokers and raconteurs, the loners nursing their beer. Westcott staff aside, each man had twenty-four hours to form up with a crew, and here and there pockets of quiet conversation attested to that purpose. It was a serious business. A few months earlier the Wellingtons at dispersal had been front-line bombers. Anyone could see that operating one of those beauties over enemy territory was no job for the casual or inept or for misfits.

I had begun to reflect on this while on leave. I drew up a list of the demons most familiar to aircrew. Those that were simple ill-luck, such as an engine failure on take off, a mid-air collision in cloud or a direct hit over the target, I crossed through. They couldn't be foreseen. They couldn't really be ameliorated. They were likely to be final. Where the outcome could be influenced by crew efficiency I withheld the pen. These were the greater part of the list. Whether they corresponded to the greater part of actual losses, I could not know. But the lottery of survival looked less like a game of pure chance.

For example, I well knew that the first and best defence against an enemy fighter was vigilance. Spotted early it could be presented with a difficult target. After that, accurate fire from the turrets might disrupt, drive off or even destroy it. Vigilance was also the key to survival over the target. Another kite on a collision course or about to bomb from directly overhead had to be detected before it was too late.

Some losses fell into the category of wilful neglect. Close formating, or just drifting too near other bombers, was asking for trouble. A shell in one bomb bay could destroy everything in the vicinity. On the other hand it was desirable to hold station in the midst of the stream . . . and never, never lose contact. Stragglers were easy prey.

Through all this, and through the forced landings, bale-outs, evacuations in the drink, through *all* extremes ran the golden thread of aircrew professionalism and teamwork. Lady Luck wasn't enough on her own. She needed to be helped and this was it. Any lingering dreams of Mosquitoes were swept aside. My sole ambition now would be to skipper a well-drilled crew, the best on the squadron, every man hand picked, utterly professional at his job and dedicated to the team.

Walking into the mess that night this noble goal receded somewhat. I suppose there were about two hundred and twenty men of all ranks on the course. Maybe a third were officers, and most had gravitated towards that small room. I reckoned that my time as an instructor made me a pretty good judge of character. But this was a lucky dip. I didn't have ten minutes or even ten seconds to interview each candidate and discover who would be dependable and who disastrous.

I paused at the bar to take stock and order a beer. Beside me were two Pilot Officers in relaxed conversation. They were both New Zealanders, both wearing a navigator's badge above the left breast pocket. I had wondered what kind of man it must take to wage war from behind a blackout curtain, oblivious to the drama and fireworks beyond. I listened out of idle curiosity.

One of them, a stocky figure with a light moustache, seemed to be the sort of tough-minded chap who knew the score. I introduced myself. His name was Bill Birnie. I warmed to him as we talked. He ran through his flying career to date, the inevitable eighteen-month progression of training courses. He seemed more than interested in my time as an instructor. He was obviously a capable individual, plain-speaking, quick-witted rather than cerebral but someone I would never have to think twice about. I asked if he was fixed up with a crew yet.

'Christ, no,' he replied with antipodean forthrightness, 'I only arrived a couple of hours ago.'

'Well,' I said, 'I'd like you to team-up with me, if that's all right.'

He held out his right hand, and the first member of my crew, a vital one, was in place.

Later that evening we found a second. Rob Bailey was a wireless operator with the rank of Pilot Officer. It was the rank that caught my eye. Only very few w/ops won a commission so early in their careers. Bill, for whom radio transmitters, morse and the rest were not totally foreign ground, was better placed to discuss Rob's time at radio school. I just listened and took in the uniform and the fact that Rob clearly knew his stuff.

He hailed from Croydon. He was tall, slim and blessed with the dark, aquiline looks that women tend to admire. With such advantages a degree of dash, a little flamboyance might have been only natural. In fact, he was a serious and very contained individual. This was no bad thing. Undisciplined thoughts and a cavalier mentality were no use to a w/op. But, truth be told, I saw in Rob someone above the common run of his trade. And that, I suppose, was how I compared myself to the other trainee pilots at Westcott. That, I suppose, was how I wanted the entire crew.

Bill and I met at breakfast the next morning. He was full of good ideas about the qualities we should look for during the day ahead. I asked him to shop around for a bomb aimer.

At ten o'clock the trainees assembled in a hangar. The three of us stationed ourselves on the periphery from where we could observe the proceedings. Already, there was a lot of movement and noise. The Chief Flying Instructor, W/Cdr Lind, stepped forward and had to call for quiet. He made the customary welcoming speech. I'd heard so many, I'm afraid I didn't take in much of this one – Bill, too, I think. He seemed more concerned to survey the potential bomb aimers within our purview.

W/Cdr Lind told us we had to the end of the day to complete our choice of crew. As soon as he finished speaking everything erupted ten times worse than before. Bill, who was obviously enjoying himself, shouldered his way into the crowd and disappeared from view. Five minutes later he emerged with a bronze-skinned giant in tow. This was Flight Sergeant Inia Maaka, the first Maori I'd ever met and, I knew immediately, the only bomb aimer for me.

'Just call me Mac,' he said, eyes sparkling, 'Everyone else does.' His was a voice full of droll humour, and his sentiments those of a natural team man. He said he had volunteered like most air bombers (their official title) hoping to fight this war as a pilot. He won a place on an Elementary Flying Training course but it wasn't

64

ABOVE: Dusk on the Prairies, and an Airspeed Oxford refuels at Penhold.

ABOVE: Success! The author (right) and six new Sergeant Pilots show off their wings at completion of their SFTS course.

LEFT: Author at the controls of an Oxford.

RIGHT: At Chedburgh to convert to heavies, left to right: Tubby; Norrie; Rob Bailey; author; Mac; Geoff; Bill.

BELOW: John Aitken and ND782 U after her 47th op. Days later she was crashed by a rookie pilot and only flew again at CU and LFS.

BELOW: Author in the cockpit of HK574 R, in the company of Rio Rita. She's dolled up in a Mexican hat, platform shoes and what looks strangely like Y-fronts worn inside out.

ABOVE: The first by night: an oil storage site at Fôret d'Englos on 9/10.8.44. Poor initial marking and the MC's demand for a 2-second undershoot contributed to some scattered bombing.

ABOVE: The first by day: a straightforward and uneventful trip to Lens marshalling yards, 11.8.44.

LEFT: Smoke, dust, confusion and, somewhere down there, enemy tank formations: Hamel, 14.8.44, the final army support op before the heavies returned to Germany.

BELOW: Formating on Mepal lanes on the return from Hamel: two AA Lancs snapped by Ron Mayhill in U-Uncle. The furthest is HK574 R with the author and his crew on board.

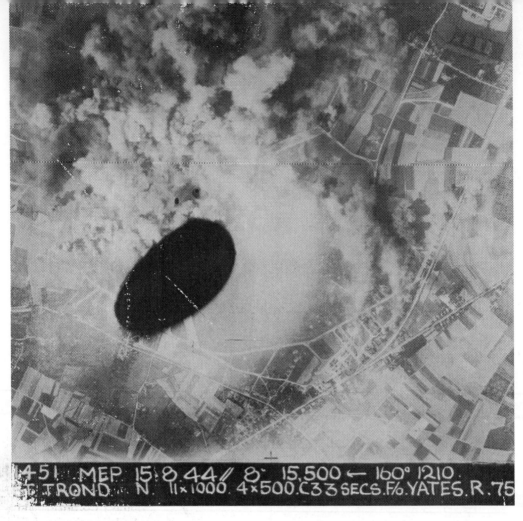

451 .MEP 15.8.44/ 8· 15.500 ← 160° 1210.
ST TROND. N. 11×1000. 4×500.C33 SECS.F/O.YATES.R.75

'. . . . . for the intrusion of a large thumbprint.' The daylight attack on No.1 Night-Fighter Wing, St Trond, 15.8.44.

RIGHT: All smiles for six of the crew after the St Trond raid. The seventh, Geoff Fallowfield, took the photograph.

`1519 MEP 25/26.8.44/NT 8 17.500 ←325° 0104`
`RUSSELHEIM. N1 1×4000 13×4.28SECS. F/o YATES R 75`

LEFT: Fire and darkness 1: Russelsheim, 25/26.8.44, a long hard night with enemy fighters taking their toll.

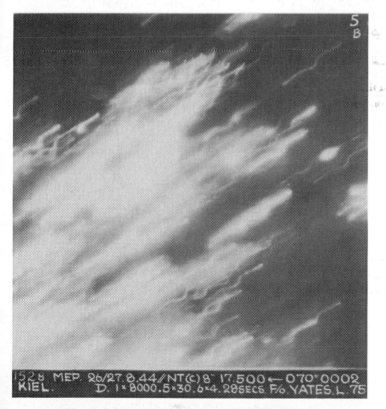

`1528 MEP. 26/27.8.44/NT(C)8 17.500 ←070°0002`
`KIEL. D. 1×8000.5×30.6×4.28SECS F/o YATES.L.75`

LEFT: Fire and darkness 2: Kiel, 26/27.8.44, another costly night for Bomber Command and a lively one for the author and crew.

RIGHT: Coming away from the débâcle at Doudeneville on 8.9.44, seen from the mid-upper turret.

BELOW: The infamous raid of 5.9.44 on Le Havre's old town.

LEFT: The last of the Le Havre raids: the attack of 10.9.44 on troop concentrations at Alvis, Montvilliers. Notwithstanding the wide distribution of TIs, Mac was credited with an aiming point.

BELOW: HK574 R at dispersal with groundcrew in attendance.

BELOW : Target photograph of the Kamen raid, 11.9.44. Moments after this was taken HK574 R was hit by flak and the author wounded.

BELOW: Staff and patients at Littleport. Author is back row centre with designs on Sister MacDonald. S/Ldr McCurry on his left. Bottom centre: Ron Mayhill, DFC; to his right Dave Moriarty, CGM.

RIGHT: In the midst of
the stream: looking back
from the astrodome with
at least thirty aircraft
visible in a typical,
daylight gaggle.

BELOW: In the first wave
of the attack: bombs begin
to impact on Walcheren
Island, 28.10.44.

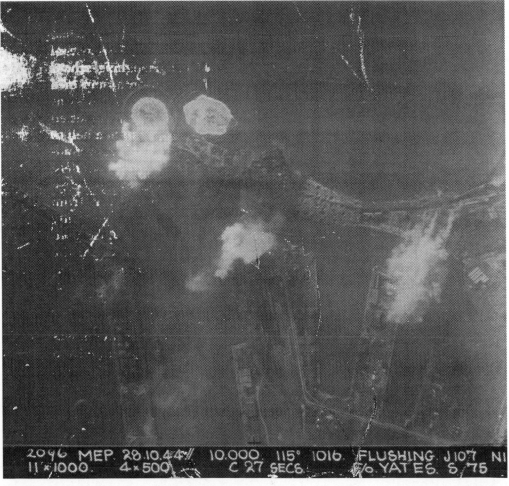

2046 MEP. 28.10.44// 10.000 115° 1016 FLUSHING J107 NI
11×1000. 4×500 C 27 SECS. F/o YATES. S 75

to be. Bombing school followed. But he clearly loved the job and there wasn't a hint of second best.

As he talked, my impressions of him became ever more favourable. No Englishman I'd met was so sincere and guileless about himself. Mac was simply a stranger to the inner tensions and vanities that make liars of the rest of us. He was mightily proud of his people who, I thought, must be formidable opponents in war if they were all like this chap. I began to see in him a military paragon. He had the heart of a lion. I don't think he was afraid of anything or any man. He had no need to be because he was built like a bunker. I felt that his loyalty would be a rich prize, if one deserved it. He was just the sort of chap one imagines walking steadfastly into the enemy's fire for the sake of his comrades. Well, the skies over Germany were fiery enough. Mac would be an example to us all.

Now we needed only two air gunners to complete the set. Mac wandered off, parting the scrum effortlessly. He returned a few minutes later with two extremely youthful Englishmen, introducing them as Sergeants Fallowfield and Close.

Geoff Fallowfield was a Londoner and still only eighteen. He had a bubbling, extrovert personality and an irrepressible sense of humour. He was a devotee of the 'always leave 'em laughing' school of human relations. Everything began and ended on a quip or a smile. He was made for the role of crew comedian. But there was more to him than that. A steely underside occasionally manifested itself. He was a competitive character who would fight like hell to avoid coming off second best. And he might need to. As a mid-upper gunner he would be perched just above the RAF roundels, an inviting target for an enemy fighter.

Norrie Close was younger still, by a month. He was from Wetherby in Yorkshire. Despite his youth he was a tough, gritty character – essential qualities for a rear gunner. From their exposed and freezing-cold turrets these men looked straight down the cannons of any fighter coming in to attack. They had to grit their teeth as the tracers ripped past, and pay the devil back with interest. The dangers were accepted as part of the job. But rear gunners took more than their share of casualties.

The one saving grace of their position was that if the aircraft was going down, the turret could be revolved through one-hundred and eighty degrees. The occupant could literally tumble out backwards and start counting. How often the rear gunner was the sole survivor by this means, I cannot say. All in all, the mid-upper gunner had the more enviable task.

Compared to Geoff, Norrie was a pensive lad with little to say for himself. But then, compared to Geoff, we none of us had. Norrie, though, didn't need to say a lot to tell me he was totally loyal and thoroughly dependable.

So there they were, my crew: a straight and level Kiwi; a ladykiller; a Maori warrior; and two young lads as different as chalk from cheese. In each his own way, I was proud of them all. I only hoped I would be worthy of their trust and loyalty.

We began training together on ground exercises. We had to get used to one another and to being part of a six-man unit. I was gratified by the effort and enthusiasm from everyone. A workmanlike team began to emerge. After two days we were taken to a satellite airfield at Oakley to meet my flying instructor, P/O Walker. And then it was time for the ride out to dispersal.

The Vickers Wellington Mark X (or the Wimpey as it was affectionately known) was a formidable jump from an Oxford. It was powered by two 1,500 horsepower Hercules radial engines. The ceiling was just over 15,000 feet and cruising speed one hundred and sixty-five mph. The nose and tail turrets housed a total of six .303in. machine-guns. At this stage, it was a misnomer to call Geoff a mid-upper gunner. That would have to wait until we converted to four-engine bombers. But in the Wellington he would man the front turret.

For the first few hours, though, I was in the hot seat. Once familiar with the cockpit layout the rest came fairly easily. The boys had a free ride while I flew three hours of circuits and bumps. Then we off-loaded the instructor and accelerated down the runway. I lifted off as captain of the aircraft and of my crew for the first time.

It had been a long, winding road from those days when my old pal, Cyril Downing, used to leave me wide-eyed at his escapades as an air gunner. Stationed in the turrets now were two lads no older than Cyril was on his last home leave. How I wished them a kinder fate than his. Still, we would train . . . and train hard. That was all we could do. The rest was a matter of luck.

We took up a Wellington nearly every day the weather permitted. Sometimes instrument flying occupied us, sometimes cross-country. Usually, these were dual (instructor-accompanied) flights. Quite quickly, though, we progressed to four-hour, cross-country solos. We flew well out over the North Sea and gave Bill plenty of practice with the Gee-box. This was a navigation system utilising timed radio pulses from three home-based ground stations. Their signals appeared as lines on a cathode-ray tube. By reference to charts marked with special grids the aircraft's track and position could be fixed with considerable accuracy. The system was a vast improvement over dead reckoning. But the limiting factor was its range. The radio pulses were good for only four hundred miles.

The focus of our training moved to the bombing range. Our bomb bay was kitted with smoke bombs, and Mac's instructor, F/Sgt Joy, came along to guide him in techniques at high and low level. Geoff and Norrie were introduced to cine-camera gun (CCG) exercises by their man, F/Sgt Bunn. The CCG was no Browning but with a bit of imagination it could be aimed like one. The first targets were drogues. Later the boys progressed to fighter affiliation. This elevated the target to a Hurricane in mock attack, realistic in every aspect save that we were never shot down.

Fighter affiliation also brought P/O Walker back on board to demonstrate the corkscrew, the approved method of evading a night-fighter. I thought I'd seen all there was to see and flown most of it myself. But this was quite different. P/O Walker seemed to be wrestling with everything at once: column hard forward; throttles open; left rudder and aileron. With amazing violence the Wellington swung down, round and bottomed out. A thousand feet later and making no attempt at a more fluid development, he heaved back the column and applied right rudder and aileron. The aircraft swung up, round and topped out. As the airspeed fell away he repeated the sequence two, three, four times. Our path and attitude scribed a giant corkscrew through the air. We poor innocents just groped for something to hold on to and grieved for our insides.

The technique was highly strenuous and tough enough to master in daylight when I could focus upon a clear horizon. At night the only point of reference was the seat of my pants. Both feet parted company from the rudder bar. Only the straps prevented my head from hitting the roof of the cockpit. But at least I could anticipate my own activity at the controls. The rest of the crew had no such advantage and surely found it hard to love the names of Junkers and Messerschmitt.

The manoeuvre was initiated on a gunner's shouted warning, 'Fighter coming in from port. Corkscrew, corkscrew!' As the stomach-churning began, and if they could articulate any other useful sounds, Norrie and Geoff were expected to give a running commentary on the Hurricane's progress. When the commotion had subsided normal flight could resume. In theory, this part was uncomplicated. The corkscrew was murder on the digestion. But if performed correctly it didn't alter course one iota.

I couldn't help but look at the Westcott flying instructors from a professional standpoint. They were not teacher-flyers like my ex-colleagues from South Cerney. They were not imbued with the same pride and motivation. Most of them were selected from tour-expired aircrew. Almost all were decorated. After the intensity and comradeship of life on a front-line squadron, instructing must have seemed like a world of shadows to them. Finding their work boring and without satisfaction, I think many merely went through the motions.

The heart of the problem was that OTUs were within the aegis of Bomber Command which, of course, had a primary and more preoccupying purpose. There was a second-best feel to everything. The aircraft were all hand-me-downs. Many of them were patently clapped out and, often, poorly maintained.

This would have been an intolerable state of affairs within Training Command. Life had its hazards there, too. But the accident rate in some OTUs was appalling, with up to twenty-five per cent of aircrews losing their lives. Both Commands taken together, accidents killed five thousand aircrew and injured three thousand more before the end of the war in Europe.

Between flights we attended classes on ground subjects, sometimes individually, sometimes as a crew. At last, the lurid details of German flak, searchlight and night-fighter tactics, ditching procedure and escape practice came to the fore.

Some Air Ministry desk pilot with an over-active imagination had the idea of pitching crews into the English countryside in the hours of darkness. Rendered mapless, fugitives under the law and forbidden all contact with the natives, we would learn something of escape from enemy territory. One dark, March evening the boys and I were ordered on board a truck and blindfolded. It was eight p.m. The truck trundled away and, seemingly an age later, arrived at a very quiet spot. We were set free. The police and Home Guard were looking for us, we were told. We must evade them and find our own way back to Oakley before dawn. Then the truck drove off into the night.

'Well, Bill?' Mac enquired, 'You're the bloke who tells us which way to go.'

'A piece of cake,' Bill replied with authority, 'All we want is a roadsign.'

At this point in the war, with the risk of a German invasion something of the past and the Allies fighting their way across France, roadsigns had made a welcome reappearance. We sauntered down a narrow lane and soon found one. But it had been uprooted and lay uselessly upon the ground like some beast in *rigor mortis*. Evidently, another crew with mischievous intent had been this way already. Bill was outraged. Left to him, no fate would have been too unkind, no punishment too draconian for them. Geoff, on the other hand, correctly divined the whole exercise to be one big joke. He slipped into his Max Miller role and, gradually, the funny side of things took over.

For a time we stumbled around quite lost. Then we found a farm-house. A democratic debate followed: did we want to see our beds that night, or not? The vote was six to nil. Orders were duly set aside and our purdah forsaken.

I knocked on the door. The hall light flickered on. The door opened by six inches and the face of an elderly woman peered out. She, in turn, was confronted by six staring, male faces and six flying jackets – surely the crew of a German bomber, desperate men shot down and on the run. She froze, wide-eyed. I tried to reassure her in my most calming tones. I knew that Geoff, just behind me, must be itching to help with a couple of one-liners. I prayed that he wouldn't click his heels or force through his teeth the words, 'Get on viz it, Schickelgrüber'. But somehow even he sensed the over-riding need of the hour and shackled his tongue.

No doubt relieved that we hadn't already forced her back into the hall, waving Lugers under her nose, the poor woman regained some composure. Rather shakily, she gave us directions. We thanked her. Each party hurried away, we to the pitch black lane, she to her tele-phone or, possibly, her bottle of gin.

Next, we found a pub. I think every one of us could taste the beer just by looking at the place. There was never the least hope that self-denial would carry us safely past. The boys sat down with the locals while I ordered six pints of best. By closing time the landlord had drawn a detailed map for us. We set off in the highest possible spirits and, six miles later, caroused our way into the guardhouse at Oakley.

We weren't debriefed on arrival or asked how, given the injunc-tion against talking to the outside world, we smelt so unmistakably of alcohol. The sum total of escape experience gained was nil. But no one could deny it was entertaining.

Shortly after this our flying programme switched to nights. I had two hours dual, then flew solo with my crew. Night after night we practised take offs and landings or we flew five-hour cross-countries topped off with bombing on the local range. Night flights were always strictly weather permitting. But five hours was ample time for conditions to deteriorate. This happened from time to time. Very occasionally, we were sent into the air when it was never advisable in the first place.

We took off at ten p.m. one night with a gale blowing already and rain lashing at the windscreen. Even as we climbed away we were given a heavy buffeting. We reached our specified altitude with no improvement. The cloud was unremittingly thick, and I had no recourse but to fly by instruments.

Over the North Sea, inbound but still two hundred miles from land, the airspeed indicator fell quite suddenly to zero. I guessed that the pitot head was solid with ice. That left me with the artificial horizon, the altimeter, and only engine revs to gauge my airspeed. I informed the crew, then brought the Wellington down to 3,000 ft, hoping that the pitot head might thaw out. It didn't. The cloud didn't improve, either.

An hour passed. Bill's latest Gee fix indicated that we were nearing the coast of East Anglia. Rob raised Oakley control and explained our problem. Visibility was zero there, too, and landing out of the question. 'You're the last Oakley aircraft still airborne', they told Rob. It wasn't much consolation. Five minutes later came instructions to head for the emergency runway at Woodbridge on the Suffolk coast. Together with Carnaby in Yorkshire and Manston in Kent, Woodbridge operated the FIDO system (Fog Intensive Dispersal Of). It employed a continuous line of heat-generating burners along each side of the strip. This was reputed to be three miles long and the wreck-strewn dispersal ten times normal area. The intended clientele were bombers returning from target damaged and unable to make base. But on such a night as this everyone was welcome.

Rob contacted Woodbridge control to tell them who we were and why we were coming in. Bill gave me a new course to steer. At 500 ft we broke through the veil of cloud. Before us, to our relief, lay two parallel lines of flaming gas burners. They stretched magnificently into the distance like some stupendous setting for a Wagnerian opera. We received permission to land. The crew took up their safety stations.

I couldn't risk over-estimating our airspeed and stalling on the approach. It would have to be low, fast and engine-assisted. I guessed a speed of one hundred and forty mph, lowered the undercarriage and applied twenty degrees of flaps. Between the rows of fire I throttled back hard and waited for the speed to diminish. I hadn't allowed for the flames, though. We sailed on and on in the heat and turbulence that they generated. But as is the way with everything that, as they say, goes up, eventually the Wellington stalled and came down to earth. We were still carrying a lot of speed. It took an eternity to bring the aircraft to a standstill. When it was done, cheers erupted from every corner of the aircraft.

It was a great moment, and it told me that the crew possessed a real sense of solidarity now. If I had listened more closely, though, I might have heard one note of apprehension beneath those cheers. As far as I knew, this was the first brush with trouble for any of the boys. It was not an easy christening but they all performed creditably. I thought it augured well for the future. But for one of them the future might have darkened appreciably that night, and become more difficult to face up to.

This incident was against the backdrop of a black harvest of accidents in the Oakley circuit. The recurrent cause was collision, almost always at night. It was cruel and useless waste, even denying its victims the soldierly memorial of 'killed-in-action'. Some of it must have been preventable. The lives lost were no less precious for being those of trainees.

In fairness, our instructors continually urged us to watch out, and not just for errant Wellingtons. Enemy fighters were said to prowl the circuit in search of easy prey. We heard of no firm sightings but I was always keyed up for evasive action or an overshoot if a kite came out of nowhere to touch down. Norrie and Geoff were our eyes. I reminded them constantly, although the 'Yes, skipper!' that they fired back relaxed by degrees to a 'Y-e-s, skipper.' Whether this was meant to imply calm efficiency or a certain familiarity with the skipper's obsession, I could never quite decide. Either way, the boys did the job.

One evening we were briefed to participate in a Nickel raid. Nickel was the code name for a leaflet drop. The target was Paris. It was not an operational flight, of course. But it was exactly like one in terms of preparation. The aircraft were fuelled and loaded, and at 2200 hrs the crews were trucked out to dispersal. Filled with anticipation, we climbed aboard and waited for the go-ahead. The weather was atrocious. For thirty minutes we sat at the ready, listening to the rain beat relentlessly against the fuselage. Then word arrived that everything was scrubbed for twenty-four hours. The following night we were not called to Briefing. Some other crew took up our Wellington and bombed Paris with paper. We were consigned to the humdrum routine of a five-hour cross-country.

On 14 May we flew another cross-country, concluding with fighter affiliation. It was our finale in a Wellington. Two days later W/Cdr Lind conducted me through yet another Chief Flying Instructor's test. Then we left No. 11 OTU for a week's leave. The NZ boys disappeared in the direction of London. I headed home with an Above Average assessment in my logbook and a strong sense of satisfaction with each member of my crew.

From here we had two more, very brief courses ahead of us, one to convert to four-engined aircraft, one at a Finishing Unit. Then would come the long-awaited operational posting. This leave, then, was the last before we began our tour of duty. Though precious, the days passed swiftly and unremarkably. The familiar, sweet rhythm of home life was not disturbed. Raw nerve ends were not exposed, anxieties were not shared. The order of the day was that quiet forbearance which other peoples ridicule but the English know to be the mark of true character.

Towards the end of the week, I received instructions to report to No. 1653 Heavy Conversion Unit at Chedburgh, about six miles from Bury St Edmunds. The time had come when we must part, for all we knew, never to meet again. I said goodbye first to my sister and then to my mother. They were both tearful, and didn't manage many words. My father, who was easily the most sentimental member of the family, kept a tight check on his feelings throughout. Perhaps his mind went back thirty years to his own leave-taking for service with the Royal Army Medical Corps. He went to the Dardanelles in 1915 and saw all that war could do to flesh and bone. Now his own son stood in uniform before him, hand outstretched. He shook it firmly. But not finding in that the expression of his heart, he kissed my cheek.

'Don't forget your mother, son. A letter every week means a lot to her,' he said. But it was as much his way of telling me to take care until I could return for good to the family home.

An old idea occurred to me. 'I'll do better than that. I'll drop my letters down our chimney. That's a promise.'

It *was* a promise, of sorts. In a few weeks I would have my hands on a four-engined, front-line bomber and I knew exactly where to fly it at the first chance.

The rail journey to Chedburgh was tedious. It seemed that whenever I boarded a train, down poured the rain. Damp and depressed, I reported to the guardhouse in late afternoon. I bumped into Bill in the mess. The sight of him, with his bustling enthusiasm and no-nonsense manner, cheered me instantly. He said he had travelled up from London with Mac. Both Geoff and Norrie had arrived but of Rob there was as yet no sign.

As we left the dining room that evening Rob finally bowled in. True to form, he had found it difficult to disentangle himself from his girlfriend's arms, and missed his train. I told him not to worry about it. At least I had a full crew again.

Chedburgh was equipped with Short Stirling Mk 1 and Mk 3 bombers. At our first visit to dispersal we were awestruck by the Stirling's lunging demeanour and mammoth proportions. We walked under and around it, gazing incredulously at the huge wings, huge wheels, a huge bomb-bay and the four huge Bristol Hercules VI engines. Compared to the Wellington, everything was oversize. I sat at the controls a good twenty feet above the ground, feeling as if I was perched on the church tower at home. The Hercules engines developed 1,635 hp each, giving a maximum ceiling of 17,000 ft and a top speed of two hundred and fifty mph at 10,000 ft. For all this size and power, the bomb load was relatively light, with a maximum range of 2,000 miles.

Four-engined aircraft required the attentions of a Flight Engineer, bringing the crew complement to seven. Mac, Geoff and Norrie had, basically, recruited an English flight sergeant in his early thirties named Denys Westell. There was a tendency for the crew to select itself. This was contrary to my original expectation but it worked well in practice. So, when I met Denys it was more or less a formality.

I was struck immediately by his gentle, almost unworldly disposition. He was clearly a man of many personal qualities, among them kindness, modesty, self-effacement. But not one of them was warlike. He might have been a curate in some quiet, rural backwater. And here was I, inducting him into the brief and violent career of a bomber crew with all its pressure, rough-hewn comradeship and uncompromising language. It occurred to me that the shock might be too much for him.

But Denys proved me wrong. He was completely unflappable. I never heard him complain, never heard him swear. Privately, he must have thought me an ogre. But he accepted the skipper's not always kindly interventions without a murmur. The boys nicknamed him Tubby, an affectionate reference to his undeniably rotund physique. He didn't mind and the name stuck. We quickly forgot that he'd ever been called anything else.

The course took some time to get going, largely because weather conditions were so miserable. It was eighteen days before we flew.

In the interim we woke up one morning to the biggest possible news. It was 6 June 1944 and the long-awaited invasion of Normandy had begun. Bomber Command now had the urgent task of supporting the invasion forces in addition to attacking the enemy's supply capacity. For the moment, the area offensive against Germany's towns and cities was set aside, a development not lost on future aircrew.

At last, on 20 June, we took up our first Stirling. With the course now properly underway I could see how inexact was the whole concept of conversion. 'Introduction' might have been a more accurate term. There was just enough time to form a passing acquaintance with the aircraft, but little more. I found it to have few vices. However, there was a marked tendency to swing off line under take-off acceleration and on landing. One had to work at the throttles to keep it straight on the runway. But, oversize or not, the Stirling was transformed in the air and was a delight to fly.

After four hours of dual instruction I was sent off for another two hours of solo take offs and landings. This was Tubby's first prolonged experience of flying. He found it arduous. He became extremely familiar with the insides of the RAF's greaseproof paper sick-bags. But he bore the discomfort and embarrassment with his own, peculiar brand of mild-mannered stoicism. Within a week we were again flying five-hour, night cross-countries concluded with fighter affiliation. Tubby surely dreaded the moment Norrie would rasp, 'Corkscrew to starboard'. But as we spent more time in the air his digestive system caught up with the rest of him and the problem gradually went away.

Tubby's job as flight engineer chiefly entailed monitoring the performance, oil temperatures and fuel consumption of the engines. He had the responsibility of identifying any dangers from this quarter, making running repairs and, ultimately, of recommending a return to base if the situation warranted it. He also had a role in the take-off drill. As I opened the four throttles he placed his hand behind mine. At maximum revs and with the speed building down the runway, I removed my hand and left him to screw down the throttle locks. I was then free to employ both hands for a clean lift off the runway.

To these I added one more duty. On the final approach at night it was helpful if Tubby called out the airspeed. That left me free to concentrate on staying in the 'green' of the flight path indicator. It also meant that Tubby was kept on his toes every bit as long as the poor pilot.

Well past midnight on 12 July we succeeded in Stirling Mk 3 LJ444 where we had failed two months earlier in a Wimpey. We rumbled down the runway with a bomb bay full of leaflets and took off for Paris. Our attacking force comprised three aircraft, all Chedburgh Stirlings. Twenty-one totally green and nervous novices were off to make their literary contribution to the invasion, and to thumb their noses at the enemy in the process.

We didn't have the benefit of target indicators or a master bomber. We didn't need them. The skies were clear and the Parisian appetite for night-life rendered the blackout less than absolute. The Seine curved unmistakably through the city in a sensual arc. There were a few searchlights but no flak or fighters, thankfully. We would not have been the first trainees to die on a nickel raid. Mac sent his leaflets showering down to be picked up by the eager hands below. The Allies, we had just informed them, were coming to liberate Paris. It was as close as we were likely to get to all those French girls who the British Army could expect to encounter in the flesh, dammit.

We completed our last cross-country from Chedburgh on 17 July 1944. We had notched up a grand total of twenty-two hours flying by day and nineteen by night. Whoever was in charge of such matters had obviously decided that forty-odd hours was enough. It wasn't. We felt that we were being processed like pork in a pie factory.

Thankfully, we would not be flying the dear old Stirling operationally. It's bombing height, generally 10,000–12,000 ft, was meat and drink to German gunners and its serviceability record was poor. It had been largely withdrawn from front-line duty in favour of the Lancaster and the Halifax. In fairness to the Stirling, it never let us down though I doubted its capacity to stay airborne if one of its engines failed on take off. But now we were going to fly a truly superb aircraft. Our posting to No. 3 Lancaster Finishing School at Feltwell in Norfolk was on the mess notice board. On 23 July we left Chedburgh aboard an RAF bus, and reported to Feltwell that same day.

I soon discovered that everything that had been said and written about the Avro Lancaster was true. Some products of the hand of man have that uncanny capacity to pull at the heartstrings, and the Lancaster was one such. Everything about it was just right. Its muscular, swept lines were beautiful to look at. It flew with effortless grace and had a precise, weighted feel. It made the pilot's job easy. You could throw it all over the skies if you had the inclination and some physical strength. It had tremendous power from those four Rolls-Royce Merlins. At 25,000 ft, its ceiling was vastly superior to the Stirling's. And it was fast, only a whisker short of 300 mph. In every department it outstripped all other four-engined aircraft of the time. At 20,000 ft the standard bomb load of 14,000 lb was equivalent to that of two Flying Fortress B-17s.

Early in our course at Feltwell I had the opportunity of a direct comparison with the much-vaunted American aircraft. Flying Lancaster R5674 over 'bomber country' one morning we spotted a B-17. We came up from behind and formated a few yards to his starboard. I feathered the starboard outer airscrew and kept station with no difficulty at all. A couple of minutes later, with all my boys waving like crazy, I restarted the engine and peeled off. The Yanks would have been perfectly entitled to report us. Perhaps they didn't relish the publicity.

We flew R5674 virtually uninterrupted through the course, having soloed after two hours in it. Sadly, on the night of 18 December when we were well into our operational tour, this same Lancaster collided with another Feltwell kite, R5846, at Hockwold on the downwind leg of the circuit. Fourteen young lives were extinguished in an instant.

After eight hours and thirty minutes of day-time flying and four hours and thirty minutes at night we were deemed ready for front-line activity. But these meagre hours were in no way adequate. I had driven everyone as hard as possible in pursuit of crew efficiency. Team spirit and discipline were good. But there was still work to do. For example, Tubby had logged only fifty hours in the air, hardly sufficient given the close engagement of pilot and engineer.

In general, such a state of affairs must have contributed to the high loss-rate of aircrew early in their tours. Better standards, better crews, better bombing would have flowed from even another twenty hours in the air. As it was, for us (and, no doubt, for everyone) the learning process would have to extend into operational flying.

We duly received our posting – No. 75 Squadron, Royal New Zealand Air Force, operating within 3 Group Bomber Command from Mepal, six miles west of Ely. Our last day at Feltwell dawned on 4 August. Later that morning we were to travel by RAF bus to our new home. I met Bill in the mess, devouring his breakfast with a will. A New Zealander on his way to a famous New Zealand squadron, he was in an ebullient frame of mind and more determined than ever to get on with it and do a decent job. William George Birnie never lacked spirit.

We gathered outside the crew room with Mac, Norrie, Geoff and Tubby to await our transport. Rob hadn't turned up. No one had seen anything of him since the previous evening. Our bus was ready. The duty officer checked off our names from the roster. A telephone call was made and, after a lengthy delay, returned. I approached the duty officer and asked what was going on.

'You'll have to go as you are', he replied.

'But my wireless operator . . . What's the matter with him? Has he reported sick?'

'Sorry, your wireless operator is scrubbed. You'll have to pick one up later.'

It took a moment to adjust to what he had said. I felt leaden inside. How could it happen, I asked myself . . . all that work together and now this. The boys boarded the bus. No one spoke. I followed them and the door was closed on Rob Bailey. We never heard another word from or about him.

CHAPTER SIX

FRENCH FOR BEGINNERS

Seventy-five RNZAF Squadron became an integral part of Bomber Command by accident rather than design. In 1938, the New Zealand government decided to order thirty of the very new Vickers Wellington Mk 1c bombers. This required dispatching a contingent of aircrew to England to fly the Wellingtons home and that, in turn, required training before they could do so. The first Flight of six signals airmen arrived in England in February, 1939. In June of that year, they were posted to the New Zealand Flight at 75 Squadron, then based at RAF Marham in Norfolk. They joined just two other New Zealanders already there.

With the declaration of war, the New Zealand government immediately waived its purchase of the Wellingtons. There followed a request to the New Zealanders that the Flight at 75 be maintained and, indeed, expanded into a new and uniquely Kiwi squadron. This was agreed, and on 4 April 1940 No. 75 RNZAF Squadron was established at Feltwell as a component of 3 Group, Bomber Command and allotted the identification letters AA.

The first operational flight was a few days earlier on 27 March. It was a Nickel raid on Hamburg involving three aircraft. On 21 May, the squadron suffered its first loss amid much bravery and self-sacrifice over Dinant, Belgium. Gallantry was no stranger down the ensuing years. Numerous decorations were awarded, the highest a Victoria Cross for some magnificent wing-walking over the Dutch coast to put out a petrol fire. The last aircraft to be lost was on 24 April 1945. At the end of hostilities in Europe the squadron had flown 8,017 sorties, more than any other in 3 Group, and recorded the fourth highest number of raids throughout Bomber Command. In the process it dropped 21,600 tons of bombs and laid 2,344 sea mines. In making this mammoth contribution 193 aircraft were lost, the second highest rate of loss of any Bomber Command squadron.

The winning of that Victoria Cross is worth recounting, not simply because of the dazzling and totally unpremeditated valour of the deed but because of the humbleness of the hero, Jimmy Ward, and the sadness of his passing not long after.

It goes back a long way, to early July 1941 when I was practising loops in my Tiger Moth and my head was still full of Stanford Tuck and Cobber Kane. An unassuming sergeant from Wanganui, New Zealand, named J.A. Ward, arrived on station at Feltwell on 22 June 1941. He was a day short of his twenty-second birthday. Seventeen days later he already had five raids under his belt and was about to embark on his sixth, to Münster. It was the squadron's second visit there in three nights.

The pilot and captain of the aircraft was a Canadian, S/Ldr R.P. Widdowson. Ward was second pilot. They took off at 2310 hrs on board a brand-new Wellington Mk 1c. It was one of ten Wimpeys from the squadron in a total of forty-nine going to the city. The trip out was uneventful. Widdowson and his crew bombed successfully and turned for home. They crossed the Dutch border still without incident. But as safety beckoned in the form of the Dutch coast and the silvery black North Sea, a volley of cannon shells smashed up through the fuselage. The rear gunner was hit in the foot. But he saw the attacker, an Me 110, long enough to get off a burst. It was accurate. The fighter flipped over and fell to earth, trailing a plume of smoke. The Wimpey was saved from a follow-up attack. But it was in a parlous state. Half the rudder was shot away, the elevators damaged, hydraulics ruptured, flaps gone and the bomb doors had fallen open. Worse, a petrol pipe feeding the starboard engine had been severed and the slipstream blasted fire into the night. The fabric over the wing and fuselage was burning away steadily, exposing the pale bones of the Wimpey's geodetic grid.

Widdowson ordered preparations for a bale-out and sent his second pilot out of the cockpit. As an afterthought and surely not expecting much success, he told Ward to try to put out the fire. The young man from Wanganui duly passed the instruction to the navigator and w/op. All three began tearing at the fuselage fabric. Ward shot a jet from the fire extinguisher through the resultant hole but the slipstream was too strong. Then he seized upon a canvas engine cover (which was only on board to raise Widdowson's seat squab because the height adjuster was jammed).

'Think I'll hop out with this', he said with startling simplicity.

Horrified by his all-too-obvious sincerity the others protested as loudly as they could. It was useless. Ward was absolutely intent on climbing out onto the wing. He could, he said, stuff the canvas into

79

the hole where the blaze was seated. The other two only persuaded him to clip on a parachute and rope himself to the navigator's chest.

He went out via the astrodome into the teeth of a roaring, icy gale. Somehow he held on to the cover whilst punching and kicking through the fabric skin to gain purchase on the airframe. Hand over hand, step by step, keeping his body as close to the aircraft as his chest-pack would allow, Ward strove on. Down the fuselage and across the starboard wing he went, clinging like a spider, until he reached the gaping hole beside the engine.

The heat was intense. Flames still blasted past him. He let go one hand from the airframe and thrust the canvas down into the hole. He held it there until he could take the pain no more. But as soon as he withdrew his hand the slipstream began to work the canvas out of the hole. Ward had another try. Again the heat beat him and this time the canvas was free and past him before he could move, billowing into the black.

He could do no more and, anyway, the flames were much reduced. Tiring fast, Ward began the slow, return journey as he had come, defying the gale to slip back through the astrodome into the relative safety of his crewmates' arms. The fire died away not long after, partly through Ward's efforts but also because most of the combustible fabric was already gone. Even so, the Wimpey kept flying. Widdowson put her down at Newmarket at 0430 hrs. Given the damage to the hydraulics he must have been delighted when the undercarriage came down and locked. But rolling along the flarepath he discovered that the brakes were shot. A barbed wire fence on the airfield perimeter finally brought a halt to the night's heartstopping events.

The very next night the squadron went back to Münster yet again. There was no wing-walking this time, though.

For his supreme airmanship Widdowson was awarded the DFC. The rear gunner, Sgt Alan Box, received a DFM. The brave navigator who had roped himself to Ward was Sgt L.A. Lawton. Later he would win the Air Force Cross. But, of course, the hero of the hour and of the whole squadron was Jimmy Ward. His extraordinary courage was recognised at the highest level and a Victoria Cross recommended, to the wild acclaim of everyone on the station. It was approved in August.

After this Jimmy was given his own captaincy. His eleventh raid was to Hamburg on the night of 15 September 1941. Over the city his Wimpey was hit several times by AA fire. The w/op and rear gunner managed to parachute but were soon taken prisoner. Jimmy

Ward, VC perished on board with the other members of his crew.

Through that one action over the Dutch coast Jimmy became, in effect, a mascot for the squadron. Number 75 Squadron was becoming renowned as a press-on, some might say a chop, outfit. Jimmy's unselfish example gilded an otherwise stark reputation. It was a reminder that heroism lies among the unassuming and the ordinary like water in the rocks. The VC was Jimmy's but it brought pride to every airman at Feltwell. Really, he should not have died. Fate should have shielded him. Instead, he was laid to rest with his three boys in Ohlsdorf Cemetery, Hamburg.

This, then, was the proud history of the squadron to whose roll our lowly names were added on 4 August 1944. We were part of an effort to rebuild. Two weeks earlier 75 had sustained a record loss of seven Lancasters out of twenty-six sent against a synthetic oil refinery at Homberg. A town that was once synonymous only with an unfashionable felt hat had become 75's bogey, more feared than Essen or Berlin. But July still had a bitter harvest in store. Three consecutive raids on Stuttgart over four nights cost four more losses. Then at dawn on the 30th another crew went down over the Normandy battlefield. Forty per cent of the squadron had been lost in little over a week. Morale would bounce back with amazing speed. It always did. But for a while, a sense of ill fortune and mortality must have pervaded everything at Mepal.

We were assigned to B Flight under S/Ldr Garth Gunn, a New Zealander (as were the A and C Flight Commanders and the Squadron CO, W/Cdr John Leslie, AFC). Garth was looked upon generally as able but very demanding. Before coming to Mepal he was an OTU instructor and this similarity in our backgrounds may have been the reason I always found him perfectly approachable and helpful. In any event, he soon set about repairing the damage of Rob's departure. He located a spare w/op in the pool and duly introduced me to one Warrant Officer S.A. Bain, also late of New Zealand.

Archie Bain was twenty-eight years old, balding, diminutive and with a robust cast of mind and a ready wit. He also had some valuable operational experience. He had flown fourteen trips on another squadron before the fifteenth to Nuremberg on 30 March 1944 ended on a wide, sandy North African beach. As Archie sketched out the story I became convinced that he was the man for us. For two months he had laboured across several hundred miles of Algeria and Morocco before crossing the Strait of Gibraltar. The Navy afforded him a berth back to England. He refused the usual survivor's leave, insisting on returning to ops as soon as possible – but with another squadron, preferably 75. Group HQ could not object to a New Zealander seeking transfer to the New Zealand squadron, and granted his request.

At the time I didn't ascribe any significance to this relapse of the usual, fierce squadron loyalty. But Archie was the most superstitious person I ever met. I am sure that during those final, tortuous hours on board his Lancaster P-Peter and in the hard days that followed, he nurtured a growing obsession. Squadron, skipper, target, aircraft letter . . . all were cast out like malevolent spirits. No echo of that night could be allowed to return. The new posting was his assurance of a fresh start.

No doubt, Archie would have felt very much more assured had he joined an experienced crew. Everyone knew that flak and night-fighters had no mercy for rookies. The evidence mounted all the time. Two replacement crews who arrived the day before us were soon logged FTR (Failed To Return). The skippers were F/O Brunton and F/Sgt King. After just a week at Mepal, and on their first raid, F/O Brunton and his men were shot down whilst carrying out army support at Mare de Magne. Both gunners were killed and the bomb aimer taken prisoner, but F/O Brunton and the others crossed Allied lines. Before the month was out F/Sgt King and his crew failed to return from Stettin. All but the skipper perished.

Bomber Command spread the fruits of operational wisdom via a familiarisation flight for every new skipper. This deposited him amidst a senior crew for his first op. He was there just to look, listen and learn and to carry back the lessons to his own crew. It came to be called the 'second dickey flight'. In Jimmy Ward's day five such trips were deemed necessary, and navigators had to do the same. But losses proved unsustainable and one, pilot-only, trip was substituted not long after.

As my turn approached, all I could think was, 'This is the moment of truth. This is my baptism of fire. Am I up to it?' Any bravado that I had displayed beforehand melted away like snow in the midday sun. Outwardly, I tried to maintain an air of calm and quiet confidence. But, goodness knows, my stomach was in knots and from time to time my knees felt weak. The Battle Order for the night of 8 August was posted on the Flight notice board. There was my name together with the crew of F/O John Aitken in Lancaster U-Uncle. The target was a large petrol storage complex at Lucheux in northern France. Clear skies were expected and so were night-fighters.

We were trucked out to dispersal as the light was fading. I followed the crew on board. They were all very young. John was the eldest at twenty-one. There wasn't much room for an extra man. I began to realise that the second dickey could be a burden to his hosts, no doubt the more so for being as keyed up and restless as I undoubtedly was. It didn't help to be doing nothing while the others were immersed in activity. I kept out of the way, anxious to get going but fearful of the possible consequences. The checks were interminable. Eventually, though, there was some action. The Merlins coughed into life, and the crackle from forty-eight exhaust stubs swelled to a single, glorious pitch. Pre-taxi checks followed. Then we swung out to join the long line of Lancasters snaking towards the take-off area. Yet more checks, pre-take-offs, ratcheted up the tension.

Finally, we were poised beside the flight caravan. Life had certainly taken a serious turn. The joy of flying which I had discovered over Stony one July morning long ago, and which I had cherished ever since, was far removed from this. For the next three hours I would have not an ounce of influence over my fate.

John brought the Merlins to full revs. Every panel and rivet was vibrating. The tailplane was dancing. Then the caravan flashed a blessed green and John released his hold. Even as U-Uncle gathered momentum and bore us aloft I began to feel happier. By the time we eased into our climbing turn some sense of adventure, of a voyage of discovery, had returned. I could not explain this sudden conversion but it was extremely welcome.

We crossed the French coast as the stars were beginning to show. Straight ahead of us the horizon was aglow. Searchlights positioned along the banks of the Somme were swinging back and forth, their beams criss-crossing in vain. At least we were safe from their grasp tonight. Some distance on, though, flak burst in the path of the bomber stream with more deadly intent. We flew through unscathed, nothing coming close. In no time, it seemed to me, we were running in to the target, bumping along in the slipstream of those ahead.

Already, Lucheux seemed to have been thoroughly clobbered tonight. Fierce fires were burning. But into their bright centre the Pathfinders dropped yet more red TIs (Target Indicators). The slowly-articulated words of our bomb aimer drifted over the intercom, 'left . . . left . . . steady,' ending with a shouted, 'Bombs going'. We scarcely needed telling. To the accompaniment of a loud and rapid 'thump, thump . . .', U-Uncle bucked like a stag and shot upward four or five hundred feet. That took me by surprise. I had no idea that the aircraft would respond so positively.

John held U-Uncle straight and level until the photo-flash burst below. There was no point in hanging around now. We banked away from the target and turned on to a homeward course. Looking back from the astrodome I saw a pall of smoke rising to 10,000 ft. Thousands of tons of *Wehrmacht* petroleum were burning. Surely, it was the end of the Lucheux petrol dumps.

Over the Channel John said the magic word: 'coffee'. It was a signal to relax a little. I poured eight cups from our flasks and carried one to each man. The stuff tasted awful. But this was a regular ritual for homeward-bound crews, a celebration of being past the worst, of adding one more to the total. The second dickey, an old hand now, had special reason to celebrate.

We touched down on the Mepal flarepath at 0133 hrs after two hours and fifty minutes in the air. I had witnessed a well-drilled crew in action. Indeed, the whole show was impressive. The marking was amazingly accurate, the bombing concentrated. I'd had my first taste of searchlights and flak but saw no night-fighter activity despite the warnings earlier. Indeed, it had all been quieter than I expected. To my surprise it was reported that three of Mepal's twenty aircraft were engaged by enemy fighters. Two of them took some damage . . . but no casualties.

After de-briefing I thanked John and complimented his crew on a highly professional performance, especially the engineer who, to accommodate me, had been on his feet for almost the entire trip. Next came the canteen and a hugely unrationed breakfast of eggs and bacon. Then, at last, I could return to my hut and my narrow, welcoming, steel-framed bed.

For some time I lay awake as the excitement and tension left me only slowly. I told myself the boys would be glad to see me back. It was necessary to distil the night's events, to arrive at a useful appraisal for their benefit. Maybe it was the rum issue and the white blockbusters dished out by the medical orderly, but I couldn't focus my mind. As if on a conveyor belt, the images and sounds of the raid revisited me: the rushing air; the hypnotic drone of the engines; the searchlights scanning ceaselessly; the smoke-strewn flight path; the fury on the ground; the shout of the bomb aimer as his load tore free; and the turn for home . . . sweet, safe home.

Finally, the pills and plain mental exhaustion took over. I lapsed into a deep sleep. But then, I did not know that the following night I would fly again, this time with my own crew.

That morning I was at B Flight when Garth Gunn received the customary telephone call. He closeted himself away to draw up his contribution to the Battle Order, matching crews and serviceable aircraft. A little later he called me over.

'Well, Yates,' he said, 'no doubt you and your boys want to get on with it. I'm giving you S-Sugar for tonight's op. She's a lucky lady. Look after her and she'll get you home.'

S-Sugar had already returned her crews from fifty or so targets. She held the squadron record though, probably, there were older kites which had been transferred to the station from other 3 Group squadrons. Old kites did not always handle particularly well. But since my only experience up to this point was training aircraft of dubious mechanical integrity, that was hardly my most pressing concern.

Bill rounded-up everyone. He told them to grab a quick bite to eat – there was an air test to fly. We cycled out to dispersal (none of us owned a car, whilst I couldn't even drive). We boarded Lancaster Mk 1 LL866 S-Sugar and were lifting off the runway before two o'clock. We were only airborne for twenty minutes. But in that time each crew member completed his individual checks. We touched down fully satisfied with the aircraft. Back at dispersal I signed Form F700 to that effect and hopped on my cycle. I passed a Matador bowser which had been reversed under the starboard wing of another Lanc.

'How many gallons?' I shouted.

'Same as yesterday', came the reply.

That sounded good to me: another shallow penetration into France. Since April the combined air forces had been under the direction of Eisenhower. Their function was tactical support of the Allied invasion. Virtually every day, RAF and USAAF bombers pounded petrol and oil dumps, marshalling yards, ammunition dumps, railway junctions, anything that German forces were using to keep supplied. Such targets weren't exactly soft. But neither were they in the same category as Berlin, Hamburg, the Ruhr or anywhere else in the Third Reich. As beginners, we had every reason to be grateful.

The tannoy announced Briefing for 1800 hrs. Feeling very apprehensive, we entered a room filled with raucous babble. I guess the worst fears and pent-up nerves of one hundred and twenty young men had to find some kind of outlet, and this din was it. Cigarettes played their part, too. The air was thick with smoke, to which the crew of S-Sugar lost no time in adding. It was our only calming device. But my stomach still felt like a lead balloon and the palms of my hands were sweating.

Then, as if a conductor had lifted his baton, the shouts and the chatter subsided. To the accompaniment of scraping chairs we all stood. The Squadron Commander, W/Cdr Leslie, known to a few as Jack but to most as the CO or Wingco, strode up the centre aisle with his briefing officers in train. Two MPs guarding the platform withdrew in deference as he stepped up. He pulled back the curtain from a huge map of western Europe. One hundred and twenty pairs of eyes narrowed on the black ribbons marking the courses and the large, red arrow at their conjunction.

'Gentlemen,' the CO said with dispatch, 'your target for tonight is a fuel storage depot at Fort d'Anglos.'

It was Forêt d'Engles if you were French, and it was on the northern outskirts of Lille. The *Wehrmacht* had buried its fuel tanks under hundreds of tons of concrete which 5 Group would go in first to break up. We were to follow behind and incinerate the place with 1,000-pounders and incendiaries. The Intelligence and Met. Officers and the section leaders supplied the detail. A Master Bomber would control the raid, his deputy on hand to take over if necessary. A small force of Mosquito Pathfinders would mark with red target indicators before the main force was called in. The weather forecast was good, both over the target and for the return to base. There should be little opposition beyond an odd night-fighter. We were to take off at 2150 hrs and bomb at 2315 hrs from an altitude of 12,000 ft. Our cameras would be given a 24-second delayed fuse.

'Right, chaps,' said the CO in winding up, 'It should be a piece of cake. Synchronise your watches. Be ready to board your transport outside the crew room at 2100 hrs. Take off as usual at one minute intervals. Good luck. See you in the smoke.'

So that was it. The crowd dispersed. The navigators and bomb aimers stayed to study the map. Most others sauntered away to their respective messes for an early supper. But I was anxious to sit quietly with my crew for a few minutes. With the possible exception of Archie, they were now experiencing the personal doubts and fears that beset me twenty-four hours earlier. I knew that as soon as we sped down the flarepath, they would leave their nerves behind. All their energies would be concentrated on the job in hand, and I told them so. My two gunners were barely nineteen years old. I reassured them that if they needed support from the others, it would be given. But they were no longer boys, but men like the rest of us.

We had all been trained to perfection. We all knew what was expected of us.

That was what I told them. There followed several seconds in which no one spoke. I think that in that moment the bonds between us all were stronger than ever.

Bill and I made our way to the Officers' Mess. John Aitken saw us come in and shouted, 'Good luck, Harry. Just remember what I said and you won't go wrong.'

'Good luck, John', I replied, making every effort to appear calm. The truth was quite the contrary. I couldn't face the prospect of food. Even Bill picked over his meal without much appetite. We pushed away our plates and lit a cigarette instead.

At 2030 hrs the crew room was a scene of total chaos. Parachutes, harnesses, flying gear, navigation bags, rations of chocolate, chewing gum and flasks of coffee, everything was scattered wildly over the tables and on the floor. Aircrew were darting about the room like men possessed, picking up one thing and putting down another, talking at fever pitch: 'Where the hell are my goggles?' . . . 'Who moved my bag?' . . . 'For God's sake, stop mixing up your gear with mine!' . . . and so on. If the heroes of the German Night Fighter Wing had seen this they would have laughed all the way to their cockpits. But before the first transport arrived the place was cleared. Seventeen crews of 75 Squadron were kitted to fly.

I checked my own gear slowly: flying boots; gloves; helmet; Mae West; harness; parachute; escape kit; and the most important item, my leather and sheepskin flying jacket from Red Deer. It was 2100 hrs and time to call the crew together. We heaved ourselves into a truck and it droned away on to the perimeter road. A few people smiled and waved at us. I didn't recognise them but gave a thumbs-up all the same. We rolled to a standstill at the first dispersal.

'Anyone for S-Sugar?' cried a female voice from the cab. Taken aback, I replied, 'That's us. But don't be in such a blasted hurry.' It was ten minutes past nine as we climbed aboard and began our checks. I spoke to each of the boys. They were all ready to go. I glanced at my watch again and, with a nod to Tubby, punched the booster coils. The airscrews whined and spun. Wisps of blue smoke spurted from each exhaust stub. The sequence, as always, was port inner, then starboard inner, port outer and, finally, starboard outer. Another cockpit check to test the magnetos at zero boost, a wave to the groundcrew to remove the chocks, a final thumbs-up and I taxied out to the perimeter track.

We tagged on to the queue of Lancasters, dramatic in the fading light, engines throbbing, moving slowly towards the take-off runway. The moment came nearer. The pilot in front of us opened his throttles and thundered away. I turned on to the strip and ran up the engines on full brakes, checking things one last time. S-Sugar shook and strained with anticipation. The seconds dragged out until the control caravan gave us our green. I released the brakes and we were away. We were going to war.

It was ten minutes past ten as I banked at 300 ft to begin the slow climb up through the circuit. Half an hour later at 10,000 ft Bill gave me a course and we left Mepal behind. All around in the darkening sky were dozens of Lancasters and Halifaxes bound, like us, for Fort D'Anglos.

Out over the Channel, the gunners requested a test firing. 'Yes,' I said, 'but don't forget Jerry can see your night trace. Keep your eyes skinned.'

There was a pregnant silence. And it was true, tonight of all nights they hardly needed reminding of their duty.

We crossed the French coast at 12,000 ft. Bill gave me the approach course for Lille. A few searchlights fingered the sky aimlessly. The flak was light and sporadic. In the near distance we saw a shower of brilliant red TIs floating down. A moment later we heard the Master Bomber calling in 5 Group to drop their tall-boys. Dead on time and track we commenced the run-in to the target with bomb doors open. Mac was sizing-up his first drop. Everything seemed fine. But when the Master Bomber's voice sounded again it was to specify an undershoot by two seconds. This was a tall order even for an experienced bomb aimer. Mac began some furious mental arithmetic. He did not want to kick off his tour with a dummy run. But then the Master Bomber thought better of it and ordered a fresh marking. A second shower of TIs floated down, this time bright green.

'Hit the greens, please. Hit the greens', he said, very matter-of-factly and quite devoid of the tension which gripped me.

Lying over his bomb sight Mac was forced into more last-second adjustments. The next words were his as our bombs and incendiaries thumped out of the racks and S-Sugar wrestled to gain height. I closed the bomb doors and held the aircraft straight and level for the photo-flash. As I dived S-Sugar away we saw massive fires below us. From his gun turret Norrie gave us a blunt, Yorkshire assessment of prospects for Fort d'Anglos.

'Well alight, is that. That's had it. I bet it's warm down there. I

88

wouldn't fancy being a fireman in that lot.' He was still going on about it as we flew over the Channel. I don't think he'd talked so much in the whole of the previous six months.

We landed at Mepal after two hours and forty minutes of flying. All seventeen aircraft from Mepal returned safely. The raid was somewhat marred by the marking fiasco but there was no doubt in my mind that the target had burnt. As regards my crew, with the exception of Mac we'd had an undemanding opener. They all performed well. The tension was gone. We were happy, excited and ravenously hungry. After de-briefing we bolted to our respective messes for a king-size breakfast. It was only egg, bacon and chips but it tasted like prime sirloin. I climbed into bed at two o'clock and, this time, went out like a light.

It was the morning of 11 August. Bill tugged at my arm as we walked through the mess door. An eager scrum surrounded the notice board. Such interest could have but one cause. We walked over and stood on tiptoe behind the others. Yes, the squadron was flying again. We had been allocated the Aitken crew's U-Uncle. Briefing was at 1300 hrs. That could only mean a daylight raid, and it didn't give us long.

Bill and I met the rest of the crew outside the briefing room. It seemed busier and noisier than ever. We took our seats at the back. As before, Jack Leslie and his entourage strode up to the platform. As before, he unveiled a map with a ribbon marked route into northern France and launched into his address.

The target was the marshalling yards at Lens, an important artery for supplies to the enemy's hard-pressed troops in the Falaise Gap. Our bomb load was to be eleven 1,000-pounders and four 500-pounders with high explosive and delayed fuses. We were to bomb from 15,000 ft. The time on target was 1630 hrs, take-off time 1430 hrs. Over the Channel, we would be joined by two hundred Spits to provide cover in to the target.

In winding up, the CO told us that this was an all-out effort by 3 Group. Every squadron would be deployed. Seventy-five was putting up twenty-two aircraft, our maximum on the day. His closing remarks were, 'I know you'll all do your best. But I want you to really burn this place. See you in the smoke.'

Those last five words were to become very familiar to us. Some of Jack Leslie's more gung-ho briefings could be strong meat. Exhortations to blast this and burn that and descriptions of the enemy as vermin or bastards left no doubt about the CO's fighting spirit, or the commitment he required from his men. But he always signed off with the same amicable, rather enigmatic tag. That was his style.

So it was to be France again, in daylight with an awesome fighter escort. With air superiority truly established over the Normandy battle area, fighter cover was the expected thing. Weather permitting, the skies were filled every day with Spitfires, Typhoons, Mustangs, Thunderbolts, Lightnings, Mosquitoes and, yes, Beaufighters.

I no longer gave much thought to piloting such wonders myself. That belonged to a distant past, a world of dreams and fables. The source of my pride now was real: the professionalism; teamwork; and boundless enthusiasm of my crew. And besides, I was flying a Lancaster, in its way as inspiring and as much a privilege to pilot as anything in the skies.

The one thing to which Lancaster pilots could not lay claim was formation expertise. The Yanks were the masters of this art. Their Flying Fortresses and Liberators flew daylight, deep-penetration sorties protected from the German border only by the formation and their own gunners (five per ship: upper; lower; two waist; and rear). The waves of *Luftwaffe* fighters exacted a terrible toll until Mustang P-51B escorts arrived in early 1944.

Bomber Command had abandoned daylight raids in mid-1943. The switch back was unheralded and swift with minimal opportunity for pilots to practise. Some Groups introduced formation leaders differentiated by white distemper on the tailfins. But I do not recall 3 Group doing so yet. Certainly, 75 eschewed all thought of a tight and disciplined formation until much later. Keeping a fully-laden Lanc on course in a stream of several hundred others was already quite demanding enough. But we did aim at a more concentrated stream. If flak was negligible it made good sense. The cover provided by escorts was more effective. Our firepower was multiplied. German fighters were denied the gift of a straggler. All the same, our early efforts were undistinguished, rarely more so, I would think, than on the trip to Lens.

I lifted U-Uncle off the Mepal runway about seven from the end of the order. As we climbed in the warm, afternoon sunlight the full justice of the term, 'bomber country', was revealed. Above neighbouring Witchford, beyond to Waterbeach and into the distant haze the sky was aswirl with the dark shapes of heavy bombers, hundreds of them, rising inexorably in their circuits. We had climbed to little more than 7,000 ft before the early ones detached themselves to fly south. Bill gave me a course, and we joined an extenuated gaggle above the peaceful fields and towns of southern England.

Out over the Channel our escort appeared as if from nowhere, high above us. Looking down on the disorder below, those boys must have felt like cowboys on the range trying to control an unruly herd of cattle. In the event, it made no difference how unruly we were. Lens was not important enough for the *Luftwaffe* to risk a confrontation. A few light AA guns offered some half-hearted resistance. But the German aces relaxed, no doubt, over a quiet – and safe – game of chemmy in the mess.

The marshalling yards came up on track, faintly visible through the ground haze. Mac unloaded his bombs, and watched them down into the centre of the target. It was 1633 hrs as the photo-flash burst. We banked away with no regrets about the lack of drama. Our escort turned north with us, still weaving white trails of condensation, probably still hopeful of a scrap. If so, they would return to base disappointed. Over mid-Channel I looked up through the Perspex to find that we were alone.

We entered the Mepal circuit at just before six o'clock. Control brought us down in a matter of minutes. Number three was in the bag. If only the next twenty-seven could be so easy.

The next day, the glorious 12th of August, saw hectic activity among the Mepal ground staff: the bowser crews, erks and armourers, and the innumerable personnel in humble or exalted posts who made the place work. Evidently, another maximum effort had been demanded by 3 Group. But this time Bill and I scoured the Battle Order in vain. Garth Gunn had stood us down. Perhaps he thought three sorties in as many days was enough for now.

At Briefing, seventeen aircrews were detailed bombing sorties to Brunswick, Russelsheim and Falaise, while six more would lay mines in the Gironde estuary. But F/O Yates and his crew spent the evening peppering the dartboard at The Three Pickerels, a favourite watering hole of both Mepal and Witchford crews. At nine-thirty the noise of Merlins interrupted our game. We took our drinks outside to toast our colleagues. One hundred and sixty-one of them took off from Mepal that night. The seven from P/O Mulcahy's crew disappeared without trace. Their aircraft was P-Peter, something that would have interested Archie. He couldn't know then that the loss of this P-Peter would, in a few days, bring him ashen-faced to the door of its replacement.

For the moment, though, operations in support of Allied forces

91

in France continued unabated. They were much needed. For three months now the 3rd Canadian Div. had been pinned down in the Falaise Gap by a massive detachment of von Kruge's *Panzers* with supporting ground forces.

The afternoon of 13 August saw one of the less glorious chapters in the 8th Air Force's war. Their B-17s were sent to bomb tank formations at Hamel, a strategic crossroads in the mouth of the Gap. Since the Allies occupied positions on three sides of the enemy the utmost accuracy was required. The B-17s bombed short, however. It was our side who took the punishment, and the Germans the advantage.

On 14 August, Bomber Command was charged with setting matters aright. To drop so close to Allied troop placements was risky with visual marking, even in the clear skies that were anticipated. A blind bombing aid named Oboe would be used instead. Developed in 1942, Oboe utilised pulsed signals from a pair of English transmitters, their point of intersection being the aiming point. Its accuracy deteriorated with distance due to the earth's curvature. But Falaise was well within limits.

The final adjudicator was a Master Bomber. He would call in the eight-hundred-strong main force only if totally satisfied that the yellow TIs were accurate. To maximise concentration our bombing height would be just 7,500 ft. A Spitfire escort would provide cover *en route* and counteract any spoiling tactics by enemy fighters over the target.

At 1.30 p.m. the Bedford crew truck slowed to a halt.

'R-Roger', announced the WAAF driver.

R-Roger, the samba dancer. The newest artform at this time was undoubtedly the painting of aircraft insignia. Everyone admired the American talent for adorning B-17s with improbably pneumatic young ladies in diaphanous robes. Not to be outdone – well, yes actually, to be completely outdone – some Mepal fitter more familiar with a monkey wrench than an artist's brush had let loose his carnal fantasies on poor R-Roger. The result was . . . unusual. Rio Rita we called her, after the song of that name. She certainly didn't stimulate my imagination. But I suppose there was a chance that an enemy pilot coming in to attack might be laughing too much to draw a decent bead on us.

At 2.05 p.m. I returned the waves from the band of onlookers gathered as always by the caravan, and we steamed off down the runway. At 90 knots R-Roger was ready to bear us and her bomb load of eleven 1,000-pounders and four 500s aloft. We reached our required height quickly and joined the gaggle on the first leg to the south coast.

Our escort arrived thousands of feet above us, weaving their sinuous, mesmeric patterns and shining in the afternoon sunlight like diamonds. I couldn't comment upon their opinion of us. We were distributed all over the sky again at first. But some suggestion of orderliness had developed by the French coast. Not formation flying exactly, but it was progress.

Visibility was indeed good. In the countryside south of the shattered city of Caen I saw afternoon shadows among the mottled browns and greens and the linear grey of the long, straight Falaise road. Small groups of charred buildings, mostly farms, dotted the landscape. The farmers had survived four years under the Nazi heel only to be burnt out by the fires of liberation. Others trod through their broken homes, not people at all in the ordinary sense but soldiers busy at their anti-tank and machine-guns, artillery pieces and mortars.

A few miles further on the evidence of soldiering became more apparent. I saw no enemy armour concentrations, no obvious signs of battle at all. But smoke and dust began to obscure the ground. It thickened rapidly until the confusion was alarming. Mac's reference points disappeared. In places even the horizon was obscured. The Yanks' problems of the previous day were understandable now. I wondered if Bomber Command had been hasty in stepping into the breach.

At least there were no enemy aircraft around. The pontoon buffs of the *Luftwaffe* clearly preferred wagering their *pfennigs* to their lives. We came in wholly focused on the job, on track and, at 1550 hrs, on time. Then, as if by prior arrangement with the *Wehrmacht*, the smoke parted over a few cratered fields where the TIs glowed yellow. I opened the bomb doors. Mac, prone over his bombsight, began his instructions. They were short-lived. A shower of reds appeared on the same ground. The Master Bomber rattled new orders over the R/T 'Do *not* bomb the yellows. Do *not* bomb the yellows. Drop on the reds, please.'

'Hold it steady, skipper', said Mac, concentrating more deeply than ever, his right hand poised to hit the release switches. Two, three, four times he said, 'Steady', lengthening the second syllable with each repetition. Then came the first of the quickfire thumps from the bomb bay and the words that all aircrews longed to hear, 'Bombs gone and looking good. Bomb doors shut.' Twenty-four seconds later we could go home.

That evening a message of congratulations from 3 Group HQ was pinned on the mess notice board. The marking *was* accurate. It transpired later, though, that in the confusion some Canadian troops had fired yellow identity flares. The Master Bomber acted promptly. But some seventy kites bombed on these, bringing death or injury to sixty-six men.

When the Allied troops attacked, the area became a killing field. Ten thousand German bodies were strewn across the battle ground, so numerous that the victors had to step on and over them to progress. Forty thousand prisoners were taken.

We didn't know it then, but with this victory the secondment of Bomber Command to Allied ground forces in France was brought to a close. For 3 Group that would herald a return to night ops over Germany. For myself and my crew it was nearly, but not quite, the end of the honeymoon.

The *Luftwaffe* had begun the war with an enormous numerical advantage in fighter aircraft. But, with one exception in the autumn and winter of 1943 when it threatened to defeat the Flying Fortresses of the 8th Air Force, the war years saw a steady decline in its effectiveness *during daylight.*

The saviour of the 8th Air Force was the product of an experiment by Rolls-Royce. It became the Allies' first long-range fighter and it was the magnificent, Merlin-engined Mustang P51B. Equipped with drop-tanks and capable of flying at 455 mph at 30,000 ft, it could escort bomber formations deep into Germany. And when it got there, it could blast the *Luftwaffe* out of the skies. From February 1944 the Mustang began to arrive in great numbers. The defenders' losses mounted alarmingly, almost doubling through spring. Then came D-Day and the battles over Normandy, during which well over a thousand more German fighters went down. German factories continued to pour out aircraft. But aircrew experience had become a commodity in short supply. As the year wore on, the pilots scrambling the Me 109s increasingly included novices with only one hundred and fifty hours of flying under their belts. The fighting strength of the *Luftwaffe* in daylight was, if not yet broken, plainly heading that way.

Though accounting for only five per cent of German fighter numbers, the *Nachtjagdgeschwader* (Night-Fighter Wing) was another story. An RAF bomber stream spread across the night sky was a more amenable place to seek a kill. Furthermore, advances in armoury and airborne radar instituted in the last months of

1943 gave the night-fighters a clear and durable tactical edge.

No, daylight sojourns to *la belle France* with a few hundred fighters riding shotgun held a powerful attraction for me. I was hoping for plenty more of the same when at 6.30 a.m. on 15 August 1944, I was shaken from my sleep to be told that ops were on with Briefing in ninety minutes. Bill and I cycled to the mess, indeed we raced (I think I won by a wheel). Whatever else the day would bring, a breakfast of orange juice, coffee, precious eggs with a generous helping of bacon, toast, marmalade and real butter awaited us and would receive our attention first.

The dining room buzzed with speculation. Where would it be today? Surely not the Falaise Gap again. And why get us out of bed at such an unearthly hour? The answer was under wraps and under guard in the briefing room. All we knew for now was that we had another date with Rio Rita.

The rest of the crew were waiting for Bill and me outside the briefing room. We were getting the hang of these occasions now. We had even staked a claim to a particular row of seats at the back of the room. All faces turned as the CO pushed through the door, ahead of his entourage. He stepped up onto the platform, took hold of the curtain-pull with his left hand . . . and paused. A smile spread easily over his face. 'You're going to like this one,' he said.

He swept back the curtain decisively. We all drilled our eyes at the lowest point of the ribbons. Not France but Belgium!

> 'We're going to knock hell out of No. 1 Night Fighter Wing at St Trond, seventy miles due east of Brussels. It's home to two crack squadrons. That's two bloody good reasons to make every bomb count and put them out of business for as long as we can. There will be a standard bomb load of 1,000- and 500-pounders, some with delay-action fuses to keep those buggers on their toes. If they or anyone else gets off the ground first, an escort of Thunderbolts will oblige their curiosity.'

Every man left that room thoroughly fired-up. There wasn't a word of dissent, not a groan nor even so much as a sigh. We liked this one not just for the sake of our own, immediate futures but for the many who had fallen victim in the past to No. 1 Night Fighter Wing. It is hard to credit that just the top three aces shot down more than two hundred and fifty RAF bombers between them, roughly the equivalent of ten squadrons. Over one hundred and twenty of these were credited to Major Heinz-Wolgang Schnauffer while Colonel

Werner Streib and Captain Manfred Meurer claimed sixty-six and sixty-five respectively. These were the observable kills. Often aircraft escaped the attack only to come to grief in the Channel or on landing in England. The real toll exacted by these three men will never be known.

While St Trond (the French version, actually in Flemish it was St Treuden) was to be a 3 Group effort, eight more Dutch and Belgian fighter airfields would be hit simultaneously by other Groups. The strategy was obvious in retrospect. But we had no thought beyond the present as we ran through our pre-taxi checks on board R-Roger. The erks pulled at the chock ropes and waved us off to the perimeter track. So poised in flight, on terra firma the Lanc was a trifle flat-footed with 13,000 lb in the bomb cradles. But just for her to be there at all, bombed-up, fuelled and mechanically A1 was a testament to the phenomenal, daily effort of hundreds of unsung heroes at Mepal.

By 9.55 a.m. the full squadron strength was taxiing in line astern, aircrews milling, Merlins growling and the very earth shaking. For us there was never a prouder or more patriotic spectacle. Quite a crowd had gathered by the control caravan to witness it. Whether it was the spirit of the occasion or the fine weather that drew them, I cannot say. But thirty or forty ground staff turned out, including several WAAFs, some holding up sheets of white paper with messages no doubt along the lines of, 'Saloon Bar, 2000 hrs'. Even in all this, men and women still managed to pursue contemporaneous, non-RAF interests.

A more august company lined the balcony of the Watch Office (or control tower). These were the senior officers who, with the exception of the A Flight Commander, S/Ldr Lin Drummond, DFC were not flying. By choice, every one of them would have been in the cockpit that day. But the Battle Order was incontrovertible. All that was left was to scan the parade through binoculars and champ around for a few hours until the squadron's return.

The leading Lancaster of S/Ldr Williamson swung on to the runway, received a green and roared away. Hardly was he airborne than number two was rolling down the strip. The Mepal spectacular, extraordinary yet routine, was in full swing. In fifteen minutes the last of the nineteen was up and climbing through the circuit.

The same, stirring ritual was being conducted all across East Anglia, the home of 3 Group. Over at Witchford our neighbours, 115 Squadron (identification letters KO), were joining the party. There was a bond between 75 and 115 which mostly took the form of friendly rivalry. We vied with one another in operational effort and serviceability. But in times of relaxation the crews drank in the same pubs. On ops we generally shared the same targets and the same risks. Of the latter it should be noted that 115 was in the unenviable position of suffering the heaviest losses in Bomber Command, the only squadron to exceed 75 in this doleful measure.

We rose into a fine, summer sky with a scattering of cirrus at a great height. Some heat haze restricted forward visibility a little as the stream formed. We were not far behind the leaders. As ever, Bill beavered away behind his blackout, though Lord knows why in daylight. I couldn't keep out the cruel thought that on such days only a single navigator in the lead bomber was actually necessary. Anyhow, Bill gave me a course of 135° to the Belgian coast. From there we would fly just south of Brussels before turning on to our final, outward leg.

The Thunderbolts came in from the south and wheeled around to effect the promised umbrella. We skirted Brussels, surely lifting the heart of every Belgian in the streets below, if not of their occupying masters. Bill gave me the final course change. I banked R-Roger gently to port. Somewhere ahead lay St Trond, its aces already forsaking lunch in the dining room for the cramped and cheerless safety of a bunker. At Briefing we were told that the airfield had three runways that intersected to form a small triangle of grass. This, smack in the middle of the airfield, was the designated aiming point.

Now we were at our bombing height of 15,500 ft, I searched the horizon for the target. Woods and fields in manifold shades of green unfolded below, dotted among them ancient, grey Flemish villages. Then, quite suddenly, out of the haze and directly ahead, the black-angled form of an airfield came into sight. I dropped my left hand down to the bomb door lever. Mac's instructions floated over the intercom. They were hardly needed. This was easy work, and there was no opposition. The red TIs dropped dead centre in the triangle, glowing brightly. As we passed above the boundary the string of bombs from the lead aircraft impacted. The earth erupted in smoke and dust, then repeatedly so as more bombs struck, smothering the aiming point in turmoil. Already there was a degree of spread, visiting ruin upon the runways and beyond. Everything was mayhem.

Our own bombs broke free with the familiar series of thumps. R-Roger kicked upward, her wings flexing with the lift. A feeling of lightness returned to the stick. This moment was always so exhilarating, I had to resist the temptation to chuck the kite all over the sky. But the camera run – honest, dull, straight and level stuff – militated against such unprofessional conduct. Mac, though, *was* enjoying himself, jubilant as his bombs curved into the triangle. From his turret Norrie watched the descent, too, but saw the bombs land wide. Were they ours or someone else's? Only the photograph could tell us for certain.

With the photo in the can we left St Trond to its torment. As we turned, the pounding confusion was at its height. All around the aiming point was obscured by billowing dust clouds. The rest of the airfield was a honeycomb of craters. For now, No. 1 Night Fighter Wing would add no more kills to its tally.

As we left the target area three Thunderbolts came alongside, wings waggling. I returned the gesture, and they peeled away. The same sense of euphoria and satisfaction surely filled the hearts of every Allied airman in those skies.

Once we could relax a little I decided to walk through the aircraft to see what the boys thought about the raid. I engaged the automatic pilot (affectionately dubbed 'George' after the saintly dragon slayer) and picked my way past Tubby. Bill looked very surprised when I drew back the curtain, then amused at the novelty. But Archie, ever alert for disaster, froze half out of his seat. His jaw dropped into the bomb bay, or somewhere lower.

'Skipper!' he exclaimed, no doubt expecting to see me clip on my parachute and disappear through the emergency exit, 'You . . . what . . . who's flying the aircraft?'

'George', chipped in Bill.

Profoundly unenlightened and trying to come to terms with the sudden arrival of a second dickey on board. Archie repeated, 'George . . . George? Who the hell's George?'

A Lancaster could be a wonderful place to explore the wilder shores of human nature. However, my wanderlust had waned rather, so I left Archie to roam his rocky cove alone. Instead, I called Mac up to the cockpit for a lesson in straight and level flying, part of a survival procedure we'd worked out.

The following day we examined the photograph, perfect but for the intrusion of a large thumbprint. That and the rising clouds of dust had almost obscured the aiming point from our camera lens – but not quite. Mac had got it right and R-Roger's message to No. 1 Night Fighter Wing had been neatly delivered.

So that was raid number five, another run over occupied territory and, again, under the protection of a fighter escort. Ordinarily, a rookie crew's first five flights were reckoned to be the most dangerous phase of the tour. The flood of French targets after the Normandy invasion made things much, much easier. It gave rookies like us the opportunity to sharpen our skills and our teamwork. That was a real blessing. But I just had the niggling feeling now that our blessings might be coming to an end.

We did not fly on the 16th. Originally, we were among eighteen crews rostered for a daylight raid on another tempting, tactical target in northern France. It was scrubbed. Attention switched to a smaller, second operation scheduled for the hours of darkness, an attack on the Baltic coastal town of Stettin. This was expanded to a much larger effort. But my crew and I were stood down by our Flight Commander and so spared a long and arduous haul.

At nine o'clock the first of twenty-three aircraft roared down the Mepal flarepath. *En route* to the target a few fighters were in evidence and one, a Junkers 88, was damaged. But all 75's Lancasters returned safely. Flight Sergeant Cooper and his crew had entrusted themselves to R-Roger's continuing run of luck, and were rewarded. However, Stettin also escaped serious harm. The bombing was scattered and produced no great concentration of fires. Successful or not, though, it marked the squadron's return to Germany, a distinctly sobering thought. The high jinks over St Trond already seemed a world away.

CHAPTER SEVEN

P-PETER

It was the morning of 18 August, a superb summer's day. I was chatting with a couple of fellow pilots in the Flight Office. Garth Gunn put his head round his office door and called me over, 'Maintenance has been sending us a lot of new kites since that bastard of a trip to Homberg. One's flown in this morning. It isn't squadron practice to pool new aircraft so I thought you and your boys could use this one as a regular.'

I was astonished at such largesse only two weeks and five raids into my tour. Maybe it was another case of the Flying Instructors' Benevolent Society. Anyway, I didn't need to be told twice. Within the hour the seven of us were in our flying gear, just standing on the dispersal pan and gazing up at HK557, our own beautiful, matt-black Lancaster B1 – ours! She didn't have her 'handle' yet. Only the Squadron markings, the famous AA, were painted on her sides. The single aircraft letter would be added some time later, once we had flown an acceptance test.

'We'll have it ready for you,' said the ground crew NCO who was standing with us, 'not even a green from the caravan stops my boy when he gets a brush in his hand.'

That set off the boys with a few letter jokes of their own: L-Love, F-French and downhill from there, each contribution more ribald than the last. We boarded the aircraft cackling like geese all of us, that is, except Archie. To him an aircraft letter was no laughing matter.

The cockpit was pristine. Not an inch of Perspex or a single dial harboured a scratch or smear or a speck of dust. Every Lancaster cockpit smelled good. But there was an indefinable and delicious scent of factory newness about this one. It had yet to be anointed with the unmentionable filth that was apt to swill around during a bad trip, of course, or the kerosene with which the erks disinfected it the next morning.

I settled into my seat and reached forward to the column, then, with my right hand, down to the four throttles. It all felt right. Sitting behind me and facing his panel on the starboard side Tubby asked if I was ready. We began the ritual of pre-start checks. Fifteen minutes later I gunned the port outer to swing us crisply round to the perimeter track. The difference between a brand-new machine and an old warhorse like S-Sugar or Feltwell's venerable R5764 was evident as soon as we were in the air. She was taut and responsive, a lovely aircraft. I couldn't ask for more – except, of course, that she should be lucky.

Luck and a Lancaster were our daily bread in those far-off, momentous days. We loved the one and couldn't expect to live without a large slice of the other. We all carried a keepsake, a sign of our trust worn around the neck or pocketed next to the heart. It could be the ubiquitous rabbit's foot or a rosary, letter, St Christopher, coin, photograph, playing card . . . Mine was probably odder than most: the wishbone of my favourite hen, Blackie, whose demise enriched the family table on Christmas Day 1942. This hallowed relic was garlanded by my mother with a sprig of dried lavender which she fixed by means of some black wool. I never left the ground without it. And there was no doubt that luck had proved a true and constant friend.

At the end of our acceptance test on 18 August, with Blackie's wishbone pocketed in my jacket and thoughts of home in my head, I determined to fly HK557 there and then to Stony Stratford. This would fulfil a promise I had made to my father in mid May as I left the house for Chedburgh. It might even make amends in another way. For I had not written to my mother every week as she so desired.

In fairness, Mepal that August was a pressure cooker by day and night. The blockbusters and the tension and the remorseless daily round were hardly the stuff with which to reassure an anxious mum (censorship notwithstanding). But she had no such problems in her many writings to me. There was always the simple stricture to eat properly and take care of myself. There was the family and the gentle foibles and follies of people we had known all our lives. And there was one other person whom she had only just met. My new girlfriend, Eileen, had called by. A nice, dutiful girl, thought Mum, to have given up her war work to care for a convalescent parent. But she was strangely unforthcoming about whatever it was she used to do. The whiff of a state secret hung in the air and Mum wanted to know *more* (actually, Eileen had been a telegraphist at Bletchley Park, the unit charged with de-crypting enemy communications, and was bound to total secrecy when she left just after D-Day).

So it was that in the middle of lunch one fine summer's day the house was positively shaken to the foundations by a fast, thunderous, low-flying intruder. Utter chaos ensued. My father leapt to his feet, knocking his chair backwards.

'You know who that was, mother!' he yelled.

He struggled over to a window then, seeing nothing, to the one in the kitchen. My mother and sister, Joan, were already making for the back door, calling for him to follow. Dad bolted after, only to halt in the doorway. He ran back in again and, not thinking to take a spare cloth from the dresser, stripped the parlour table in ten seconds flat.

White ensign in hand, he raced through the back door onto the tiny patch of grass to see us looming large from the direction of the allotments. We roared low overhead with the cloth thrashing about wildly, the dog barking and the women alternately waving or blowing kisses, and hopping up and down as if they were on hot coals. This exuberant performance was played out again for our third and final pass.

They watched us climb away and make two steep turns. Then, wings waggling, we grew small in the distance. It was over. Dad put his arms around the women's waists. My sister kissed his face, which was wet with tears. When the sound of the engines was lost to them they returned indoors and, for a while, could find no meaningful words to speak.

We flew HK557 back to Mepal for her appointment with the painter and the moment when the seven dead of P/O Mulcahy's crew would bequeath us their aircraft letter, the unwanted P-Peter.

After lunch I cycled alone to B Flight dispersal. It was no great distance. After a couple of hundred yards I could see the painter at work. Though not completed, there was no mistaking the shape of the letter. Utterly dismayed, I leant the bicycle against a tyre and walked around the aircraft. P for panic, I thought, once Archie gets wind of that.

The armourers were waiting for the painter to finish. Their trolleys held no g.p.s, just the massive, dark green cylinder of a 4,000-pound cookie and the rest, incendiary canisters. Tonight would be our first with either. The entire squadron had guessed from the fuel load that the target was in Germany, another first for us. I cycled away with a deep sense of foreboding.

The immediate problem was Archie. If his pronouncements were to be believed he must be given no time to brood. I didn't want to lose a second skilled w/op and have to take an unknown, last-minute replacement on the trip. Fortunately, Archie had seen a Battle Order listing only our kite's serial number. For now I was the only crew member who knew the damned letter. But it was still early. Briefing was almost three hours away. I decided to break the news first to my two gunners.

There was something more troubling me as I rode back. What if by some appalling coincidence tonight's target was Nuremberg? How would we ever get Archie on board? And even if we did, what sort of state would he be in? What would it mean for his and our operational efficiency?

I found all the boys sitting idly in the sun, sucking on grass stalks and discussing matters of blissful unimportance.

'No sign of the paint pot', I lied. It didn't prove difficult to draw Geoff and Norrie aside. 'Look,' I said, 'there may be a job for you two later. We're flying a P-Peter tonight.'

'But . . . what about Arch?' said Geoff, quick to see the danger. We each slid our eyes in Archie's direction. He, in turn, was watching us.

I continued, 'We'll keep him in the dark for now. But he'll find out sooner or later. Just make sure you're both around when he does. I'm giving you the job of getting him in the truck *and* the kite. Pick him up and throw him in if you have to.'

As I left Geoff and Norrie to their ruminations with the others I heard Archie's voice, 'What was all that about?' 'Bloody night-fighters, what else!' Geoff replied with brilliant invention.

Six o'clock and Briefing arrived. We took our seats amid the usual bedlam. Geoff, who seemed to have a talent for conspiracy, leaned over to me, his right hand close to his mouth.

'Hasn't got a clue, skipper', he murmured.

The CO came through the door, behind him Garth and his opposite numbers on A and C Flights, the Navigation, Signals and Gunnery leaders, the Intelligence Officer and, bringing up the rear, the Met. Officer. One hundred and seventy-five aircrew, so many young faces, rose as one man. Jack Leslie asked us to sit. He swept away the curtain. Yes, everyone knew we would be gazing on Germany. But hearts were thumping hard while we took in the meaning of the ribbons and the stark, single red arrow. A deep groan welled-up, but not from me. I could have cheered and punched the air. From the back of the room the target's name was not legible. But I was familiar enough with the Fatherland to know that Nuremberg, bless it, was somewhere else.

'Gentlemen, your target for tonight', the CO said, provoking a chorus of despair, '. . . is Bremen.'

Briefing lasted one hour. All the assembled officers made their contributions. We absorbed the details of the bomb load, the fuel load, weather over the target and on our return, take-off time and time on target, the colour of the TIs to be dropped by the Pathfinder Force, the Master Bomber's call sign, the number of main force bombers detailed to participate, the diversionary raid on Berlin by Mosquitoes, and 4 Group's simultaneous activities all over the Ruhr. Bill was given the routes, Archie the callsigns for the night. To wind up, the Intelligence Officer spoke of the importance of Bremen and, in particular, its giant Focke-Wulf plant. He gave us the latest information on the strength of German defences, using a map with large areas marked heavily in red both on the approaches and around Bremen itself, like a ring of steel.

Jack Leslie said he'd see us in the smoke, and the room began to empty. As after our first Briefing on the Fort d'Anglos raid, we stayed in our seats. I wanted to talk over something – not the aircraft letter but a still grimmer subject.

For a while now we'd been pooling ideas about crew procedure if one of us was hit by shrapnel or cannon fire. In an emergency even the wounded may have to lend themselves to other disciplines. Far better that this should be predetermined rather than driven by the heat and confusion of events. So we each set about giving one other crew member a survival guide to his job. Archie made sure that Bill could operate the r/t and tap out a mayday on the w/t. Bill, however, turned to Mac for cover. Like every bomb aimer, he was already trained in map reading and the use of H2S navigational equipment. The gunners could interchange at will and, of course, Mac also knew his way around a Browning though I doubt if he could squeeze himself into Norrie's rear turret. But he was more useful elsewhere.

If I was the one incapacitated, the only option for the rest was a bale-out. But someone would have to hold the aircraft straight and level while they evacuated. That took courage and selflessness. Many captains had perished in the performance of this duty. Mac was the obvious candidate, both from the point of view of experience (he had at least attended an Initial Flying Training course) and his undoubted strength of character.

So he became my last-ever flying pupil. I had put him in my seat during the final, homeward leg of our early operational flights. He had exceeded my expectations. The gigantic leap from a Tiger to a Lanc was accomplished with some alacrity, not that I asked too much of him. There was no aim beyond that he could trim the aircraft and hold it straight and level for two or three minutes. But that might be enough to save six precious lives.

The unlucky seventh in these deliberations was, of course, oneself. Such a candid assessment of one's future was entirely contrary to the pervasive culture of optimism. The attitude among most aircrew was and had to be, 'it could never happen to me'. Even when this was assailed by the reality of a kite on fire a few hundred feet away, the response shifted only as far as an unconscionably grateful, 'thank God it's *not* me'.

References to death itself were invariably euphemistic. You went down or for a beer (a burton), or bought it, got the chop, met the Reaper, had your time or your number came up. Such talk meshed neatly with all the technical jargon and airfield slang. There was a spurious toughness to it. But in reality it was simply self-pacifying, almost comforting to call death by another name. We weren't especially clear-eyed on the subject. To us, it only seemed right to face facts and do something for our pals for a time when nothing could be done for ourselves.

At 2000 hrs Bill and I found the others in the locker room and in disconsolate mood. Archie's flying gear lay unattended.

'Sorry, skipper,' he said, drawing himself up, 'any other kite, but not that one.' Six men, all standing taller than poor Archie, pressed towards him. 'Never!' he reiterated.

'Anyone for P-Peter', shouted the driver of the Bedford as we jolted to a standstill. Archie landed on the concrete, followed in quick order by the six of us. I walked my inspection while the others shuffled him to the ladder. After a pause Mac launched himself into the aircraft, whistling innocently. Tubby and Bill followed, then me. I turned to find Archie still rooted to the spot with the youngsters at his elbows. I have in mind a picture of him still, as pale as death, eyes unblinking as if in shock. I thought he might faint and certainly that he wouldn't make it on board. Geoff and Norrie were all ready to force the issue, just waiting for my word. Whether Archie knew this I cannot say. But with a massive effort he reached forward, grasped the ladder and hauled himself up. I made way for him. He was a true hero.

Behind the Perspex of the cockpit an incongruous, sleepy warmth remained from the heat of the day. Tubby and I ran through the checks. I started-up the four Merlins one by one, revving each for him to record oil pressure and magneto drop. When all was done I called up each crew member for the all clear on their individual checks. Archie sounded dry of mouth but I could rely on Bill to watch over him now. It was time to roll. I waved to the ground crew to remove the chocks. We taxied to our place in the queue, the newest kite, the proudest aircrew on the squadron. Our turn beside the caravan arrived. I wound up the motors. The deafening roar of more than five thousand horses and that urgent, shaking anticipation engulfed the senses. As it always did, the green came as a blessed release.

I called out, 'This is it, boys. Here we go.' In full fury P-Peter surged down the runway. Beautiful, beautiful thing though she was, she still swung to port like every Lanc I ever flew. I advanced the port outer throttle to keep her straight, and then progressive right rudder. But she was past the renowned point of no return soon enough and asking me to pull back the column. Then we were riding the air and on our way.

The time was 2132 hrs. I knew that about now my father would be walking home from his evening at The Case Is Altered. His mates would have stood him his ale on the strength of our beat-up. He might look up at the dying light in the sky as he closed the front door on the world. But he could know nothing of his son's work this night.

As we climbed in the circuit the sun was pale above the horizon, throwing long shadows across the landscape of East Anglia. At 10,000 ft we joined the stream on its first leg, flying eastward and out of the golden light. A few minutes later we crossed the coast, with Cromer looking serene and at rest. I said a quiet farewell to my beloved England. Those same feelings would have filled the hearts of Geoff and Norrie, watching from their turrets. With luck P-Peter would bring us home in five and a half hours. Cromer would be in darkness, its people asleep in their beds. But, first there was Bremen.

We continued our climb out over the North Sea. It was a ghostly feeling to know that we were already appearing on German radar screens. At that very moment orders were in transmission to coastal flak batteries and to scores of night-fighter airfields (happily, not including St Trond this time). At 12,000 ft we broke through light cirrus cloud into a darkening and already starry sky. But more wondrous than that was the sight of four-engined bombers breaking cloud all around, rising as one and with one immutable purpose.

With so many aircraft in the sky I reminded Geoff and Norrie to sing out the second anyone moved too near. Even as I spoke, I looked up through the Perspex roof to see the angular shape of a Halifax slide silently across. There was no more than two hundred feet of separation. Its pilot and crew could have no idea of our presence.

We crossed the Dutch coast at our bombing height of 19,000 ft. Flak ships were sending up a light fire, but it was spent harmlessly thousands of feet below our altitude. Forward visibility gave more cause for concern. Good for miles, it was an open invitation to every German night-fighter.

Again I went on the intercom to Geoff and Norrie, 'For Pete's sake, stay alert for fighters.' They both snapped back, 'Yes, skipper.' They knew the danger well enough.

Archie knew better than anybody and he wanted to go on watch as well. He took the astrodome. On the horizon ahead he and I saw a veritable forest of weaving searchlights. I don't know what palpitations they gave him but worse was on the way. As we began our approach flak burst across the sky, not light anymore but formidable, indeed, a seemingly impenetrable wall of it. We'd seen nothing like this over occupied territory, nothing at all. The realisation came to me how very inexperienced and vulnerable we still were, really just a crew of six rookies and a veteran convinced he was going to die. At least we had a brand-new, A1 kite that would give us every possible chance.

The flak was, in fact, aimed not at the main force but the PFF boys whose TIs were flaring green on their descent. We were late in the stream, still a few minutes flying time from Bremen. Mac had been engaged in releasing our bundles of 'Window' into the night. Now Tubby took over, freeing Mac for the drop.

Window was the code name for a brilliantly simple anti-radar device. It consisted of thin strips of black paper coated on one side with aluminium foil. I have heard it called angel hair, a much more apt and descriptive title. Each strip appeared as a blip on German ground and airborne radar screens. Showered in their thousands from every bomber, they created a white storm of confusion. Introduced to a puzzled *Luftwaffe* over Hamburg in July 1943, Window began as a total success. Enemy pilots were thrown back on their own devices (which the more adventurous preferred anyway). But they soon learned that the snowstorm was stationary on their screens while bombers moved steadily and predictably. With experience they discounted the foil and, as before, targeted the intruding force. In the absence of anything more effective,

Window continued in use. But it was no cloak of invisibility and that, surely, was what we needed right now.

From thousands of feet above us the night-fighter pilots released their own flares. They floated down on parachutes, illuminated the sky all around in a deathly-orange glow. We were denied the sweet black of night. I could see at least two dozen Lancasters to both port and starboard, all as naked as at noon. We passed so close to some of the flares, they lit the cockpit with a brilliance that made me shield my eyes.

On the tail of the flares came the fighters. While I was still nursing my vision, coloured tracers ripped horizontally across our path. The intended victim was to port. The tracers cut into her flanks. Returning fire from both turrets, she heeled away into a port corkscrew. I looked for the aggressor but saw nothing. Nor did my gunners, revolving their turrets in a desperate bid to sight him first. He must have zipped right past us. Maybe he had dived in pursuit of the other kite. Maybe he was already somewhere else in the stream looking for his kill. In any event, this time it wouldn't be us.

We were now well into our bombing run with Mac lining up his sights on the TIs. Bremen presented an incredible sight. Raging storms of fire engulfed vast areas. Tremulous explosions rippled out from their epicentres in a second or less as each cookie struck. God knows what it was like to be down amongst that lot. It was no part of our job to think about it. At this point our minds had to be concentrated on the approaching bottleneck and the proximity of other bombers. This was as dangerous as any phase of the attack, and perhaps the moment of greatest vigilance. There were few reprieves from a falling bomb and virtually none from collision.

The defenders reacted to the bottleneck, too. It concentrated their targets and presaged a switch to ground fire. We left the fighters behind. Seconds later we were enveloped in a box barrage of heavy flak. Two bombers were hit in front of us, one of them already a fireball sinking fast. Then, as if some invisible hand had thrown a switch, we were snared by a radar-controlled searchlight. Its blinding power flooded the cockpit, bluish-white, the colour of fear. In a moment every available searchlight was swung on to us. We were coned, naked and, no doubt, exposed to a thousand pairs of eyes on the ground watching, hoping for the first sign of distress.

The batteries wasted not a second in pumping heavy shells up into the cone. There was no future for us as things stood, and only one possible way out. But even as I pushed the column forward there was a huge explosion under the aircraft. We yawed and shuddered to port. I was lifted into my straps and my hands left the column. Lumps of coarse metal followed the shockwave, peppering the kite from nose to tail.

I grabbed at the column again and pushed P-Peter down into the light. Nothing fancy, I went for speed. But she felt soggy. We didn't break free and those damned gunners were throwing everything up at us. More metal rattled into the fuselage and wings. I was operating on luck and instinct. The intensity of the master beam completely obliterated the instrument panel. There was no indication of attitude, altitude or airspeed. There was no Bremen burning below, no world beyond the perspex. There was nothing but aching light and the convulsions from shellfire.

I stamped on the starboard pedal. What did it matter now if the tailplane fell off? Barrelling downward at God knows what speed, P-Peter began to bank. The gravity felt savage. But the light did not follow. We were re-united with darkness and we were free. Breathless and sweating, I pulled at the column until the aircraft was straight and level. We had lost 4,000 ft and, I think, all our remaining illusions. We were beyond the TIs but still over the burning centre of the city. The stench of cordite swept through the aircraft.

Mac came on the intercom, 'Would you like me to drop the cookie here, skipper? Or do you want to go around again?'

Humour! The man could afford to joke at a time like this.

'Christ!' I said, 'get shot of it now.'

In all the commotion I had forgotten the open bomb doors, the four-thousand pounder and full house of incendiaries. One flak splinter would have blown us and everything in our vicinity to pieces. Mac hit his switches and we executed the camera run.

Obviously, we'd taken a hell of a mauling. But my concern now was for the boys. As soon as we cleared the target area I called each one on the intercom. To my relief none had been hit. Asked how he was doing, Archie replied, 'All right. Yes, all right.' There was a palpable note of surprise in his voice.

Our talk was interrupted by a high-pitched yell from Norrie, *'Skip, fighter coming in from port. Corkscrew NOW.'*

From Geoff, in steely confirmation, 'I see it, skip.'

I hurled P-Peter into the void again, twisting down and round as tightly as possible. Both gunners blazed away. The kite juddered with the recoil. But the German pilot didn't flinch and held to his curve of attack. As we swung up, a stream of incendiary shells scorched by my window. Then he was gone into the night. I eased the kite back into normal flight.

Norrie came on the intercom, very fired-up by his first combat, 'By Christ, another couple of seconds and I'd have got him. It warmed me up a treat, though.'

'I said you'd feel better when you lose your virginity', replied Geoff obliquely.

An aircraft was going down in flames to starboard. Perhaps it had fallen victim to the same fighter. We flew on, hoping for a respite. Bill gave me a course to take us over the coast between Emden and Wilhelmshaven.

Then Tubby interjected, 'Skipper, the starboard outer's losing oil pressure.'

'Probably flak-damage. How long will it last?' I asked.

'It won't. You'll have to feather it now.'

I looked out to my right. But before I could move a muscle, a tongue of flame licked over the wing, then more of them, brighter and intensifying with every second. I stared in horror. After all we'd been through tonight, we were going to be burnt to cinders! I turned off the petrol feed, throttled the stricken engine back hard and feathered the airscrew.

Confronted by the awful probability that we had only seconds left, I shouted into the intercom,

> 'All crew members, this is the skipper. We have a fire in the starboard outer. Parachutes on and take up stations to abandon the aircraft. But for God's sake don't go until I tell you. Stand by.'

The flames were massively bellowed by a gale of over two hundred mph. They were shooting far out from the trailing edge of the wing. The chances of extinguishing even a modest blaze were only fifty/fifty. That was the hit and miss nature of a Graviner fire extinguisher, one of which was built into each engine. With a decent inferno you could forget it and reach for the parachute. This one certainly looked half-decent to me.

Anyway, it was our only hope. I pressed home the Graviner switch and waited. Nothing happened. The blaze grew unchecked. Tubby and I watched helplessly. Looking across and past where Tubby stood, I thought he spoke under his oxygen mask though the intercom was silent. I don't know why, but I had the strongest impression that he was reciting, 'The Lord is my Shepherd . . .'.

I am afraid our immediate fate rested with me. Should I give the order now and get everybody out . . . or try to blow out the fire in a vertical dive? This was a well-known, last throw of the dice. But it was not guaranteed to succeed, and escape against the G-forces would not be possible. Equally, the wing could simply melt through and that would be that.

I tried to weigh the risks dispassionately but my instincts were to go for the dive. Baling out truly terrified me. For one thing, leaving via the hatch above my seat afforded an excellent opportunity to collide with the mid-upper turret or, failing that, to be chopped in two by a tailfin. If somehow still sound of body I would be ripped away into tumbling chaos, counting and praying for the canopy. Then would come the interminable drop in the biting-cold air, fear of the murderous attention of fighters and, of the rest, who knows?

Even so, it was clearly more important to cling to life than to an aircraft. We would jump. At the end of it all, probably, would be capture, a sound beating, maybe, and internment as PoWs – but we would jump.

Then, to my astonishment, I saw that the fire wasn't spreading so rapidly. The flames weren't shooting so far into the night. With excruciating slowness they began to draw inward to the engine. I wasn't alone in these observations. First Norrie then, as safety stations were deserted, the others came over the intercom. There were shouts of encouragement as the flames reduced to a fizzle, and unfettered cheering as they spluttered and died away. With a bit less clutter and no main spar the whole crew would have been dancing for joy. Instead there were just clenched fists, slapped backs and exultation. The boys thought it was the Graviner. Tubby, I am sure, thought it was the psalm. But I knew it was the Lady herself, crewing lucky number eight, who had worked her fabled magic again.

Lifted beyond belief I went on the intercom, 'All right boys, excitement's over. We're going home. Got that, Archie?'

There was more cheering and then we got down to nursing a damaged kite home on three Merlins. To the wonderful Lancaster this was no problem at all. Once trimmed and with engine revs adjusted she held height easily. We lost airspeed and manoeuvrability, of course, and would be vulnerable if a fighter appeared. We all prayed hard that none would.

We expected a flak barrage as we crossed the German coast. But other than an impressive display of searchlights to starboard over Wilhelmshaven, all was quiet. Minutes later we crossed the string of islands that run parallel to the coastline, giving Borkum a wide berth. Out to sea, Bill gave me a new course. I began to feel that we would make it.

There was time to reflect on the crew's performance. It had been a fiery introduction to the Fatherland. We were entitled to ask if every German op would be like this. But through it all the boys had been superb. No skipper could have asked for more. Archie deserved special praise. He had dragged himself on board in the unshakable belief that he was already a dead man. Heaven knows what thoughts went through his head at times. But he uttered not a word of protest. He didn't freeze or withdraw into himself. He was simply dedicated to doing his duty. In the process our faith in him was restored. More important still, his faith in himself, lost on that terrible night over Nuremberg, had returned also.

As we neared the Wash, Archie established contact with Mepal to inform them of our condition. Control offered us a landing at Woodbridge with its three-mile runway. The choice was mine.

I asked Archie to ascertain visibility at base. At Briefing, the Met. Officer had warned us of possible, heavy ground mist on our return. I didn't fancy stooging across misty Albion on three engines, looking for a clear strip. The right answer came back.

'Tell them', I said to Archie, 'we are coming in to Mepal. We have half-an-hour to go and P-Peter continues to handle well.'

However, there was one factor to which my burgeoning confidence did not extend, and which I kept to myself. What would happen when we lowered the undercart? Hydraulics were peculiarly vulnerable to the scatter-gun effect of flak. The bomb doors had closed over Bremen but that didn't guarantee the integrity of the rest of the system. It could be slowly bleeding to death even as we flew the Mepal lane. Then again, the hydraulics might be intact but a tyre shot away. I could only wait and hope.

As promised, the Mepal beacon beckoned us from several miles out, with the flarepath twinkling beyond. We were given priority landing. On the downwind leg of the circuit I reached for the undercarriage lever. There was a disquieting pause. Nothing seemed to be happening. I was already adjusting inwardly to this final twist of the knife when, much better late than never, that lovely, solid thump resounded through the aircraft. The green indicator lit up. The cart was down and locked.

The rest, pretty routine stuff, was up to the pilot. With the exception of Tubby, the crew were at safety stations. I turned P-Peter through ninety degrees to face the flarepath at 700 ft. The drill was: come in fast, apply hard left rudder and throttle back the port outer engine to counteract yaw. We came over the boundary on half-flap at one hundred and fifteen knots and in the green of the glide path indicator. As we sailed down the centre of the flarepath I asked Tubby to close the throttles. P-Peter eased down like an elderly aunt feeling for her favourite armchair. It was certainly no three-pointer, but it would do. A spot of engine-juggling and some judicious braking brought her down to taxying speed. We were home.

The CO greeted us from the control tower with an abrupt, 'Good show, young Yates.' We taxied past the fire tender, sent out to save our skins but, thankfully, given no work this time. It was seven minutes past three as we completed the shut-down procedure at dispersal. The ground crew hastily threw chocks under the wheels, then stood back to gape in disbelief. I could almost hear them saying, 'Blimey, a brand spanking new kite five minutes ago, and now look at it.' One of them proffered cigarettes as we clambered down the ladder. We were eager to see the damage. But the Bedford driver was in a hurry to pick up another crew. So we climbed aboard, chattering like sparrows.

Of course, Archie gave us hell.

'I knew this would happen,' he told anyone who would listen, 'I *knew* it. Every damned P-Peter is jinxed.'

His language was as uncompromising as ever. But the tone was not the same. There was something in it, a brightness, that was missing before. I looked into his face as he spoke. The fever had fallen from his eyes. Archie Bain had recovered his belief in good fortune as well as bad.

It was half past four before the crew room, de-briefing and break- fast had done with us. After a few hours' solid sleep I awoke with one idea in my head, and dressed hurriedly.

I cycled out to dispersal alone. It was evident from a distance of fifty yards that my beautiful Lancaster had taken a fearful beating. The starboard outer was an ugly mess, the nacelles perforated by shrapnel and charred by fire. The wing behind was reduced to blackened and twisted sheet and fretwork, crowning a hole large enough even for Tubby to wriggle through. I walked slowly around, counting each hit by rocket or flak. It took some time. There were sixty-four, many as big as a football. I climbed aboard. Daylight streamed into the fuselage from unexpected places. Debris littered the floor. How it was we all came through without injury I just couldn't imagine. But of all those contorted lumps of Essen steel that ripped through P-Peter's skin, not one had so much as dented the Elsan. Every item of essential on-board equipment survived intact and in working order. Getting home might have been a lot more complicated otherwise.

Outside I found the ground crew's hut shut up and deserted. That answered the question of my heart. There was no point in taking spanners and wrenches to this lot. The airframe was too extensively damaged. P-Peter was a write-off.

Number 75 Squadron had dispatched twenty-five Lancasters to Bremen. All returned safely though three were damaged. The other two were not badly shot-up and were ready to go to war again in a day or so. But my aircraft, with which I felt a real affinity despite the brevity of our acquaintance, would never lift another bomb.

I saw Garth later that day.

'One op!' I complained, shaking my head to make him understand my sense of personal loss and, perhaps, as a bit of an apology.

He just smiled philosophically and said, 'One more towards the thirty'.

CHAPTER EIGHT

DEUTSCHLAND,
DEUTSCHLAND . . .

The Bremen raid was followed by several days of foul weather over Germany and France. Having recommenced its great offensive on the cities and industry of the Third Reich, Bomber Command was now forced into inactivity.

For us seven it was a welcome breathing space. We'd been swept along in a whirlwind of briefings, bombs and breakfasts ever since our arrival at Mepal. How strange now to find time on our hands and a change in tempo about the place. The grinding pressure quickly dissipated. Our day/night routine returned to normal. After a few days life became almost leisurely. But it would be wrong to say it was more enjoyable. Even at the height of operational activity the atmosphere at Mepal positively buzzed with liveliness and humour. Of course, it was a different story the morning after losses. But that was still the exception. In general, our lives were boisterous, full and content.

The RAF did much to encourage this. One way was to pander to its aircrew. Every wartime comfort was provided for us (save, of course, the impossible one that two hundred young males most desired). But milk, fruit juice, sugar and eggs – real ones, not the powdered variety – were there for the asking. The medicos toned us up daily under infra-red sun lamps, and fed us capsules of halibut oil (the richest-known source of Vitamin A, deficiency in which causes night-blindness). On terra firma we were excused all but the most essential duties. The Officer class even avoided the menial ones altogether. They were accorded the services of a batman, not yet seen as a manifestation of an anachronistic class system.

Such five-star treatment did beg the question as to whether some indulgent, Bomber Command brass hat had said, 'Oh, let's spoil 'em. They're not long for this world.' Dead right. Thirty raids and pass the egg powder, please.

It was 23 August before we boarded a Lancaster again. We rumbled down the runway in W-Willie which had the nickname The Paper Doll. We lifted-off into conditions surely little better than on the continent. But it was only an exercise in daylight fighter affiliation for the benefit of our two gunners.

On the 25th it was Bill's turn. We boarded dear old S-Sugar for a three-hour H2S cross-country. Number 3 Group had been the last to convert to Lancasters. But when the first of them arrived at Mepal on 13 March 1944 they did at least carry an improved H2S airborne radar set. This airborne radar had entered service early in 1943 and, initially, it had given a rather poor picture. But it was thought worth persevering with as an addition to Gee. The latter, of course, was susceptible to jamming and limited in range, neither a consideration with H2S. The system functioned via a high-speed scanner housed in a blister aft of the bomb bay (where once was the mid-lower turret). It pulsed radar waves to the terrain below. Echoes provided the navigator with a map: a blur for built-up areas, a strong outline for major features such as cliffs or rocky islands, and a clear contrast at the shoreline of sea, river or lake. Even in ten-tenths cloud the location of seaports and of towns on wide rivers was remarkably accurate. In certain circumstances blind bombing became a real option. Blind marking, the technique of dropping TIs through solid cloud (the Paramatta method), became a regular exercise for Pathfinders. But H2S had one major drawback: German radar defences intercepted its signal very easily. The track of an incoming bomber force was quickly plotted and night-fighters directed in to the stream. For this reason navigators operated H2S over enemy territory under a strict injunction to keep things very brief.

Conditions were tailor-made for H2S as we flew S-Sugar northward along the East Anglian coastline. At 11,000 ft we broke through ten-tenths cloud into brilliant sunlight. We gazed across the cloudscape and bathed in the warmth, all of us save Bill who toiled over the images on his cathode-ray tube and bathed only in the weak orange light of his compartment.

Fifty miles from home on the final leg we re-entered the murk, bumping down into clear air again at 1,200 ft. H2S or no H2S, it seemed to me that such unremitting gloom should preclude any ops tonight. In any case after a lengthy cross-country we could expect twenty-four hours' rest, especially Bill.

The first of these presumptions was knocked down as soon as we swung onto our dispersal pan. A Matador stood at the ready and snaking in from the perimeter track was the bomb train. The fifty-fifth op was approaching for 75's record-holder.

When those first Lancasters had arrived back in March, LL866 S-Sugar was among them. At 1935 hrs on 9 April 1944, she had lifted off for 75's maiden Lancaster raid. Eleven of them were sent to attack railway yards at Villeneuve-St-Georges. They had all bombed successfully in clear weather, though one had been damaged by friendly bombing and landed at Ford, a fighter station conveniently situated on the coast across from Selsey Bill.

I have the most tenuous of connections with the Villeneuve raid. The last of the eleven into the air that night was ND768 F-Freddie with P/O Armstrong and his experienced crew on board. The wireless operator was F/Sgt Leslie Edgerton, a very lucky man. A few weeks afterwards he was taken ill with German measles and dispatched to hospital. On 22 May that same F-Freddie and crew, completed by another w/op, went FTR on a Dortmund raid.

Knowing nothing of this, a fully recovered F/Sgt Edgerton returned to Mepal resigned to the fact that his crewmates would have completed their tour, but nevertheless hopeful of hearing something of them. In fact, nothing was offered. He managed to discover that they were logged FTR, but that was all. As a pool w/op he went dicing with scratch crews to the end of his tour, flying a number of the same raids as me.

We did not know one another, but thirty years later our children married. It was not until the fiftieth anniversary of VE day in 1995 that the coincidence of our Service records came to light. In all that time he still harboured hope that even one of his old mates might have been a PoW (as were around one in seven of all aircrew shot down) and returned to New Zealand at the war's end. But by referring to Norman Franks's excellent history of 75 Squadron, *Forever Strong*, I was able to inform him that no one on board F-Freddie survived. Such is the way of things.

It was the way of things, too, that by the end of May 1944, five of the eleven Villeneuve Lancs had already been lost. But S-Sugar flew on, topping two hundred and fifty operational hours and forging her name in the squadron's affections. We could not know, though, as we climbed down the ladder on 25 August, that Lady Luck trailed behind us. S-Sugar would not return to dispersal again. I would be the last pilot to bring her home.

We headed straight for B Flight Office and its notice board. To my surprise our names were on the Order, uncontestable in black and white. My second presumption of the afternoon fell in flames.

As Bill said with some indignation (but, hopefully, no prescience), 'They damned well want their pound of flesh today.'

The reason was that this night would be another maximum effort for the squadron. The week's lull had produced a high level of serviceability. Twenty-eight aircrews were rostered to fly. We weren't given S-Sugar, though. That fell to P/O Snow Barker and his very experienced crew. Our old friend HK574 R-Roger, the samba dancer, would carry us on our seventh raid.

By evening the cloud cover had broken. The sun was fading in the western sky. The moon, which was still in its first quarter, hung pale above us now. Later it would silver the clouds and give us no refuge from hunting fighters.

At twenty past eight I nodded towards Tubby, and pushed the starter coil. The port inner turned over and crackled into magnificent life. How things change. Only a week ago we were going through the identical procedure with the newest kite on the squadron. Now here we were back on board a hoary veteran, running up the engines, completing our checks, girding ourselves for a second trip to the skies of Germany. Would it be as daunting for us as the raid on Bremen?

'Your target for tonight,' the CO had announced more than two hours earlier, 'is the Opel Motor Works at Russelsheim, near Frankfurt. The motors in question are V2 rockets . . .'

Everyone jeered at the mention of another target deep in the Fatherland. This time I jeered with the best of them. Russelsheim was well-defended. Two weeks earlier ten of 75's kites, in a force of two hundred and eighty-six Lancs and Hallies, had experienced its fury. Pilot Officer Mulcahy's doomed P-Peter was one of them. The force was disrupted and Opel escaped. So we were going back. But a similar loss rate tonight could claim twenty-one more lives.

For the survivors it would be a long night. The round trip was over fifteen hundred miles – eight and a half hours in the air. It would be 0100 hrs before we even began the run in to target. Seven hundred Lancasters and Halifaxes would execute a saturation attack, bombing in layers from 17,000 to 21,000 ft, and in three waves. The first and second waves would be heaviest to ensure that ground defences were totally saturated. It would all last only twenty minutes.

My pre-taxi checks complete, I spoke to each of the boys over the intercom. They were ready. Next to Mac, Archie was the calmest man on board. Freed from the burden of his Nuremberg experiences, he was changing before our eyes into a man of irrepressible, even cavalier, optimism. The pendulum had swung too far, of course. But better that than what had gone before.

I signalled to the waiting ground crew. The chocks were pulled away and we rolled off to join the long procession around the perimeter track. A few places in front an aircraft veered off the track. Mud churned up as the wheels sank. The kite stopped, blocking our way ahead. We and a dozen or more crews could only wait while the seconds turned into minutes. Nerves, already strung taut, became unbearably so.

It was critical for the engines to be kept running at or above eight hundred rpm. Low rpm invited oiling and a very loud bang when, still short of take-off speed, you crashed off the end of the runway. Jack Leslie, of course, knew the danger as well as anyone. He hared over in his Jeep and leapt out, arms waving manically at the ground crews. Duly galvanised, they hauled the errant bomber further infield. We began to roll forward again.

R-Roger's Merlins were revving sweetly enough as the caravan flashed us our green. At three thousand rpm and maximum boost they propelled us down the centre of the flarepath. As ever, my inner tensions and anxieties fell away once the kite began to feel light. It was exactly 2100 hrs as we cleared the boundary, wheels up and heading for the clouds.

Behind the blackout, pencil and calipers in hand, poor Bill was already at work on his charts for the second time that day. All but the first outward leg would be flown in darkness. He could look forward to utter exhaustion well before we sighted the Mepal beacon again.

As twilight faded to darkness the stream turned to the south-east on its second leg. Below us at about 7,500 ft the cloud tops reflected the moonlight for miles into the distance. One almost gasped at the austere beauty of it all: the arc of opalescent pink above the western horizon, the silvery whites and soft greys of cloud tops darkening beneath to charcoal and, intermittently visible far below, the North Sea rippling with speckles of light.

In the midst of beauty, though, lay the seeds of danger. We climbed upward through cold air. Long, white trails of vapour strung out far behind every aircraft to port and starboard. There had been talk about how hazardous this phenomenon had proved to USAAF bombers, indeed a giveaway during their daylight operations to German targets. But I had not witnessed it before. It was a disturbing sight. If air conditions remained unchanged the consequences hardly bore thinking about.

119

We crossed the Belgian coast and flew on in a south-easterly track. The cloud cover started to thin again, but not yet our contrails. North of Liège two aircraft exploded ahead of us within a minute of each other. The night-fighters were out there, somewhere. My thoughts returned to St Trond and the ruin we had perpetrated ten days earlier. Slave workers by the thousand could shift a lot of earth in ten days. If No. 1 Night-Fighter Wing was operational and looking for revenge, we were well within range now. But in any case there were several other night-fighter airfields in the area. Over to port the beacon of one was flashing its message, almost certainly an interception course for the swarming Me109s and 110s, Fw190s and Ju88s with their forward and upward firing cannons.

We skirted west of Koblenz. The cloud cover was no more. Carnage was taking place all around. Our route was marked every few miles by a blazing aircraft falling to earth. Fighter flares hung in our path by the score. Those that passed closest lit the cockpit so dazzlingly, I just hung on to the controls and flew.

So many combats were taking place now, so many aircraft blowing up (no doubt some of them German), that I asked everyone but Bill to join the gunners on watch. Mac went into his forward turret, Archie into the astrodome and Tubby stood at my side. Bill, meanwhile, was busy behind his blackout, building up the track on his charts. Each change of course, it was hoped, would sow doubt and confusion among the ground defences as to our eventual port of call. So it was that past Koblenz we swung due east, then towards Stuttgart. Finally, on a course of 325°, we headed north-west for Russeisheim.

There were ten minutes to go. We were at our bombing height of 17,500 ft. I could see no more evidence of contrails, thank God. Straight ahead the Pathfinders' first green TIs were going down, followed immediately by reds. Although hundreds of searchlights played all around, the AA batteries were still. Ground fire there was, but of chandelier flares in support of the circling fighters.

The first, huge explosions erupted in the midst of the ground markers. I opened the bomb doors and waited for Mac's now familiar, coolly-delivered words. In the darkness ahead dozens of aircraft packed the sky. The turbulence was bad, begging the question as to how close we might be to one of them.

'Steady, skip', said Mac – not, I hoped, in criticism of the rough ride. Then came the thumps and the unrestrained leap upward and those two wonderful words, 'Bombs gone'.

We continued to bump and bore along for a twenty-eight second camera run. Before it was completed there was a tumultuous explosion right in front of me. Dense smoke and fire swirled past. By pure, wonderful chance R-Roger flew on, steady as a rock. Not a single piece of shrapnel ruptured her skin.

With the benefit of a rear view, Norrie shouted, 'Scarecrow! It's a bloody scarecrow!'

Strictly speaking, he should have averted his eyes from any such fireworks. But a scarecrow was special. This mythical beast was thought to be a ground-fired shell which exploded in a ball of fire and took on the vague but apocalyptic form of a blazing bomber falling to earth. In fact, no such shell existed. But aircrew believed otherwise. Most thought they had seen one sometime. The consensus of opinion was that by creating these burning 'bombers' the enemy hoped to sap our fighting spirit. It was all of a piece with Lord Haw-Haw's propaganda. 'Resistance is useless,' it told us, adding as an aside, 'and don't believe the losses reported by your Air Ministry.' The latter simply denied their existence, so implausible did it seem that Jerry should fall back upon a non-lethal piece of pyrotechnic theatre. But the seven of us were now willing believers. Psychological warfare was a lot friendlier than the real thing. If we had to get clobbered, we were only too pleased for it to be a spoof.

We dived out of the target area, picking up speed steadily before levelling out at 14,000 ft. Bill gave me a course of 260°. We left behind the burning motor works but not the fighter flares, through lanes of which we still flew – and not the danger which was everywhere. A kite passed extremely close to port. No scarecrow this time, she was trailing vivid orange flames from her side. I thought I could make out a figure still at the controls. But his aircraft was sinking fast and could explode or go belly-up at any second. In our own fire a week earlier I had told the boys to jump only on my word. We had to give the Graviner time to do its stuff. This one was a fuselage fire, and surely offered no grounds for delay. If the skipper was giving his crew the chance to get out, nobody took it while Tubby and I watched. But we did not see how the agony was resolved. This time Norrie had obeyed the gunner's code and kept his eyes off the flames. He was rewarded with the sight of a faint, approaching blur.

'Fighter portside! Corkscrew starboard! Go!' he screamed. His guns opened up, with Geoff's joining the fray almost immediately. I hurled R-Roger down and round with all my might. Tubby, who had just thrown out the last of the Window, wasn't strapped in yet.

He simply hit the roof, hands scrabbling for any kind of hold. Incendiary shells streamed past us. Our gunners replied to the point where the attacker, a twin-engined Me110, peeled away below our starboard wing. By the time turrets were turned he was away, apparently unscathed. But so were we.

'Missed the bastard', raged Norrie, having hosed the fighter all the way in to no effect. 'Why didn't I get him? He should've had his f****** chips.'

Geoff, much the more insouciant character, was unperturbed. 'Not chips, mate,' he said, 'German f****** sausage.'

'You mean he'll be wurst back in the mess', cut-in Archie in appallingly buoyant form. 'Wurst . . . ?' he repeated hopefully.

Such an intervention would have been unthinkable a week earlier, though the absence of strangulated groans told me that I was alone in grasping his meaning (alone also in having had a pork butcher as a Home Guard CO).

All this was interesting but, frankly, not professional and the captain was obliged to tell them so.

I decided to lose more height. The contrail problem could return as we flew north, and the antidote was warmer air. Before we crossed the Rhine south of Koblenz we saw two more bombers engulfed in fire, drifting slowly down. They exploded on impact with a dull red glow followed by briefly-flickering yellow and then nothing. We crossed into Belgium south of Bastogne, still under the treacherous full moon, still nervous of enemy fighters. As we approached La Capelle, Bill gave me the final course for Mepal. That precipitated a gradual change of mood. We descended through light cloud and levelled at 6,000 ft. Visibility was good. Moonlight played on the English Channel. We began to feel more relaxed. No, we began to feel good. This had been another demanding raid, a night of the hunter. But we had not been snared. Each man had turned in a solid performance, especially Bill who must have been ready to drop. Tubby distributed the coffee and biscuits. By the time the Thames estuary shone below, the boys were well into their repertoire of unrepeatable ditties. Well, you know, the relief, the relief . . .

We were held up for some time while Control brought home to roost some of its other birds, no doubt one or two in need of priority. Dawn had broken as I taxied to dispersal and switched off the engines. Seven tired but exhilarated young men climbed down the aircraft ladder, eight and a half hours older and more battle-hardened than when they took off.

The raid appeared to be a success and, indeed, production at the Opel works would be hampered for many weeks. But the mood at de-briefing and in the mess was subdued. Two 75 crews had not come home. The time in which they might have landed at another field had passed without news. It only remained to log them FTR. One, alas, was Snow Barker and his boys in S-Sugar on their twenty-fifth trip. The other was F/O Alan Flemming's crew in their N-Nan, known as 'Round Again Nan' because the exacting and courageous bomb aimer, F/Sgt Vincent, had earnt himself a reputation for calling a dummy run. They were flying number twenty-four. Nothing would be heard of any of them again.

In our heads we all knew experience was not an invulnerable armour. There were no guarantees, however well we did our job. Even so, we worked away diligently to chalk up another op. We had to believe that with each one our survival became a little more secure. The loss of not one but two very good, experienced crews assailed that belief and made us doubt ourselves more than did ten thousand German scarecrows, real or imaginary.

On a brighter note, we learned that there was indeed a priority landing. The beneficiary was the admirable Irishman, F/Sgt Eldrid O'Callaghan, who wobbled home minus both ailerons and a few, not insubstantial pieces of wing, the result of a suicidally gung-ho evasive manoeuvre. For his airmanship he would be awarded the DFM.

Life on the squadron was nothing, as I have said repeatedly, if not intense. But to appreciate this to the full, you need to be shaken into wakefulness by your batman at midday, when you only climbed into the sack at seven. And you need to hear the insistent words, 'Excuse me, sir . . . EXCUSE ME, SIR . . . but ops are on tonight and you have an air test to fly at 1300 hrs.'

Regrettably, I couldn't shut out his voice. Against the expressed desire of every tissue and bone in my body, I got out of bed, dressed, on my bike and over to B Flight Office. Bill was already there, looking even worse than I felt. We squinted at the notice board. Yes, there were our names again, this time rostered to fly quite a new kite on the Squadron, HK562 L-Lucy. Briefing was at 1700 hrs.

Although produced on an assembly line from identical parts, each Lancaster had its own distinctive character. No two flew quite the same. There was always an idiosyncrasy somewhere. It was as well for a pilot to acquaint himself with this before he headed for the Fatherland, and the time to do it was the air test. We gave L-Lucy a thorough once-over. She pleased us all and certainly handled well, which was my main concern.

By now I reckoned I was pretty familiar with the Avro Lancaster. This wasn't difficult. It was free of any vices worthy of the name. For the squadron hotshots, and there were always a few who fancied themselves in this department, it was rather dull and, if anything, too simple to fly. But trips like Russelsheim weren't made any easier by coaxing an enervating machine through the skies. The Lanc suited me just as she was.

I signed Form 700 declaring L-Lucy serviceable and headed with Bill to the mess for a late lunch. Then, while the ground crews laboured over refuelling, re-arming and bombing-up, I crawled back into bed and slept fitfully.

At five o'clock we were ensconced in our usual row of seats at the back of the briefing room, smoking like men possessed. The maps were spread before us. Speculation buzzed.

'Eighteen hundred gallons, six-hour flight, twelve hundred miles . . . that spells the Ruhr to me.'

'Spells trouble wherever they send us.'

'Hamburg's possible . . . or Bremen again.'

'Nah, rubbish. They've found some nice, quiet corner of Berlin where no one's ever 'eard of ack-ack guns.'

Jack Leslie opened the door to the Briefing room. Quiet descended. We stood as the line of officers swept past. The CO mounted the platform and paused while the MPs quit the room. He looked tired and more serious than I had seen him before. Was the grievous strain of sending out his crews over Germany, in the clear expectation of losses, taking its toll? Looking at him then, I thought it extraordinary if it did not. Certainly, he had reacted to the Barker and Flemming losses by placing himself at the head of this day's Battle Order.

When, from the vantage point of seven decades of life I think how we respected and admired the CO not merely for his rank but for the style of his leadership, I am astonished by his tender years. Of course, we were all young, and nearly all younger than him. But at twenty-five he would be considered hardly more than a boy today and kept well away from a post of such life-and-death responsibility. Of course, we are not now in the fifth year of total war. Life-and-death responsibilities are rather fewer and further between.

With a deft flick of the wrist, the CO uncovered the wallmap behind him.

'Gentlemen,' he began, as always, 'the target for tonight is Kiel.'

And, as always, the gentlemen responded with groans, the only democratic expression in Air Force Life. But one bright spark shouted out, 'Sir, can we be excused? I promised to meet my girl-friend at eight o'clock.'

The groans transmuted into cackles. The CO smiled broadly, shot a glance at the wag's Flight Commander and replied, 'You're very welcome to bring her along.'

A robust and approbatory gale of laughter swept across the room. The tension, his as well as ours I think, fell away. The CO turned to the business in hand, the attack on the Reich's largest naval facility. We learned of its vital significance to the German war effort. Intelligence reports showed two cruisers currently in dry dock and a number of U-boats under maintenance. A miscellany of lesser naval assets, large warehouses filled with stores, and dozens of huge cranes lining the wharves were there to be smashed. But the Intelligence Officer also spoke of the rows of sailors' houses stretching back from the docks. These would be hit, too, we knew. But the suggestion was that they constituted a worthwhile target in their own right, not a view likely to be shared by many of us who had to do the job.

Kiel was, of course, a regular subject of Bomber Command's attention. A month earlier, an attack by six hundred and twelve bombers managed both to be concentrated and a surprise to the ground defences. The port and U-boat yards were seriously damaged and the city paralysed for three days. But that was the first main force raid on Germany since the Normandy invasion, an advantage that was gone now. A hot reception was guaranteed.

The weather over the North Sea and the target area was forecast to be good. The moon would be full again. We would be bombing at midnight precisely and from a height of 17,500 ft, the same as for Russelsheim. Twenty-one of 75's kites were to be part of a force of four hundred Lancasters and Halifaxes from 3 and 4 Groups. It would approach the target from a course of 070°. Six of our kites, including L-Lucy, would drop an 8,000 pound high explosive block-buster and a complement of incendiaries. The rest would carry a 4,000-pounder plus incendiaries. A Master Bomber would control the raid, calling in PFF Lancasters at one minute to midnight to mark the target with green indicators. Reds would be employed as secondary markers if the Master Bomber so required. The leading squadron aircraft would take off at 2000 hrs, the last twenty minutes later.

The CO brought Briefing to an end with his usual *bon mot*. This time he meant it literally. He would be in the billowing, grey plumes above Kiel in more than spirit. That wasn't always the case, of course, and I still hadn't quite worked out what he meant the other times. But as I followed everyone out into the warm light of evening, contemplating this mystery, I closed the door on a room now empty of everything *except* smoke.

At 1930 hrs we were kitted-up and waiting outside the crew room for our transport. It droned to a halt. The driver, however, was a pretty English rose in the uniform of a WAAF. All seven of us clambered into the truck at once, lugging our flying gear over the tailgate and finishing in an undignified heap of parachutes, boots and curses. She flashed us a smile. She'd seen it all before. Each of us, of course, would have given a month's leave to see just a little of her, preferably later in the local.

Geoff, as ever, said it for all of us, 'Gentleman, your target for tonight . . .'

Tempting thought though this was, we had a prior engagement with a lady called Lucy. Besides, Mac seemed almost as taken with the idea of getting up close to that 8,000-pounder, twice the size of anything he'd sent hurtling at the enemy before. The first such blockbuster was dropped on Essen on the night of 10 April 1942. Not a sophisticated piece of engineering, it was basically two 4,000 lb cylinders joined in-line (the final development in this type was the three-cylinder, 12,000 lb HC bomb, first employed by 617 Squadron in a costly attack on the Dortmund–Ems Canal on the night of 15 September 1943).

At 2032 hrs I checked my watch and held the brakes on. The flarepath burned brightly ahead of us. Only the leading aircraft had set off down it and was just lifting off into the evening sky. Conventional wisdom had it that being high in the take-off order was a bad thing. It meant stooging around, burning up precious fuel until the last aircraft had joined the party. It reduced the margin of error. But, anyway, here we were at number two. The caravan flashed us a green. We were away, deafening the knot of bystanders. I held L-Lucy down until the last moment before hauling her over the airfield boundary. With wheels and flaps up, we began our climb in a wide orbit, finally coming back over the airfield to set course.

The evening sun was low on the western horizon, shooting rays of light up through the few, ragged clouds and casting long shadows across the fields. England, my England, no place on earth ever looked more fresh and peaceful to me. Now was the time to be walking that pretty WAAF through the woods and along the river bank, to the little country pub where the landlord always welcomed us. Instead, we were encased in steel and climbing to 17,500 ft, with high explosive and the sound of Merlins for company and a welcome from flak batteries and night-fighters to come.

We crossed the English coast at Cromer. The fiery orb of the sun disappeared below the horizon and stars became discernible in the heavens. One of our engines was revving slightly out of sync., producing the pulsing note familiar from German bomber incursions over England two or three years earlier. I made the requisite adjustment and settled back to search the sky for my brothers-in-arms. It had been some time since we'd seen another aircraft, despite the full moon. We crossed the Elbe estuary. Below us the clouds had dispersed. To port and starboard I could see the flashing beacons of night-fighter stations. But we were quite alone.

Bill gave me a change of course for Hamburg. It was a predetermined feint, all part of the guessing game. Then we changed course to the north-east to make a direct approach to Kiel. I could easily make out the city, the waterfront and the docks. Dozens of searchlights probed the sky. Every gunner in the area was poised to fire. Yet still no markers had gone down.

I knew something had gone badly awry. We had arrived in advance of the Master Bomber, the Pathfinders and the main force. I glanced swiftly at my watch. It read five minutes to twelve. I banked L-Lucy to take another, hard look at the city below. It was in total darkness, eerie, almost expectant.

I went on the intercom to my navigator: 'We're too damned early, Bill. There are no markers. There's nothing at all. We're the only ones here. I'm going to fly a wide circle out to the east. When the TIs go down we'll come back on course.'

No sooner had we set off eastward away from the target when the Master Bomber's voice floated over the r/t. He called in the Pathfinders to mark the aiming point. Their green TIs burst and, moments later, huge sheets of white flame erupted over the dockyards as the first bombs were dropped by the main force.

We came around, nervously approaching the edge of the stream until the gyro compass read 070° again. But we still had to negotiate the bottleneck along with three hundred and ninety-nine other bombers. We inched across to starboard. Everybody was on watch for converging aircraft, except Mac. He, of course, was in his glasshouse, no doubt hoping he wouldn't now have to call a dummy run. Next to the rear turret, the bomb aimer's compartment was the

coldest corner in the aircraft. At altitude the metal of the fuselage
had never to be touched since skin would bond to it instantly. So
cold and far from home, it seemed an unlikely battleground for a
Maori. But Mac was in his element there.

Flak had no more effect on him than freezing temperatures. The
AA batteries had come to life with the very first TI. Now a wall of
exploding shells stood between us and the dockyards. I opened the
bomb doors and flew into the maelstrom. Heedless of everything
except our position relative to the greens, Mac slowly intoned his
instructions. For the rest of us it was an excruciating process. The
flak exploded, the kite rocked and six men willed just one other to
get the hell on with it. But it was never any use trying to hurry him.
All the longest minutes of my life have been spent wishing it was
only otherwise.

The blockbuster finally tumbled into the night. L-Lucy bucked
and rocketed upward more savagely than any Lancaster had done
in my hands before. But Mac, God bless him, still felt constrained
to inform us that the bombs had gone and it all looked good, as to
his loving eyes it no doubt did.

I closed the bomb doors. We put our heads down for the camera
run. The scene below resembled a gargantuan fireworks display.
The back-up Pathfinders had been called in for the second time to
reinforce the green markers. They deposited their flares into a lurid
mass of fire, crowned by white-radiant circles spreading over the
waterfront as each cookie struck.

We flew on straight and level, impatient for the burst of the photo-
flash. The flak, which had been coming up thick and fast, eased off.
But there was no respite from danger. Orange fighter flares began
to drift down slowly, robbing us of all vestiges of darkness. We
watched and waited. The first tracers arced across the sky, and then
combats began all around us. I could see several bombers returning
fire. One, only about four hundred yards ahead, was already in
serious difficulty.

The photo-flash burst and I pushed the column forward. We were
still on our north-easterly bombing course but diving away from the
target area as fast as possible. We had three hundred mph coming
up on the airspeed indicator when Geoff yelled,

'Fighter, diving on us from port side. Corkscrew. Corkscrew.'

The German pilot must have been a single-minded devil. He had
picked us out and, for some reason, followed us a long way down.
I banked L-Lucy onto her starboard wingtip. As I heaved her over

onto the opposite side he opened fire. A few shells penetrated the fuselage, exiting downwards on the other side, but most curled away from us. He passed somewhere over the top as the corkscrew took us down. Then he was gone.

Such combats in the past had elicited a raucous commentary from the gun turrets. This time there wasn't a sound. I went straight onto the intercom. They and the others were somewhat shaken by the violence of the corkscrew, but that was all.

'I thought the bloody wings were going to come off that time,' complained Archie, who was not given to over-statement.

I assured him that the Lancaster was made of sterner stuff than that. But it was true that we had gone down faster and much further than I had anticipated. We were flying level now, though only 3,000 ft above the sea. Also, I was surprised to find myself both wet with perspiration and shivering from cold.

Unsure what to make of it, I called Bill, 'I don't like this, Bill. Give me a course and let's get out of here.'

The flight plan was to turn back almost through 180° to bring us across Denmark and out over the North Sea well south of the island of Sylt, which we knew to be heavily defended. We left behind the deathly orange flares and flew over the shadowy woodlands, villages, fields and rivers of Denmark, tranquil in the light of the moon. It all seemed very peaceful as we approached the coastline and the North Sea. Moments later, I knew something was terribly wrong. A few miles out to sea, and coming up fast, were islands that should not have been there.

I yelled into the intercom, 'Bill, there are islands ahead. One just to port, the other one to starboard very long and narrow. *Where the hell are we?*'

No answer came. Bill was lost. He was checking and double-checking but coming up with the same result. A proud man, expert in his craft, Bill *knew* there could be no islands, nothing but the cold North Sea until we reached the English coast. But even he couldn't dispute the intervention of German ground defences.

As we crossed over the east coast of the larger island innumerable searchlights flicked on. Notwithstanding the clear sky and moon-light we could have expected at least a few moments' grace. But the lights swung in our direction straight away. Worse, a radar-controlled master beam locked on, trapping us in its consuming, bluish glare. With extraordinary, indeed uncanny efficiency we had been coned, as over Bremen. But whereas there we had 19,000 ft to play with, here we had but 3,000 ft. The AA batteries burst into action, hosing light flak at us. In turn, Norrie was pumping his .303s back, aiming at the roots of the light.

I had to push down the nose, there being no other prospect of escape. But since the cockpit was filled with blinding light, there was no guide beyond or within as to how far I could go. Breathless and staring into nothing, I opened the throttles to the maximum and down we went with the terrible, rising whine of a kite in its death throes.

Light flak was more a rapier than a bludgeon like its big brother. Aimed visually at low-flying targets, it was frighteningly accurate. Aircrew knew it by the descriptive and apt title, flaming onions. It scribed a graceful, sweeping arc through the sky, slow at first, then accelerating rapidly to pass with a swish and explode with a crack of thunder. It came not singly but in a string of fire, multi-coloured, indeed beautiful were it not also deadly.

For all that, it had not hurt us. But the soldiers manning the defences thought otherwise. As soon as they heard the scream of engines at bursting point they stood back from their guns and their searchlights. They stood back to watch us hit, to savour the crump and the power of the explosion. They stood back so they could tell one another afterwards what damned fine fellows they were and how to deal with these *terrorfliegern.*

In the course of eight or nine seconds everything, even the master beam, was off us. I pulled at the column in the name of my mother's love and backed off the throttles. We scraped clear of the coastline and levelled out. We were flying westward above the mirror of the sea, beating spray. The spider had lost the fly.

I decided to stay down until we were well out of range, and set the tail trimmers back. The boys were quiet. Probably, like me, they were reflecting that 3,000 ft was not an ideal platform for night-time diving practice.

Then a despairing, northern voice broke the spell, 'Skip, for pity's sake don't listen to the mid-upper if he wants any more corkscrews. I'm shipping salt water back 'ere.'

For once there was no rejoinder from Geoff. He had tasted his own medicine. The laughter, the release of tension, the joyous knowledge that we were still in one piece and going home carried our spirits upward as L-Lucy rose into an empty sky.

It was all of thirty minutes before Bill was within range for a Gee fix. He could hardly believe what he saw on the screen. We were miles north of our intended track, heading towards the Moray Firth. Now he knew for certain that there was a failure in our navigational equipment. This banished any doubt that it was Sylt's defences we had encountered. It all began to make sense. Bill was vindicated.

The precise nature of the equipment failure was less important at this time than a course correction to take us home. Bill set to work on his charts and the Dalton computer, and soon responded with the new course and arrival time.

Tubby was satisfied with the fuel reserves, notwithstanding the extra flying we'd put in and the early slot at take off. I increased speed accordingly. But we were still all alone as the Mepal beacon came into view. At 0204 hrs L-Lucy settled gently between the two rows of flarepath lights. We expected to be the last ones home. But three minutes later F/O Martyn came in. I reckon we had done three targets that night, so goodness knows what he had been up to.

One of 75's twenty-one Lancasters had aborted but all the rest bombed and made it home. The human cost was restricted to a single mid-upper gunner with serious leg injuries. Elsewhere the blade fell more frequently. Twenty-two aircraft failed to return to their squadrons that night. Extensive damage to the docks rendered the operation a success. But, as ever, it was bought with the sacrifice of many a cherished son or husband.

The following day we went out to look at L-Lucy. We counted nine small entry holes in her fuselage, a modest score for a busy night. To Bill's satisfaction, the ground crew found that the gyro compass had toppled, evidently during our escape from the Ju88, and was reading 30° out of true.

But it didn't matter now. Operation number eight was safely behind us. To our delight, Garth Gunn gave us seven days' leave. Probably, he looked at us and saw a crew arriving early over the target and flying to the frozen north instead of Mepal. Probably, he saw a crew that was tired and susceptible to error. In any event, that same evening I walked home to Stony from the station at Wolverton, down the narrow, echoing passage to our back door and into my parents' arms.

For me, much had come to pass since the last leave. That one had been before the flak and tracers, before 75, before Lancasters, before conversion to four engines, even. There was a lot that could be said. But I think my mother preferred not to hear it. Naturally, she worried for my safety as any mother would. She would not have thanked me if, in the quiet of the evening when she was alone in the house, she had cause to ponder corkscrews and scarecrows, flaming onions and blue master beams.

On the other hand my father, moved by the same anxieties,

pressed me avidly for every detail. To make matters easier he spirited me away to The Case Is Altered. The Case was one of seventeen hostelries in the town during the war years, an average of rather better than one pub to a hundred adults. It was Dad's haunt every evening of his married life except Tuesdays which, long ago and only under duress, he had agreed to spend in the matrimonial home.

But Dad's plan for me didn't quite work out. The Case didn't see many RAF pilots. Its regular clientele of crib and dart players and grizzled old characters who would nurse a pint of mild for an entire evening was a bit short on recent operational experience. They gave us no privacy or peace. If not a celebrity I was at least a talking point, the more so for having flown a beat-up or two in the locality.

Bob Rollins, the town's Police Sergeant and a regular at The Case, warned me that folk had complained about the beat-ups. He put on his most *ex cathedra* air. 'It is my duty', he said quite correctly, 'to bring you before the appropriate authorities. Anything you may say . . .'

I must have blanched at the sight of due process because, almost at once, he began to quiver with suppressed hilarity. It quickly got the better of him. The whole pub finished up laughing into their beermugs at my expense. Then the good Sergeant bought me a drink for having been so gullible. If I didn't know before, I knew now that my beat-ups were entirely immune from legal redress.

On subsequent evenings Dad released me into the more tender care of my girlfriend, Eileen. But come the weekend, he tried again. He insisted on us walking the two miles across the fields to Calverton for a lunchtime pint at The Shoulder of Mutton.

When my sister and I were small this used to be a family treat on fine, summer weekends. Dad would leave us outside the door of the pub, children never being tolerated within. It would always seem an age until he emerged carrying a tray of drinks: shandy for my mother; lemonade or ginger beer and a packet of sweet biscuits for us; and a beer for himself. Joan and I would sit on the low wall of the pub garden, surveying the life of the village and thinking ourselves very grown-up and sophisticated. It was a simple pleasure in serene and innocent times.

Now Dad and I sat at the bar with my sheepdog, Bob, restful at our feet. I answered every question, first about my crew, then the squadron, then operational flying. He spared himself nothing. That was his wish and we were too close for me to disregard it. The only thing I did not tell him was how desperate and frightened I had felt in those damned master beams over Bremen and Sylt. I did not want him to think of me in the coming weeks and remember only that.

The boys and I reported for duty on the evening of 3 September. At the same time ten of Mepal's Lancs came home from a 3 Group raid on the night-fighter station at Eindhoven. Slight but accurate AA fire damaged three of them. But the consensus of opinion was that it had been a relatively easy trip.

Two more formidable operations had been called for 29 August. Stettin was revisited by fourteen aircraft. Six more from B Flight dropped mines in the Gulf of Danzig. Both trips were long, the Danzig op excessively so. Take-off time was 2130 hrs, the aircraft returning at 0815 hrs the next morning. But it was Stettin that claimed the casualty. This was F/Sgt King's Lancaster LM594. The crew was one of the two who had arrived with us at the beginning of the month.

Now only we remained.

CHAPTER NINE

BUT GOD DISPOSES

Mepal was inactive for thirty-six hours after our return. But on the morning of 5 September a closely-typed sheet of paper was pinned to the Flight notice board again. Our names were listed against HK596 O-Oboe which I had not flown before. In the briefing room at noon we heard the target, a name that resonates in French hearts to this day – but not for happy reasons.

The story begins with the Guards Armoured Division, the spearhead of the British Army, in its drive across northern France and Belgium. On 3 September 1944 it entered Brussels victorious. But in its wake lay a highly selective liberation. Some French coastal towns thought to be heavily garrisoned by the *Wehrmacht* were simply bypassed. To Field Marshal Montgomery the paramount objective was to drive his spearhead all the way to the German border. The task of clearing those towns militated against that. Unquestionably, the garrisons would be ordered to hold out for as long as possible. Once their outer defensive positions fell a slow and bloody battle, house-by-house, street-by-street, was in prospect. Allied manpower and materials would be tied up. Time would be lost. Pressure on the retreating German main force would be relieved.

Of course the German garrisons had to be made to quit and surrender, and not merely for the altruistic purpose of freeing Frenchmen. While the Allies were denied use of Channel ports, especially those to the east, their supply lines were anchored to the Normandy beaches, far from the front. Nonetheless, the Army would not yet launch their assaults. First, the enemy would be softened up with a well-targeted intervention by heavy bombers.

A hasty request to Bomber Command followed. The first town in line was Le Havre. A force of 11,000 men was thought to be garrisoned in the constricted and easily identifiable old town quarter. The operation would be relatively safe for local noncombatants, a prime consideration (not least because 12,000 French and Belgian civilians had already died under the Allies' pre-Overlord bombing). As with the Hamel raid of 14 August, pinpoint accuracy would be a necessity. Then, Bomber Command had utilised the Lancasters of 3 Group. It would do so again now.

One hundred and seventy-five young men gathered in Mepal's briefing room to hear that this was their next job of work. We were told how we would trigger the liberation of Le Havre and save the lives of countless British soldiers. Two days earlier warnings had been issued to the local populace by means of a Nickel raid. Unless they were German, all those who wished to leave knew they must do so. Le Havre would be ready and waiting for us well before the red TIs went down at 1600 hrs.

To all this our principal and instant reaction was relief. Bremen, Russelsheim, Kiel, the Gulf of Danzig, Stettin . . . these were dangerous places. By comparison, a brief excursion to occupied France was a cakewalk. For eighteen of the twenty-five crews it must have seemed almost too good to be true. Originally, they were scheduled to attack Dortmund, a regular and fearsome object of Bomber Command's attentions. The squadron's last trip there in May saw two FTRs, all aircrew lost.

In hindsight, the other component in our attitude to this or any raid was the total trust we put in the facts as they were presented to us. I doubt if anybody had a single insubordinate thought about them or about the safety of the local populace. Our competence did not extend to such matters. That was the preserve of high-flying staff officers at Bomber Command and the Group HQs. By the time the Battle Order was pinned to our notice board, the trigger was already pulled. Bill had his flight plan. Archie had his callsigns. Mac, and nearly three hundred and fifty like him, had 13,000 lb of explosive to drop upon the heads of German soldiery.

At 1345 hrs I pressed the button and O-Oboe's port inner crackled into life, first of the four. The pre-taxi checks were completed, the chocks pulled away. We swung off the pan and into the queue of twenty-four other kites. Even with the cockpit window closed and my flying helmet firmly over my head, a hundred Merlins produced some deafening but still, I think, euphonious music. It certainly set the pulse racing and, for me, will forever be the epitome of raw, man-made power.

Within twenty-five minutes of the first aircraft rising majesti-cally from the ground, the last had followed. The might of all ten 3 Group squadrons circled in the skies of East Anglia. And circling with them was almost two thousand tons of general-purpose bombs.

We climbed to our bombing height of 12,000 ft. The weather conditions and visibility were perfect. We flew over the fields in which a Norman king once seized the English crown. We crossed the coast above the town that lent its name to the battle. On the other side of the water Le Havre awaited us, along with our own small and unwelcome place in Anglo-French history.

We were given no escort. But throughout the afternoon Allied fighters had conducted sweeps across the countryside of northern France. That was sufficient to deter the *Luftwaffe*. Unchallenged, the Mosquito Pathfinders deposited their TIs neatly into the old, eastern part of the town where the German Army was quartered. The only opposition was a solitary light AA gun. I thought then that one gun was a very poor show. It contrasted starkly with the British Army's story of certain and desperate German resistance.

All the way in, the stream was tighter than on my previous daylight raids. Now, on our bombing run, everything looked good. Fécamp came into sight to port, and the Seine estuary ahead. Below us, visible in every detail to the naked eye, lay Le Havre. The Master Bomber carried a heavier burden than usual that day. But he came through on the r/t as composed as ever, 'Come in, Main Force,' he said, 'Bomb the reds.'

We followed the first wave. I saw their bombs falling with remarkable accuracy as, indeed, we all knew they must. Mac began to line up for the drop. That familiar voice and those same old, spare phrases guided my hands and feet. Then the Master Bomber – the MC to us – cut in again. He wanted a fresh marking and ordered the Pathfinders to drop green TIs. Mac, however, already had the aiming point square in his sight. He was too single-minded and downright stubborn to heed the descending greens. Fifteen brisk thumps and O-Oboe's simultaneous struggle upward told us that our work here was done, bar the camera run.

The photo turned out to be a good one. All the evidence pointed to a highly successful operation. The aiming point was well saturated with very limited spread or creep-back. Bomber Command had done everything demanded of it, and lost no aircraft. If the Army's pre-raid intelligence was good and their assessment of the likely effect of the bombing accurate, there would be little now to stand in their way. Le Havre could be liberated.

We spent the evening in the Plough and Harrow talking to some of the Witchford boys. We all thought the same. It was a job well done. We wouldn't be going back. We could not know that the raid had been flawed in the planning and consigned to failure and obloquy before a single aircraft lifted off.

By morning a cold front had moved in. Flying was curtailed. Garth detailed us to take up a new Lancaster 1 for an acceptance test when the opportunity arose, but it was early afternoon before we could board. We landed to find the ground crews and armourers hard at work again. The weather had improved, not much but enough: ops were on. We hurried over to the Flight Office. We were not included among the twenty-four crews on the Battle Order, and Briefing was already in progress. Our plans to while away the evening over a pint in the local were not interrupted, except by the distant glory of Merlins at take off.

The target was the German Army HQ at Harquebec, close to Le Havre and evidently part of the same army support effort. The crews reported a very concentrated raid with no opposition. Over in the old town fires were still smouldering. All twenty-four aircraft returned safely.

On the morning of 8 September we flew an air test in a Lancaster 1, LM276 which had just arrived on station and flown only the Le Havre and Harquebec ops. It was lettered S-Sugar and was the successor to the fallen squadron record-holder. A vacant letter wasn't always guaranteed to new kites. By this stage of the war most squadrons probably boasted more bombers than there were letters in the alphabet. At one stage Mepal accommodated thirty-five, of which at least eighteen had to share letters.

We landed to find the Matadors and bomb trolleys trundling around dispersal again. This time we were on the Battle Order, to fly S-Sugar. Twenty-three crews gathered in the briefing room at midday. The grapevine forecast a run over occupied territory. But no one could have predicted the CO's actual words.

'Gentlemen', he said, 'your target for today is an enemy troop concentration on the outskirts of Le Havre.'

There were gasps of astonishment from the floor. Troops! What troops? What the hell was all that about two days ago?

This time the drop zone was different: the district of Doudeneville, some distance from the old town. But take-off time, flight plan, bomb load, bombing instructions and time on target were all identical. The rationale was also broadly the same. The enemy's capacity to fight was not broken, but another seventeen hundred tons of bombs was the way to change that. So, back we would go.

The one significant variation – ever the variable – was the

weather. The heavy stuff might have left East Anglia, but only to drift southward across the English Channel. By the time of our arrival the target area would be buried under two miles of dense and turbulent cloud. None the less, the Army couldn't wait. The op must go ahead, regardless of the difficulties. And if that meant sending us in below the cloud base, a bombing height of only 3,000 ft, so be it!

In the event not even this meagre distance was obtained between the German guns and some of those who managed to bomb. As we made our approach the cloud base was at little more than 1,000 ft. We crossed the coast with Le Havre veiled in drifting white and grey. Some of the early aircraft at the head of the stream managed to bomb as briefed. But a handful of press-on chaps had gone down to 900 ft to get the job done, exposing themselves not only to flak damage but to dismemberment by the shockwaves of their own bomb blasts.

By the time we arrived over the target all this fun was over. No one could get a clean sight of the markers. The Master Bomber ordered us into a tight orbit of the drop zone. Round we swirled, still numbering hundreds, in and out of the rain-laden clouds as if on some mad merry-go-round. There was an imminent danger of collision and even more so from flak. The ground defences were firing from dozens of light AA guns and even ordinary machine-guns, a totally different story from the raid of 5 September. The choice of so many targets eddying on the ground radar screens, and at such inviting range, must have made the gun crews giddy with excitement.

Finally, discretion prevailed over valour. The Master Bomber took the only possible decision and aborted the raid. The defenders were left triumphant.

I turned S-Sugar upward and away, urging everyone to be alert for converging aircraft. It was a request made more in hope than expectation. Visibility was near zero. Then we topped the cloud and blissfully warm sunlight hit the perspex. The drama was past. We still had our bombs on board, of course. But soon enough the Channel was visible again, glistening silver on blue. I opened the bomb doors. Mac searched for shipping. Satisfied that all was clear he hit the switches. In this he was not alone. Bomb aimers in dozens of 3 Group Lancs around us were doing likewise, and the sea erupted into a turmoil of spray from hundreds of tons of impacting bombs.

So our total of ops reached double figures. We were only too aware that we had funked the mission, though in truth there was nothing to gain from circling Le Havre any longer, and everything to lose. Ten of the aircraft dispatched from Mepal fared better, getting their bombs away before the order to abort. Squadron records show that the remaining thirteen returned with their bomb loads intact. Well, I would never even have attempted to, and there must have been many like me. But all of 75's Lancs returned safely and so, too, did four rather special Stirlings of 149 Squadron. They were the last of these great birds to fly operationally – ironic that an aircraft found so wanting in ceiling should bow out in a debacle at 3,000 ft.

The next day, 9 September, was free of operations for 75. But that did not bestow freedom upon us. Such days required an air test at least and, not infrequently, a training flight for the navigator or gunners. The only respite from flying came with bad weather, and I do mean *bad* weather.

The weather on the 9th was made for navigators. A slab of dull grey cloud overhung bomber country, providing the ideal conditions for H2S practice. So for Bill's benefit we all climbed on board S-Sugar once again and took to the skies for a three-hour cross-country.

By this time we had been a month on the squadron and were just beginning to encroach upon the territory occupied by the senior crews. This was all a matter of operational experience, the number of sorties flown. The fact that my flying hours were several times those of the average squadron pilot did not enter into it, and rightly so. I began my tour no different to the greenest pilot with the minimum six hundred hours in his logbook. We all progressed under the same sun (or moon) and via the same risks. Such seniority as we attained was as much a gift of Lady Luck as the product of our talent. It did not do to forget this, particularly when discussing events over a beer in the mess. Those crass enough to talk-up their own bravery or expertise were invariably met with a pained silence.

In some quarters, though, my instructing days did not entirely count for nothing. There was one aircraft on the squadron provided for the non-operational use of the CO. Generally, that involved him flying it to Waterbeach for the regular conferences of 3 Group Commanders held there. One would have expected a Lancaster to be requisitioned for the purpose. But this option was never pursued. Perhaps the C-in-C of Bomber Command would have disapproved. Instead, an Airspeed Oxford was made available.

All through my RAF days I could never quite get away from the Oxford. Whenever one came within five miles of me I wound up flying the thing. And so it was at Mepal, this despite the fact that Jack Leslie was a fine pilot and, moreover, one not normally reticent at the controls. But not long after our arrival on station word of my instructing days reached his office. Bill and I were ordered to present ourselves. The CO duly appointed us his unofficial, personal aircrew and I was back flying an Oxford. He, meanwhile, took to passengering in style. This was undoubtedly the whole point of the exercise and, I suppose, only befitted the honour and prestige of the squadron.

On the morning of 10 September I flew the CO the short hop to another of his meetings. It lasted an hour, during which the pair of us basked in the glorious sunshine and chatted to some of the aircrew stationed at Waterbeach with 514 Squadron. On our return to Mepal we sauntered into B Flight Office to discover a Battle Order on the notice board and our names typed on it. We would fly S-Sugar again.

Garth introduced Bill and me to a new replacement pilot. He was an English Flight Sergeant named Bill Osborne and he would come along with us as second dickey. This was a significant milestone in our careers as well as F/Sgt Osborne's, and further confirmation of our burgeoning status.

We had an air test to fly as quickly as possible in S-Sugar. I asked along our second dickey to shake hands with the rest of the crew, whom I was proud to present as professionals every one. And they surely were. Over the past four weeks they had all performed magnificently. I knew that none of them had thanked me back at OTU and in our early ops for being a demanding so-and-so, sometimes an unreasonable one. But we had got this far, by God, and I felt entitled now to take satisfaction in the results.

A second dickey flight was an opportunity for the chosen crew to demonstrate all the arts of the bomber's war. This may sound like vanity, but there was none. There was a sense of benevolence, however, and there was patronage. For the skipper there was also an obligation to repay his peers, albeit indirectly, for the same past favour. The only selfish motive in this was the desire to do a damn good job. If as a result Bill Osborne saw fit to model his crew on us, that would be a fine compliment but one that would probably never reach our ears.

The eight of us reported for Briefing at 1315 hrs. There was little surprise from the floor when for the third time in six days the CO pronounced the name of Le Havre. After the last mess we half expected to be sent back to Doudeneville. But, instead, our attention was directed to Alvis near Montvilliers, north-east of the town. There, the *Wehrmacht* was fighting a desperate but effective, last-ditch action. The British had been halted by a powerful concentration of armour. Yet again, the call for air support had gone out. In response, one hundred and fifty Lancasters of 3 Group would bomb on green TIs at 1730 hrs. Number 75 Squadron would contribute twenty-seven of these, carrying the familiar mix of eleven-thousand-pounders and four five-hundreds, some with delayed-action fuses.

This time the meteorological forecast for the Le Havre area was good: cloudless skies with excellent ground visibility. We would be separated from the enemy's guns by 11,000 feet of clear air. There would be no repeat of that low-level nonsense.

A sweep by Lightnings and Mustangs would purge the skies of *Luftwaffe* fighters. If opposition there was, it would be restricted to ground fire.

We were geared up and on the Bedford by 1430 hrs. Forty minutes later we were cruising in the midst of the stream. Tubby invited our initiate to take the tip-up seat beside me. He sat in total absorption, more sharp-eyed and observant than ever I was on board John Aitken's U-Uncle, I am sure. In turn, we strove to put on the show that he deserved and could expect from a quality crew. If we failed there were no excuses. A second repeat-trip in so few days ought to mean clockwork perfection.

For my part I offered him the usual, sound advice such as rigid discipline on board, no chatter on the intercom, seeking safety in numbers well inside the stream and, of course, total vigilance throughout. The time to relax was when he was back in the crew truck, and not before. I demonstrated the gentle weave that was always employed over enemy territory, except on bombing and camera runs, and banked the aircraft every so often so the gunners could take a look underneath. It was like old times with my pupils at AFU all over again.

The Channel loomed calm and blue. Hastings lay to port, Bexhill to starboard. No doubt, Bill Osborne was reflecting that at last he was leaving England to fly into the fray with all the uncertainty this entailed. The people in the streets and gardens below surely watched us on our way. Four years earlier they were braced against an invasion and lived in fear of enemy bombs. Now the bombers over them were 3 Group Lancs flying to aid our own invasion. Shortly, the muffled thump of almost nine hundred tons of exploding bombs would carry to their ears.

We crossed the French coast at our bombing height and only minutes from target. Flying conditions were perfect, the sky clear apart from some sporadic, black puffs of AA fire. The bomb doors were open. Mac was over his sight, waiting for the green TIs to burst. Everything was on song.

The concentration of flares appeared on open farmland. At the MC's bidding bombs began to fall from the lead formation. Mac called out his final adjustments. Meanwhile Tubby, Bill and Archie appeared to my right, each anxious to view the spectacle below. I wasn't entirely convinced that a crew-filled cockpit was the best example to set our second dickey. But battlefields had that effect on aircrew. Even the normally incurious felt some desire to witness these momentous events. To deny oneself the opportunity was, perhaps, a denial also of one's intellectual vitality and plain, simple interest in life.

Mac released our bombs and told us they were looking good. I executed the camera run of twenty-eight seconds and banked away. Columns of thick, spreading smoke already towered thousands of feet upward, but the hard pounding continued. As we turned for home a long line of tailenders hung black in the sky, still on their bombing run. The ground fire, meanwhile, had almost entirely dissipated. Quite probably, the ferocity of the attack had persuaded the gunners to dive for shelter.

We flew across the Channel at a sedate 7,000 ft, mindful of our responsibilities. Ahead of me most of the others were skimming the surface of a slight sea, with all the taps open and not a care in the world. It was too much to take. I handed over the controls to Bill Osborne and went back to talk to the boys. From the Thames estuary he enjoyed himself flying the Mepal lane on the back edge of an excellent 75 format. When Ely Cathedral came into view I took my seat again and we peeled off to enter the circuit. Virtue, they say, is its own reward. For putting aside temptation over the Channel, Providence bestowed a (pretty rare) three-point landing upon me. We only used half the runway to reduce speed and turned off promptly to make way for the aircraft behind.

For me, that was the icing on the cake. But for Mac there was one other sweet moment. All twenty-seven Mepal aircraft bombed and all returned safely. But it was Mac's bombs that fell closest to the TIs, and Mac's photograph that took pride of place on the notice board.

After de-briefing Bill Osborne shook hands with each of us. Then he went off to fight his war, probably thinking that things were always done that way in the Yates crew. Did I say there was no vanity in any of this?

So ended our trinity of Le Havre raids. The *Wehrmacht*'s resistance in the area was broken. The British Army made no further requests for intervention there by Bomber Command. The story had begun with the Guards' selective liberation of northern France. But it did not end with the final freedom of Le Havre. For when British troops entered the town they found the aftermath of a grave event (or blunder or crime, as some may believe).

On the afternoon of the raid on the old town where the 11,000-strong occupying force was said to be garrisoned, the Lancasters of 3 Group dropped perhaps six thousand bombs with all the precision possible in those days. It would have been a blessing if every one had fallen into the sea. As it was, in the storm of destruction, in the blast and fire, three thousand innocent men, women and children died – three times the toll of the infamous assault on Rotterdam by the *Luftwaffe* in 1940.

At the time, of course, nothing was heard of this back in England. The war effort was all-consuming. For aircrew the focus was always on the next op, then the next and so on. It might seem a callous thing but we could not allow thoughts of civilian deaths into our daily lives. It was the function of 75 and every bomber squadron to carry out successful operations as directed. There was no more to it than that. It was a job that had to be done, and done within the constraints of wartime technology *and intelligence.*

In the case of Le Havre, the quality of intelligence was the decisive factor. It emerged afterwards that few soldiers were actually billeted within the town. Worse, most of the civilian population had been driven from their homes by the Germans and forceably settled in the old town area. British intelligence was clearly not aware of this. But it should have been. Le Havre was not some sleepy fishing port. It had been the subject of Bomber Command's attention regularly since 1940. With the Allied invasion it assumed particular importance. Scores of fast E-boats were based in the harbour, protected by day under thick concrete pens. At night they slipped away to loose their torpedoes at the Allied troop and supply ships at anchor off the Normandy beach-heads. Prior to 5 September, the last raid on Le Havre in which 75 participated was the great attack of 14 June. This was the second outing for Barnes Wallis's new Tallboy, dropped by 617 Squadron. Neither the pens nor the E-boats survived. The German Navy was finished at Le Havre, but not so the *Wehrmacht* – about which so little turned out to be known.

What, then, of the promised effort to warn the townsfolk of the attack? If any Nickel raid was ever flown it was singularly ineffective. More likely, radio warnings were used, possibly backed up by early marking. This method was regularly employed in France, but for open and relatively unpopulated targets such as marshalling yards. It would hardly have been suited to the geography of the old town. In any case, the appalling loss of life showed that not enough, or the wrong thing, was done. How or why one can only speculate, and resign oneself to the vagaries of war and the blasted prevalence of the cock-up.

The Le Havre story was a postcript which is interesting in two respects. First, it is a skirmish in the unending battle for how aircrew should be remembered, whether as chivalrous young men who fought and died for their country's survival or as agents of an immoral policy of mass destruction. Second, it shows how, despite the years, Bomber Command is still seen as a suitable subject for liberal excoriation.

In 1987 the BBC was planning to broadcast a documentary on the Le Havre raid. On 5 September, forty-three years to the day after the event, I received a telephone call from the BBC studios in Southampton (a city twinned with Le Havre). The caller, an assistant producer, invited me to contribute to a television documentary on the subject. The idea was to take several crew members to Le Havre to meet French survivors and families who had lost loved ones in the attack.

I was suspicious of the BBC's motives, and said so. To me, it seemed all too likely that the RAF crews would be depicted as butchers. Earlier, a Canadian film had been broadcast on British television with just such a portrayal of the RCAF. I made a few off-the-cuff remarks about the raid and the necessary limitations on aircrew responsibility, and declined the offer.

On 11 September the same person wrote asking me to reconsider. He didn't mince his words. The letter explained how he and his colleagues were 'spurred' by this country's ignorance of the raid. 'While Southampton's Blitz is celebrated, that of Le Havre is not', he wrote.

One might wonder whether he and his colleagues understood the difference between the *Luftwaffe*'s bombing policy and our very limited objective in the old town that day. If they did, they didn't let it show. Our objective and its achievement – the placement of our bombs in the precise, designated area – did not interest them. It was the unintended *effects* of the raid that connected to the bombing of British cities and it was these that were to determine the editorial line now. As the letter-writer put it, 'What I certainly did not have in mind were simply impersonal recollections about the technical success of the raid.' That, of course, would let aircrew off the hook.

Given such a predetermined critique of the RAF, it was difficult to see what aircrew could really contribute. But we had our uses, none the less, and these were embodied in the programme's three stated aims.

No one could dispute the first: 'to show . . . that the daylight raid was very much a routine, even soft mission'. The second was, 'to confirm that at squadron level there was little or no knowledge about the reasons for such a large-scale operation'. The operation was, of course, scaled to the size of the objective. As for reasons, no doubt the BBC of the '80s seethed with independent-minded folk demanding explanations for everything. I can't help but wonder whether they would have found squadron life terribly suitable, though.

The heart of it all was the third aim: 'to . . . personalise a day which saw a particularly high loss of French civilian life'. This was taking history well beyond the usual public record and plain statistic. The recollections of survivors can make compulsive viewing. The Canadian film demonstrated that. But for ex-aircrew such sorrows are unanswerable. They shift the emphasis away from the greater cause in which deaths occurred and onto the manner of them. They exploit the moral superiority of the victims. The aegis of military duty becomes a contemptible thing. There is such a strong imputation of guilt or complicity, the supposed transgressor can find himself babbling away about following orders before he knows it.

I had no desire to be set up like that. The programme-makers called again. Evidently, they had yet to net themselves a pilot. I gave them my final refusal, thereby denying myself both a day out and some decent, French cuisine at the BBC's expense.

They managed perfectly well without me. Three or four veterans, none of them pilots, took up the offer. One was very familiar. I watched in astonishment as the camera panned across Le Havre from the top of the town hall and settled upon the tanned and still-rakish face of a one-time mid-upper gunner, Geoffrey Fallowfield by name. The BBC only gave him a few moments on air. But he voiced the essential truths that we were given a job to do and wanted to free the French, not harm them. Well, I trust that my old crewmate enjoyed the daytrip and dined royally.

Naturally, the BBC people achieved their first two aims. The third was less straightforward. Although the general tenor was sadness, not anger, it seemed to me unpatriotic and highly manipulative to confront ex-aircrew with their unwitting victims. It was trial by modern liberal conscience, with no right for the defence to call its own witnesses. I hoped that the viewing public – at least, the less fickle among them – would not be taken in.

The most impressive aspect of the programme was the testimony of the French survivors. They were dignified, restrained and articulate. But, ultimately, they bore witness against the wrongly accused.

The young men in their Lancasters were not the villains of the piece that September afternoon, much less butchers. The three thousand lives were not lost to wickedness. Wherever the blame actually lay, the real culprit was incompetence . . . mundane, tiresome incompetence. And that is what makes this event so poignant and inadmissible, though I accept that for the French there are, and will always be, many other and more personal considerations.

On 5 January 1945 another French port under the control of a stubbornly resistant enemy garrison was attacked in the same way. It was Royan, situated at the mouth of the Gironde and controlling the approach to Bordeaux. The besieger this time was the French Resistance. Again, it was proposed that the RAF soften up the enemy. Intelligence reports showed that the town was evacuated of civilians. In the early morning light a powerful force of 1, 5 and 8 Group Lancasters pummelled the town almost to destruction. But lessons can be forgotten as easily as learned. Two thousand French civilians were under the bombs. More than five hundred lost their lives.

This time Bomber Command was rapidly exonerated. But the question of whether the French or the Allies on the ground were to blame was acrimoniously debated for years.

Perhaps, in all conscience, there could never have been much certainty. Perhaps these towns could never have been guaranteed clear and ready for the bombers in the sky above.

CHAPTER TEN

RIO RITA

Garth replaced the receiver in silence. Everyone in the Flight Office was watching him intently, all conversation suspended. He rose from his seat and walked over. We braced ourselves for what he would now say.

'Well,' he began, looking from face to face, 'fifteen kites go late-afternoon . . . another eight gardening tonight.'

That signalled the end of a twenty-four-hour break from flying activities. The previous day, 11 September, gales and driving rain had swept across the airfield. Even H2S practice was ruled out. Our Lancasters stood unattended at dispersal, the upper-wing, tail and fuselage surfaces outlined by a luminous halo of dancing rain. Inevitably on such a day, the mess was crowded. The air was heavy with smoke and the comfortingly familiar smell of damp caps and coats. We dried out over a game of poker or billiards, read a newspaper or caught up on letters home, and we waited . . .

That part was over now. But there was still waiting to do, this time for the Battle Orders to be posted on the Flight notice board. Bill and I were in no doubt which op we would prefer. With three late afternoon trips to Le Havre just completed it was reasonable to suppose that today's would be more army support over occupied territory.

On the other hand, mine-laying held not the slightest appeal for Bill or me. It had a vernacular all its own. It was called gardening. Mines were called vegetables. The watery targets, stretching from the southern end of the Bay of Biscay to deep in the Baltic, were inventively coded. Artichoke, Sultana and Wallflowers cohabited literally with the rather more apt Gorse, Jellyfish and Forget-me-nots.

As usual with the RAF, banal language disguised an extreme danger. Hours of low-flying in filthy weather, mostly on your own, was the norm. If you could get a fix on the enemy coast, the next thing was to release the mines at low level. But German naval captains were assiduous in taking refuge in inhospitable places, beneath mountainous coastlines or behind a picket of flak ships. No amount of cloud cover hid an incoming bomber from the latters' radar or their Bofors. If the skies were clear it was worse. There was the added menace of fighters.

Gardening was the short straw which we hoped never to draw. Imagine our relief, then, at finding ourselves rostered for the late afternoon effort. With luck we'd be safely back and in the pub before the gardening crews even lifted off from the flarepath.

Garth had given us the samba dancer, the redoubtable R-Roger, again. It would be our fourth date with her. I noted somewhat wryly that Garth and his crew were part of B Flight's contribution to the Battle Order, a disquieting sign – 75 was not the sort of outfit in which senior officers picked the easy trips. At least the CO hadn't volunteered himself. That really would have been an invitation to trouble.

R-Roger had to be air tested, for which we had precious little time. We cycled straight to the crew room to collect our gear. Half-an-hour later we were roaring over the boundary at safety speed, to head along the line of the twin Bedford canals and out towards the Wash. Half-an-hour later again we were back over Sutton Church on the edge of the field. I eased R-Roger gently down to earth. We knew she would give of her best today.

Before we were even on the crew truck there were ground staff at work on the kite. These were the men upon whose honest sweat and know-how all aircrew were totally reliant. The armourers had begun bombing-up. A radar crew was crawling through the aircraft, making last-minute checks. A Matador was standing by to off-load. As ever, Mepal's complex engine of war was working flat out and in harmony.

At 1430 hrs in the briefing room the consensus of opinion was that we were going not to France but to Germany. Always the worst kept secret on the airfield, the fuel load was known now and too heavy for a fourth trip to Le Havre.

Suddenly, speculation became irrelevant. The door swung open. One hundred and five chairs scraped as we rose to our feet, and scraped again as the CO bade us to sit. This was the moment when fear stirred in the pit of the stomach. The curtain swept to one side. A large-scale map was exposed. It was blotched with expansive, red-inked areas to show heavy belts of flak and, yes, it was Germany. My eyes, everybody's eyes, went to the arrow marking the target. No doubt, a volley of silent curses followed immediately behind.

Not the bloody Ruhr, surely? In daylight? Endless bloody flak . . . hundreds of fighters . . . nowhere to hide!

'Gentlemen,' said the CO, 'the target is Kamen, situated midway between Dortmund and Hamm. You are in hotly defended country just east of the Ruhr.'

Just east, then. But even so the groans welled up from our boots. The Ruhr, Germany's great heartland of coalmining and iron and steel-making, and the centre of its armaments industry, was defended to the absolute hilt. Only Berlin was comparable for sheer threat to life. The string of Ruhr towns was known as Happy Valley, a piece of aircrew slang that encapsulates their grim but gallant humour. The ground defences were not just in and around these towns. Great blocks of batteries – heavy anti-aircraft guns in their thousands – were strategically located across the whole region. Incoming bombers had to pick their way past as best they could. There was no easy way in or out and this was true also for neighbouring targets such as Dortmund and Wuppertal.

As if that wasn't enough, the *Luftwaffe's* crack fighter squadrons lined the country to the north and east, and were surely aching to get at a few enemy bombers. To get at *us*, however, they would first have to penetrate hundreds of Spits and Mustangs. By and large they lacked the aviation spirit to do that, but we didn't know. We knew only that today we would bomb their heartland and a fiery response seemed inevitable.

The CO's closing remarks made the boys and me sit bolt upright:

> 'In recognition of our consistently fine operational and serviceability records, Group have accorded us the honour of spearheading today's attack. All other squadrons will be advised that an AA Lanc will lead-in the first vic. This task goes to Flying Officer Yates and crew in R-Roger.'

An honour, maybe, but one I might have preferred on an easier trip. Seated beside me, Bill uttered a short Anglo-Saxon expletive beneath his breath. He was not charmed by the idea of navigating in front of hundreds of his peers.

It was the same for Mac. Competition was endemic among bomb aimers. After every op, target photos were pinned up for all to see. Each one was well eyed from a professional standpoint, and to be accorded an aiming point conferred lasting prestige. But Mac knew that wherever he put his bombs today, every damned bomb aimer in the stream would be out to better him.

Nevertheless, the CO's announcement was a fillip for our morale.

149

There were plenty of other crews who were longer on experience and no less deserving.

The CO gave way to the Intelligence Officer, then he to the Met. Officer, who forecast clear skies and excellent visibility over the target. That did not please us terribly. The Nav. Leader exhibited a blown-up photograph of the target. It was a synthetic oil refinery, the first such target since the dread Homburg raid in July. It was hidden away in dense woodland. But a tell-tale railway line sliced through the trees. That would provide Mac with a reference point. Our approach course would be 160°. The Bombing Leader was next, detailing our load: a 4,000 lb cookie and sixteen 500 lb H/Es, some with delayed-action fuses. The Signals Leader gave his men the radio back-up procedures, callsigns and our own and the enemy's colours of the day. Gp/Cpt Patrick Campbell spoke last. He was Station Commander with overall responsibility for the day-to-day administration of Mepal. Though officially non-operational, from time to time he took it upon himself to passenger and share the same risks as aircrews. Time on target, he said, would be 1845 hrs, trucks to dispersal 1530 hrs, take-off time 1630 hrs. We synchronised our watches on his countdown. And that was it. Briefing was over.

The briefing officers filed past us. Excited chatter recommenced. Crews huddled over maps, drawing the route, checking every detail. Really, this was work for the navigators and bomb aimers only. But the rest contributed what they could or just stared at the map and tried to take in the enormity of it all.

Bill and I drank a quick cup of tea in the mess before collecting our flasks and flying rations. In the crewroom all our personal belongings were handed in. I kept back only my good luck charm, old Blackie's wishbone. The WAAF who handed us our parachutes fixed me with a doleful stare. 'Don't worry, sir, *we* won't let you down', she said. They were not the most comforting words she could have spoken.

We arrived early at dispersal and sat on the grass to wait. The ground crew proffered cigarettes which we smoked pensively. This was the time one always wanted to pass quickly. Once we boarded we would be too busy to ponder our fate. But now, sitting there picking at stalks of grass, glancing occasionally towards the kite but not much at one another, it was impossible to stave off forbidden thoughts. Even the painted Rio Rita, a monument to the triumph of ambition over artistry, looked more out of sorts than usual.

The last butt was extinguished.

'All right, boys,' I said, 'let's go.'

With the pre-start-ups completed, Tubby checked that all hatches were closed and sat down beside me. I signalled to the ground crew to stand clear, and fired up the port-inner. A few minutes later all the Merlins were singing, four tireless voices in perfect pitch. I signalled again and the chocks were pulled away. Brakes squealing, we swung round to the perimeter track. The flight caravan and the tyre-blackened runway awaited us, and beyond them two and a quarter hours of flying to Kamen.

Thirty minutes later we had climbed to 10,000 ft and come back over the centre of the airfield. Bill gave me the course and we led the 75 contingent east towards the coast.

We muscled past the few kites that we found ahead of us. There was quite a bit of air turbulence so I decided to take R-Roger up to 15,000 ft. We climbed out of the afternoon sun, its light mellow now rather than bright. Summer had irrefutably slipped past. Slender shadows lay across Norfolk's patchwork of fields, mostly shorn of their wheat and barley now and awaiting only the plough. The next turn of the wheel would bring autumn. This afternoon's op completed our first dozen. If we stayed lucky we should complete our tour before the seasons changed again. Such were my hopes as, still climbing, we crossed the coast at Lowestoft and left England behind us.

Norrie came on the intercom, 'Half the RAF's on our tail, skipper . . . kites as far I can see.'

That was fine. The sky ahead was empty. We were on station at the head of the stream. Now we only needed the aircraft in our immediate vicinity to formate nearer the target. Norrie came on again, asking if he and Geoff could test their guns. The clatter lasted a few seconds, then silence except for the rush of air and the monotone of the engines.

It was known that ground radar facilities in Germany picked up an incoming force very early on. Our height, course and strength would have been relayed to the AA batteries on the Dutch coast, and a barrage planned accordingly. Had R-Roger been well back in the stream I would have been able to gauge the flak concentration ahead and, maybe, fly around it. But leading the gaggle proscribed such selfish considerations, the more so since we were the standard-bearer for a famously press-on squadron.

As we neared the coastline the first shell in the barrage arced up to explode a short distance off. Our reception committee was clearly pleased to see us and had our range. Within moments the sky was pitted with the dirty grey residue of spent shells. There was nothing to be done but hold course. One could easily believe that every gunner was sighting the lead aircraft which, initially, they probably were. But we entered clean air again unscathed and crossed the coast well north of Amsterdam.

Over Apeldoorn Bill gave me a course of 145°. Then with a note of calm satisfaction Geoff said, 'Look up, skipper.' I obeyed and saw far above us our escort shining like gems in the sunlight. They seemed incredibly distant and, indeed, were nigh on twice our altitude. But that was where the overview was effective and no more than thirty seconds away at diving speed. Looking up through the Perspex I still felt a twinge of envy at those single-engine boys. But it was a great relief to know they were sweeping our track.

We crossed into Germany in free air, without interference from below and well guarded from above. The houses of Bocholt were clearly visible to starboard. The route attempted to slide us around the main AA threats. We skirted Happy Valley in whose grimy haze lay Essen, Gelsenkirchen, Duisburg . . . names of fear and dread. Bill gave me the final outward course change, adding that we had eight minutes to go. Mac was down in his office. Tubby was throwing out Window like a man with a dozen pairs of hands. Two Lancasters that had been on our tail from the English coast now began to draw closer, one to each side. We were riding the very horns of the charge.

In the CO's book this moment belonged to the whole squadron. It was a pinnacle of collective pride. I cannot say that it felt quite like that on board R-Roger. The burden upon aircrew was heavy enough just with our operational duties and the battle to survive. It was a dangerous thought, but zeal ran these a very poor third. Of course, in military life you are not asked to approve of your superiors' decisions, only to execute them. And that is what we did.

We bisected the conurbations of Dortmund and Hamm, with its great marshalling yards. There, right ahead, was the target. Visibility was so good and the refinery so unmistakable, we could have bombed visually.

The Pathfinders had already sent down their first TIs which were burning a brilliant red in the complex. This, at least, made our intentions perfectly plain to the ground defences. As if stung by our importunity in bombing here rather than down in the valley, they hit us with everything they had. I held R-Roger at 16,200 ft on the specified course and airspeed. But the bloody flak was murderous now. Already, I was thinking about getting those bombs away and diving the hell out of here. I asked Mac what sort of run he had on, hoping for some sign that he might perform with due dispatch this time.

'Great,' he replied, 'I've got the railway line. Just keep her steady.' He sounded ebullient and not at all concerned about the dangers that preoccupied me. At least, turbulence from other bombers would be no problem. That much could be said for flying out in front.

The seconds laboured by. We pushed on through a sea of nebulous, black and grey explosions, each capable of killing us all but for an accident of timing. Yet there were no developments from the bomb aimer's compartment. It was torture.

In total exasperation I shouted, 'Well, let the bloody things go, then.' I knew I was speaking for all six of us.

There was a lengthy silence followed by the single word, 'Steadyyy', uttered in the same melifluous, preoccupied voice. A couple of repetitions later the cookie thumped out of the bomb bay, with the rest in attendance. R-Roger leapt upward in relief and so, metaphorically, did we. We were on the camera run, unsure whether to be grateful to Mac or put in for a creep-back merchant instead.

Mac himself was watching the cookie spinning and tumbling on its downward path. It exploded right among the TIs. For a second or two until the bombs from other aircraft also struck home and confused the picture, the full impact of his work was revealed. He could see the violence of the initial shockwave and the eruption of smoke and dust from virgin ground.

'Chrrr . . . ist!' he shouted. Then, as if to confirm his appetite for this sort of thing, he added, 'Bang on, skipper. Bang on bloody target.'

I gazed down at the cause of Mac's jubilation. But when I looked up again it was to see a solitary Lancaster no great distance to port and in flames. It was in a shallow turn towards us and losing height slowly. There seemed to be no parachutes in the sky. One could only guess at the horrors occurring on board. An aircraft was a recondite place in which to die. It simply blew apart as we watched. I wrenched R-Roger to starboard but we were safe. We slewed away from the pitiful remains of a brave crew and their aircraft, now no more than a pall of smoke above scattered and barely recognisable debris.

I was beginning to dislike this 'hotly defended country' intensely. It was time to put some distance between it and us. I told Bill that

I'd need a course shortly, and pushed the column forward. The airspeed rose high into the two hundreds. We had almost cleared the target area when Kamen's defences caught up with us. A tremendous explosion ripped at the air immediately in front of me. The entire nose section of my Lancaster disappeared, taking with it the front gun turret.

It is strange how the next sequence of events was so slow and dream-like. Black, acrid fumes poured through the opening . . . cordite. It stank in my nostrils. Next, a substantial chunk of black metal came through the windscreen. It was past my head before I could flinch, angling upward to smash its way out of the escape hatch. Yet in the peculiar intensity of the moment I saw, or thought I saw, it spinning slowly and even smouldering as it went. Then the Perspex windscreen disintegrated before my eyes into a thousand dancing fragments of silver. They were organised on the gale and flung full into my face.

Everything degenerated into chaos. I was in darkness. My senses were disorientated by shock and pain – most of that from what felt like dozens of blades slicing into my eyes. A roaring wall of icy air pressed so hard against my face I was fighting to draw breath. This was all so suddenly and radically different from the normal familiarities of flying, I did not immediately connect the two. But I knew I was alive and conscious and had a duty of some sort, some call upon me. And out of that knowledge came the recognition that we must still be flying, indeed, still diving and I must find the column.

I groped forward, locked my hands on it and pulled. The effort brought me to normal consciousness and razor-sharpened the pain. But through the seat of my pants I could feel R-Roger pulling out. She appeared to respond well. As the airspeed moderated I tried to open my eyes. It was an unequal struggle against the gale but there was light in the darkness.

A hand pulled at my shoulder. A voice was close to my ear, repeating something. It was Tubby telling me to pull off my flying helmet. He went away, then returned with a fistful of cloth. He turned his broad back to the gale, braced his left arm against the steel plating behind my head and began dabbing tenderly at my lacerations. Though numerous, these were all in the crescent of flesh between my flying helmet and oxygen mask.

While he cleaned me up as best he could, Tubby assured me that R-Roger was flying reasonably straight and level at a little over 10,000 ft. There was no damage beyond the nose section. All four engines were running normally and we had lost no fuel. I asked about the boys. They were unharmed, he said, though chilly (possibly excepting Norrie who, behind his turret doors, was ensconced in a heated suit).

More than once during this exchange Tubby addressed me by my Christian name. Only Bill, my fellow officer, generally made a habit of this. To the others I was never anything but 'skipper'. I had never dreamt that one day my Flight Engineer might feel obliged to extend his patronage to me in this way. I suppose that as my senior by twelve years he was fully entitled to do so.

By now I had begun to find that my eyes could still function. There were things to be done. The first of them, if we were not all to finish up as frozen corpses, was to lose height. I put our faithful, old warhorse into a shallow dive, reckoning that the temperature at 5,000 ft would be endurable. The next was to let everyone know that both I and the aircraft were still in business and we were going to make Mepal. Since the howling gale rendered the pilot's intercom useless I sent Tubby back with the news.

Bill appeared beside me, grasping his rolled-up maps in both hands for want of a quiet place to leave them.

'All right, old man?' he asked. I nodded. After some hesitation he gave me a course for the Dutch coast and retired, no doubt wondering if I could see my gyro at all, never mind its calibrations.

Then Mac arrived with an emotional pledge of loyalty. 'If we get hit again,' he bellowed into my right ear from zero distance, 'and we've got to jump, you're going out first, skipper. The boys will see to that. I'll take care of things here. But *you* are going to go!'

Well, that was the one and only Inia Maaka. He meant every word. He was a large man with a very good pair of lungs, and one hesitated to correct him. But before I could remind him that I was still captain and was obliged to evacuate not first but last, he punched my shoulder and went away. I was only grateful that he wasn't in the nose section when we were hit. The same went for Tubby who also spent much of his flight time there.

As for myself, I couldn't feel particularly unlucky. Had I been sensible and obeyed flying rules things would have been different. But my goggles had stayed where they were before take off, slung up on my helmet. My eyes were unprotected and, of course, it had to be there that trouble struck.

The eyes, dammit! Why couldn't it be the fleshy part of an arm or a leg? I always hated fishing about in my eyes for dust and dirt. Now this! Still, no amount of self-recrimination would change anything. And everything was secondary to getting R-Roger and the boys home.

I levelled out at 5,000 ft and crossed the border west of Emmerich. The cold did not improve. Airspeed was two hundred mph, still a hell of a blast through the nose and windscreen apertures. I couldn't stop my teeth from chattering. My fingers had lost all feeling. But it was hard on the crew, too. Geoff stuck it out in his turret, searching the sky as usual now the escort had quit. But as and when work allowed, Bill, Mac, Tubby and Archie sought shelter where they could, perhaps behind the rest seat or an armour-plated door or down beside the main spar.

At the beginning Archie may have had an additional problem. The aircraft's heating outlet was located down to the left of his station. It was rather an on/off affair. If on, the w/op simply sweltered. Archie responded, like most w/ops, by removing excess flying gear. Quite how casually he was attired when the ice-cold air burst in I do not know. But in that aerial madhouse anything not actually bolted down surely became extremely mobile, his discarded gear included. He must have been led a merry dance before he got it back on. One felt some sympathy for Archie. He never said so, but I always assumed that he had experienced more than one eventful trip before coming to Mepal. All in all, I think a little less excitement might have been welcome now.

It was imperative to lose more height so I went down again. We skirted Arnhem and Amsterdam, diving still, and crossed the coast. At only 500 ft we must have been an easy target for the coastal batteries. I was in no shape to hug the ground, and just hoped for luck. We got it. The guns were silent.

The evening sun was low on the horizon as we neared the Norfolk coast. It seemed like another life when last we came this way, leading the stream out to sea. My eyes remained extremely painful and, of course, the gale blew as before. Tubby recovered my helmet and goggles, and tried to put them back on me. But it was unbearable – my skin was a pin cushion. I could see into the mid-distance well enough to fly. But focusing at short range was difficult and moving my eyes from side to side in their sockets was impossible. Most of the instrument panel remained a blur.

Archie appeared at my shoulder. He had reported our condition fully to Mepal Control. We were given a priority landing. I was grateful for the news but the landing itself would require some thought. I wondered how a noseless Lancaster handled at low speed. How much would stalling speed be affected? It seemed wise to make a fast approach under power and from a lower height than usual.

I need not have worried. This was the indomitable R-Roger bringing us home. She put up with my split-arse circuit (flying parlance for no circuit at all). And she remained a lady while Tubby called out the altitude and held the throttles closed and we waited, finally, for the wheels to touch.

As I turned onto the perimeter track Archie appeared in the cockpit again. He told me that Control had ordered us to the nearest dispersal. The squadron Medical Officer would be there with an ambulance. I must wait in my seat for him to come on board.

I braked R-Roger to a standstill beside the ambulance and switched off the engines. The time was 2035 hrs. We had been airborne for four hours and twenty minutes. From a military perspective, at least, our twelfth operational flight had been success-fully completed.

The MO entered the aircraft and took a close look at my face. An orderly cleaned me up and put a dressing over both eyes. I was led by the arm down the aircraft steps towards the waiting ambulance. The CO had driven out to dispersal. He shook me by the hand whilst my crew stood in a circle watching silently. Before I could thank them properly the ambulance doors closed on me. I was driven away, not knowing whether I would see them or the cockpit of a Lancaster again.

'I'm afraid Perspex doesn't show up on X-rays, Flying Officer Yates. We have to probe for it with needles. You'll need two, possibly three operations during which we shall remove as much of it as possible.' The speaker was the senior Medical Officer at Littleport Hospital, S/Ldr McCurry.

Littleport, just to the north of Ely and in the heart of Bomber Country, was established by the RAF as a treatment centre for eye wounds. Much as in modern-day Ulster where surgeons are un-surpassed in the treatment of burn and blast injuries, Littleport was at the frontier of its speciality. Of course, it had a constant supply of acquiescent guinea pigs on which to experiment.

Many, if not most, of the cases it saw were a good deal more serious and gory than mine. A substantial proportion involved the saving of an eye or of sight as a whole. Clearly, the question mark hanging over me concerned the *quality* of my sight after R-Roger's debris had been removed. I was, therefore, already more fortunate than some of the poor devils in my ward.

157

S/Ldr McCurry did make me think, though, when he told me that some minute particles of perspex would remain. I would carry them for the rest of my life, mostly in the right eye which was the worse of the two. The prospect of some part of R-Roger and me being together unto the grave was hardly beguiling. I had formed an affection for the old girl. But this was carrying things too far.

The time arrived for my first encounter with the needle. The operating theatre was very dimly lit except where I lay, my head restricted by a padded rest. The Sister deftly deposited a drop of cocaine into each of my eyes. This dilated the pupils and helped to dull the pain of the probing to follow. Squadron Leader McCurry positioned a magnifying apparatus above my face. In a benign but authoritative voice he explained that I must look straight up and not move, not the slightest shift in any direction. Only if I absolutely had to blink should I do so. Even then I must warn him first with a grunt or somesuch, and *without* moving lips or jaw.

Then he bent over me and began working first on the right eye, then the left. It went on for some minutes, probably not very many in actuality. But it couldn't finish soon enough for me. My teeth were grinding away despite the doctor's repeated commands to be perfectly still. My fists were clamped tight. The Sister laid her hand across them to get me to relax.

When the probing stopped, the doctor straightened and said in an upbeat voice, 'Well, you've been remarkably fortunate. The largest splinter was embedded one-sixteenth of an inch from the retina of your right eye. Another fraction and your flying days would have been over. I take it you want to fly again?'

I didn't know whether to laugh or cry. Satisfied that he had inflicted as much pain as I could stand for now, the S/Ldr stepped back. The Sister's face swam in front of me again. The tips of her fingers pressed lightly into my eyes, smearing them with a copious quantity of soothing ointment. Then she bandaged me. Only the mouth and nostrils were left free. And with that I was returned to bed.

Every two days I was re-examined. A disclosing fluid was poured into my eyes. It reacted to the weep from unhealed tissue by changing colour, and this pinpointed the remaining splinters.

Meanwhile, I had become the responsibility of an endlessly attentive staff nurse. She fetched and carried for me, fed me, read to me and guided me through every aspect of the daily round.

I had only the vaguest notion of my surroundings and none whatever of how to cope, psychologically as well as physically, with

158

the deprivation of sight. Stoicism proved a poor redoubt. I tried to ignore the perpetual discomfort and forget about my next appointment with the operating theatre. But time and darkness are powerful conspirators. Privately, I began to doubt the doctor's motives in assuring me so soon that I would fly again. But worse than being grounded, a lifetime of blurred horizons stretched before me. There were a lot of wonderful sights in this world, foremost among them the face of a beautiful girl. What future was there without that?

In my ward were four or five other bandaged souls late of Fighter or Bomber Command. Some had undergone five or six bouts of surgery. We chatted and joked together as normally as we could, which wasn't all that normal. We had all been lifted clean out of operational life to a place of total inaction. We would not have been human if doubt, frustration or impatience didn't get the better of us sometimes.

As the days crawled by I yearned to slough off the yards of loose-woven cotton bandages. That, of course, required at least one more encounter with S/Ldr McCurry, for which I had no enthusiasm at all. The call came anyway and I had to submit to the same, ghastly business of pricking and scraping. If anything it was worse than before. The splinters were deeper, smaller and more reluctant to co-operate. I was returned to my bed, bandaged as before but grateful to be away from that darkened room.

A day later I was led back there again. The nurse unwound the bandage from my head and lifted away the padding over the left eye. Squadron Leader McCurry shone a pencil beam of light at me. The glare was a tremendous shock. To my intense delight I could focus and see, not perfectly, but better than I dared hope.

Outside, I found a world shining with light. It was an extraordinary rediscovery of a miracle which at any other time I would just take for granted. I was euphoric and minutely studied the most ordinary objects simply for the pleasure of doing so. My right eye remained covered, but no matter. With even partial sight came an end to my confinement and the freedom of the hospital grounds.

The house had once been Littleport Grange. It looked early Victorian, not grand but pleasantly roomy. The grounds were of similar modesty. Secluded by bushes and trees, they boasted some fine aspects, an old wooden summer house and a low-walled garden of sweet-scented roses, not at their best in mid-September but looking pretty good just then to me. The gentle art of croquet was practised by patients on the broad lawn in front of the house. I heard a Kiwi accent among the mallet-wielders. The owner was Ron Mayhill, a fellow officer from B Flight and the bomb aimer in John Aitken's crew. Like me, he had a Perspex injury, picked up on a French daylight raid at the end of August. It had been his twenty-seventh trip and a supposedly soft target.

In his ward was another New Zealander of 75 Squadron, F/Sgt D.J. Moriarty. His injury was far more grievous than Ron's or mine, and his courage at the time it happened quite outstanding.

It was the day of the Allied break-out, 18 July 1944. Bomber Command and the USAAF dispatched nearly a thousand bombers apiece to the Normandy battle area, the largest concentrated deployment of the entire war. Among 75's contingent was F/Sgt Moriarty and his crew in K-King, scheduled for the dawn attack on Cagny. It was one of many villages fortified by Rommel's men and lay five miles or so from Caen. K-King bombed in intense AA fire. Soon after, a flak splinter burst through the windscreen, penetrating Moriarty's head beside the left eye and exiting behind his left ear. Probably sensing that to bale out was to consign Moriarty to his death, the whole crew elected to stay on board. By what power of the will I do not know, but Moriarty kept flying. For ninety minutes he endured the pain and trauma of his injury and heavy loss of blood until he, K-King and his crew touched down at Mepal.

In recognition of his valour he was awarded the Conspicuous Gallantry Medal, one of only three from 75 to receive this high honour. By incredible good fortune he escaped brain damage. But saving his eye proved beyond even S/Ldr McCurry's skill.

My modest scratch troubled me less now. Another week passed then, at last, visitors were allowed. Bill and Mac came with smiles and handshakes, some chocolate and a lot of news. The best was that the boys and I would be kept together as a crew, picking up where we left off at number twelve. I had only to recover, which the CO anticipated. We could even find ourselves on board R-Roger again. Far from being scrapped, she had flown to Frankfurt only twenty-four hours after our troubles. The Mepal airframe fitters, electricians and the rest had rebuilt her truncated nose in a few brief hours.

There was darker news, too. We were not alone in taking a flak-hit over Kamen. Another B Flight crew came home with L-Lucy in a mess and their navigator, Bill Topping, injured by shrapnel. He,

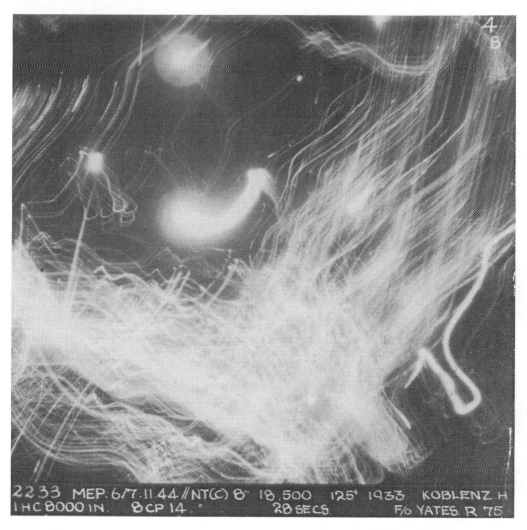

2233 MEP. 6/7.11.44 // NT(C) 8" 18.500 125° 1933 KOBLENZ. H
1 HC 8000 IN. 8 CP 14 ° 28 SECS F/o YATES. R 75

ABOVE: Searchlights obliterate Koblenz' marshalling yards from the camera lens on the evening of 6.11.44.

BELOW: ME321 N at dispersal on a wet November day, while one of the groundcrew polishes her Perspex.

ABOVE: No Perspex to polish but thumbs-up from Norrie who's all set to go.

BELOW: G-H days: at the head of the stream, formating behind a leader from another 3 Group squadron.

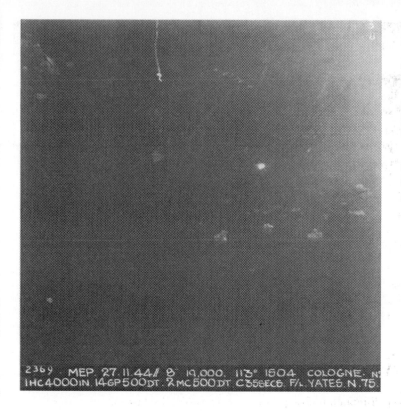

2369 MEP. 27.11.44/ 8 19,000. 113° 1504 COLOGNE. N°
IHC 4000 IN. 14 GP 500 DT. 2 MC 500 DT C 355 SECS. F/L YATES. N. 75

LEFT: G-H days: mist and murk over Cologne on the afternoon of 27.11.44. The Rhine and one of its bridges are barely visible. At the top of the picture something (not a Lancaster) trails fire downward, exploding above the city.

2468 MEP 5.12.44/8 20,000 125° 1130 HAMM N2
I HC 4000 IN. 14 MC 500 DT. 26 P 500 LD. C 37 SECS. F/L YATES. N. 75

LEFT: G-H days: cloud tops to 14,000 ft and a probable overshoot of the massive marshalling yards at Hamm, 5.12.44.

OPPOSITE PAGE: Ely Cathedral photographed in September 1944. A shining beacon on the home run.

LEFT: S/Ldr Bob Rodgers DFC, DFM, who took command of 75's B Flight after Garth Gunn's crash at Hawkinge, and on the day Garth died of his injuries.

BELOW: With Nan's groundcrew after the 30th trip. Bill Birnie in doorway, author and Geoff on ladder. Standing left to right: Norrie, Mac. Squatting: Bill Otway, Tubby, Rob Aitchison.

RIGHT: Author in Rangoon after the posting to Burma Comm Sqn.

BELOW: All seven of the author's crewmates back in Mepal village after 34 years for a Squadron reunion. Standing left to right: Geoff; Bill Birnie; Mac; Norrie; Bill Otway; Archie. Squatting: Tubby.

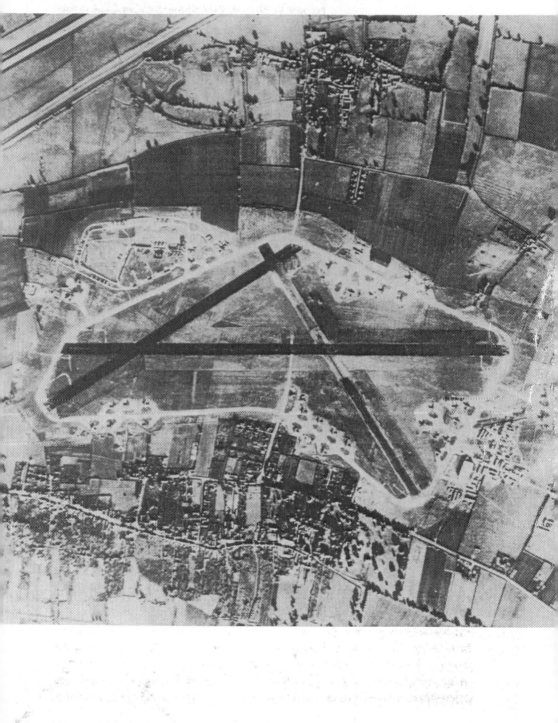

ABOVE: The remains of RAF Mepal photographed Christmas Eve, 1994. Snow cannot hide intersecting scars left by the main and No.2 runways.

BELOW: Mepal Watch Office, demolished 15.10.88 by the developer in the face of a campaign to save it.

though, was not expected to fly again and had been decorated. Then, that night's gardening sortie to the Baltic saw F/O Hadley and his crew fail to return. We didn't know it but two survived.

On Battle of Britain Sunday, 17 September, the Squadron mounted two raids. The later of these was the extraordinary and highly secretive operation in support of the doomed parachute drop at Arnhem. Only 75 was briefed for the raid and just ten aircraft participated. The target was Emmerich, south-east of Arnhem and just across the border into Germany. It was a diversionary tactic. The sealed 'bomb load' comprised miniature, dummy parachutists which put on quite a show when they hit the ground, setting off green Very flares and the sound of machine-gun fire. Tubby witnessed it from the cockpit of F/Lt Andrew's kite, one of four times he was co-opted into another crew during my absence.

The earlier operation on that Battle of Britain Sunday was an attack on enemy artillery defences in the Boulogne area. It was a softening-up exercise in preparation for an assault by Allied troops. The Squadron dispatched fourteen aircraft, one of them flown by my friend and Flight Commander, Garth Gunn. As so often in army support operations the two opposing forces were in close proximity. Accuracy was paramount. No one took the responsibility of leadership more seriously than Garth, at least I presume that was his motivation. For he bombed in good visibility from only 3,000 ft, a foolhardy enterprise given the formidable level of ground fire. His aircraft was damaged severely. Both starboard engines were hit and had to be feathered. Garth manhandled the kite back across the Channel. But they had lost precious height and would have to get down at the first available airfield.

Just north of Folkstone was the RAF fighter base of Hawkinge. The short runway was never intended for heavy bombers, certainly not damaged ones. An early touch down was their only chance. There was no possibility of going around again. Tragically, Garth came in either too high or too fast. Half the runway had gone by before his wheels touched. Still carrying a lot of speed the kite ran off the end of the concrete and into an obstruction.

The flight engineer was killed, the bomb aimer horribly wounded. Garth himself was trapped in the wreckage. One of his legs had to be amputated. He never regained consciousness, and died in the Kent & Canterbury Hospital on 21 September.

That night, after Bill and Mac had left and the ward lights were put out, I lay in my bed trying to comprehend the meaning of a life cut off like that. Garth was a determined, optimistic and gutsy character, in many ways a typical New Zealander. From the beginning he had set out not just to preach but to exemplify these qualities to the aircrew of B Flight. Yet there was a needlessness about his death and, too, the cruel irony that it commended not the qualities by which he had lived but those such as caution and self-preservation which he had spurned. He died on the altar of his own zeal.

Many a pilot was decorated for guiding a crippled kite home on just two port engines. Few of them, I suspect, had so little altitude to work with. Few had to set down on a fighter airfield. Garth was granted no posthumous award. Perhaps his actions over the target were seen as endangering to his aircraft and crew. But what he did was in the name of duty and for the greater safety of our troops. His last minutes at the controls of a Lancaster – the letter was that damned P-Peter again – demanded airmanship and courage of the highest order. Five crew members owed their lives to him as a result. Some recognition would have been just.

All the next day at Littleport I was in deep thought. I had not been prepared for the loss of a close and true friend. I found that it weighed heavily on me. In the short time I had been away from the squadron I had let fall a vital piece of operational armour. It was that forward-leaning, blinkered determination, the warlike spirit without which aircrew would undoubtedly fall to pieces. Bill and Mac were still imbued with it. To listen to them was like finding oneself on the ground, having fallen from a swing. Up above, that other life, the life of smoke-filled briefing rooms and flying breakfasts, flak over the target and the grateful descent into sleep at dawn, that life carried on without me. But here in the hospital there was only stillness and thought. Here, I realised how at Mepal I had disappeared into the role of skipper of a Lancaster crew. Now I felt myself more to be the person before all that, a country lad with his head full of flying, the son of my parents. One day soon, though, I would have to put aside this reality and climb back into the swing. Inevitably, it was a prospect I viewed with mixed feelings.

A day or so after this, S/Ldr McCurry subjected me to a third operation. He expressed his satisfaction that my left eye was clear. But the right still harboured minute particles which he could not eject. Though I would have to live with them my sight was fundamentally unimpaired. With more time and rest it should be restored to normal. Meantime, the dressing over the right eye had to remain.

That was how I greeted my parents and Joan on their visit to the hospital. For a few hours we walked through the gardens and sat talking beneath the trees. I think they had expected me to be half-dead, bandaged like an Egyptian mummy and barely able to say two words. Finding me on the mend was a relief in one way but not in another. Dad had convinced himself that the injury would bring an end to my operational flying. When I said I was to rejoin my boys he became quiet, as if made heavy by the knowledge. The farewell was not as I would have wished it. They walked away down the drive slowly and solemnly. I had disappointed them.

A couple of days later my girlfriend, Eileen, breezed back into my life. She had come with one resolute intention, and that was to cheer me up. For the sum of seven shillings I booked her two nights 'b&b' at a farmhouse on the edge of the village.

We spent our first day together on a long walk down past the confluence of the Ouse and the Lark and across the flat countryside beyond. Life had taken on a rosier hue. The following day the farmer, a bluff but kindly man, equipped me with a rather fine split cane fishing rod and a wooden centre-pin reel. His wife packed tea for us and a tartan cloth upon which to sit. We walked to the bank of the Ouse again. The weather was fine and dry, a perfect late-September day to go courting . . . and flying. Whilst we talked and watched the gaudy red-tipped quill drift lazily on the current I heard the roar of aircraft engines building in the distance. Not long after, a stream of Lancasters rose into the sky to carry the fight to the enemy again. I said nothing to Eileen but in my heart I prayed that every one might return.

When we arrived at the farmhouse that evening the farmer's wife had put two jugged hares in the oven and stewed some apples from their orchard. They had no sons of their own to send to war, she said. It would be an honour if we would share a meal with them. In those days such sentiments were not unusual. Aircrew were made well aware of the public affection for them. So we stayed and ate and did our best to repay our hosts' generosity. But we could not tarry. Littleport's doors were locked at ten o'clock sharp. Eileen escorted me back. We parted at the gates, she to leave early in the morning for her family home at Wolverton and I to resume the routine of hospital life once more.

The latter was steadily improving. I began to frequent the Plough and Harrow, just around the corner from the hospital, in the company of two other inmates. Between the three of us we had only two good eyes. We would wander down to the pub arm in arm, myself on the port station and a fellow with a bandage-free right eye to starboard. The poor chap in the middle had both eyes swathed and couldn't see a thing. This performance brought much amusement to the regulars and a free round or two to us.

Occasionally, some of the boys would cadge a lift or brave the ten-mile cycle ride through the narrow lanes to meet me in the pub. Thus, the news from Mepal reached my ears. As ever, it was a mixed bag. On 3 October Bomber Command launched its famous daylight attack on Walcheren Island in the sea approaches to Antwerp. The port had fallen in the British advance a month earlier. But Walcheren remained in enemy hands, its coastal gun batteries still dominating the Scheldt Estuary. However, much of the island was below sea level. The raid brilliantly targeted and breached the sea wall at West Kapelle. The gun emplacements were flooded and an evacuation forced. Twenty-one of 75's Lancs were in the eight waves of bombers. All returned safely.

On the night of 5 October, 75 put up no fewer than thirty-one aircraft in an abortive raid on Saarbrucken. They flew at low level across France before climbing to their bombing height of 14,000 ft. But over the target they found solid cloud and atrocious weather. Only fourteen of Mepal's crews bombed before the MC called a halt. Worse, the veteran Lancaster of F/O Alan Galletly collided with a new Witchford kite on the run-in at Wolsfeld, northeast of Trier. At low altitude, of course, nobody had a chance. In his five weeks on the station F/O Galletly, a New Zealander, had become known universally as Pop, though he was only Tubby's age.

The attrition ground on. The very next night twenty-nine aircrews left Mepal for the dangerous target of Dortmund. Night-fighters were active, with one claimed by a 75 gunner. But F/O Southward's aircraft was shot down, too. It turned out that six of the crew survived as PoWs. The skipper died in his duty of holding the aircraft steady while they jumped.

On 13 October Bomber Command issued two new directives, Hurricane 1 and Hurricane 2. Within these lay the instruction to demonstrate the extent of RAF and USAAF air supremacy. The means was to be a sharp series of maximum efforts against area targets in the Ruhr. The C-in-C gathered his forces and at dawn the next day 1,013 bombers attacked the first target, Duisberg.

What effect it had on the German High Command nobody knows. But the ground defences were certainly moved to resist, shooting fourteen kites out of the sky before they were over-whelmed. Several of Mepal's thirty-one participants were hit. Eldrid O'Callaghan's aircraft took a shell in the bomb-bay. An emergency landing at Woodbridge ensued. Jack Plummer's lost the nose just as R-Roger did over Kamen. They made it back but the skipper was frozen to the marrow. He was taken from the aircraft involuntarily gripping a truncated control column, and shipped off to Ely Hospital. For his pains he was awarded an immediate DFC.

At about this time S/Ldr McCurry agreed at last to dispense with the bandage. At first my right eye was very weak. It was strange, indeed quite difficult, to focus with both eyes. But this didn't last long. I began to feel ready for duty again and anxious to see my crew.

On 18 October the squadron contributed sixteen aircraft to a daylight attack on Bonn. This was to have a profound impact on the method and extent of future bombing operations. For the first time, a blind-bombing aid called G-H was employed to good effect.

Only a third of all Lancs were fitted with this equipment (and just three at Mepal). Their crews were briefed to spearhead vic formations of three or five aircraft. When the bomb doors of the leader opened, so did those of the non-equipped kites in the vic. When the leader released his bombs, so did the rest.

This breakthrough opened the door to operating in ten tenths cloud conditions and would shortly become a standard pattern of delivery for Bomber Command, and for 3 Group in particular.

Two days before my discharge from Littleport 75 suffered a further operational casualty. The date was 21 October and the op was a low-level, daylight attack on heavy gun batteries at Flushing, on the Island of Walcheren again. Twenty-five aircraft went from Mepal. John Johnson and his crew took up HK596 O-Oboe, the kite I had flown on the first Le Havre sortie. They were hit late in the bombing run and went into a vertical dive. Against the G-forces at work within O-Oboe it would have been impossible for anyone to get out. They impacted beside a battery. It was the sole loss among all the 3 Group Lancasters that did the trip.

The time had come to take my leave of S/Ldr McCurry and his magnificent staff. After a lifetime of benefit from their skill and dedication my rather diffident words of gratitude and a shake of hands seems barely adequate. But, really, what could ever have repaid them for the gift of sight? Besides, I was still young and in a hurry, probably awkward, too, and none too eloquent in such circumstances. And then I might have been overawed by the sheer, cold-blooded torture of the Squadron Leader's handiwork. Yet even that had one indirect benefit: I would never again be caught flying through flak with my goggles casually worn up above my helmet.

CHAPTER ELEVEN

COLOGNE AND BACK

O n the grey morning of 23 October 1944 a crew truck arrived at Littleport to return me to my flying war. It was a strange feeling to be going back after nearly seven weeks . . . good, undeniably good, but not without trepidation. One realised, of course, that only the heroic or the rash swapped hospital for cockpit with complete alacrity. Being neither, I thought that a little fear was a healthy thing and perfectly justified – we still had a formidable number of raids to survive.

Looking back at our modest tribulations to date and at the loss of so many colleagues over the same period, I reckoned our chances were about evens. On such an assessment it was best to get back into the air as soon as possible and get on with the job. Waiting around with time to kill, thinking about the odds, about pals one would never see again, about the flak and fighters and all the varied ways to get the chop, none of that was any use at all. But wait I would have to, at least for the two or three days it took the MO to pass me fit for duty and to adjust once more to the rigour of squadron life.

The boys needed no such adjustment. Their last seven weeks had been spent on pool duty, filling in for sick-listed or injured men. The pool was not a favoured locality. Aircrew could not be substituted like mechanical components. Some loss of efficiency, trust and teamwork was inevitable. The margins for error were bound to increase.

Mac, Archie and Norrie were lucky. Their services were not required. Geoff only filled in once (as a rear gunner) while Bill was called upon three times. But Tubby was most in demand. On the evening of my first day back twenty-seven crews were flying home from an uneventful raid on Essen. Tubby was in the care of a friend of mine, F/O Terry Winter, but would not land before 0930 hrs. The others bundled me off to The Three Pickerels by the river at Mepal for a welcome in liquid style. Our glasses were raised to one return

167

which was accomplished and another which was still in the realm of Providence.

Otherwise, we came together in just the same spirit as before. If there was any self-doubt showing on my part, the boys never noticed it. I was their skipper and that was that. Their trust, their cheerfulness and their enthusiasm for our shared endeavour were undiminished.

Elsewhere on the station much had changed. Several crews had completed their tours and moved on, among them John Aitken's and Eldrid O'Callaghan's. There were also far too many faces missing for the opposite reason. Five times during my absence the service police had visited the crew huts, collecting personal effects and expunging all trace of seven more brave lads.

In consequence of these things there were a lot of aircrew about the place whom I did not recognise. One was the new Commander of B Flight, S/Ldr J.R. Rodgers. He had taken-over a month earlier, on the day Garth died. He was a New Zealander and rather taciturn by nature. His post required him to be something of a communicator, however, and to this he responded with typical Kiwi straightforwardness and informality.

He stood on no ceremony in establishing first-name terms and generally making me feel welcome and at ease. He also took pains to offer some sound advice about returning to operations mid-tour:

> 'You may have done twelve trips, but think of number thirteen as your first. Don't let yourself become overconfident when you reach the half-way point. Plenty of crews think that gives them the right to relax or take a chance. Jerry would like nothing better. Don't fall for it.'

So now I settled down to wait and reacquaint myself with the perpetual activity all around me at Mepal. The squadron had about eighteen hundred staff busy grinding out the hours or the ops. As well as the various aircrew sections there were meteorological, intelligence and admin. staff of various grades, a groundcrew of seven or eight men to each aircraft, armourers, refuelling crews, airframe fitters, engine fitters, electricians, instrument fitters, spark plug testers, radar crews, w/t mechanics, truck and tractor drivers, maintenance men, gardeners, medics, cooks, and cleaners, service police, batmen and doubtless scores of others I have long forgotten. It was a large and dynamic enterprise, realised with the single objective of placing the maximum explosive in the designated, minimum area.

In recent days this had meant frequent trips to Germany. The C-in-C had embarked upon his last great Battle of the Ruhr, in fact an assault on all the familiar and well-bombed industrial towns and cities and not merely the benighted valley. The briefing room at Mepal had witnessed the CO giving his aircrew a stream of bad news: 'Gentlemen, your target for today is Saarbrucken' . . .; 'is Dortmund' . . .; 'is Stuttgart.' These and Emmerich, Duisberg (twice), Bonn and Neuss all rolled off his tongue in the first twenty-two days of October.

On the evening of the twenty-third the first of two Essen raids was executed in ten-tenths cloud. That restricted the ground defences while the escort deterred enemy fighters. The threat to the attacking force was minimal. But the bombing was evidently scattered and unsatisfactory since the very next day the order to return was issued. This time the squadron put up one aircraft fewer. Conditions were better. The attack was in daylight with built-up areas and factories clearly visible. Anti-aircraft opposition was moderate but, again, no fighters were seen. Twenty-three bombed. The concentration was good. As on the previous evening, there were no losses.

These two ops to the premier Ruhr target greatly bolstered my confidence. If Essen couldn't lay a paw on the squadron in two attempts there had to be some hope for a quiet remainder to our tour. We couldn't be gifted a milk run every time. There were going to be Essens and Colognes. But a quiet life was the thing. No more coning, no more fires in the starboard outer, no more shattered perspex . . . just a series of unremarkable take offs, bombings and landings and machine-like efficiency on board until our thirty was complete. Plenty of crews sailed through in this way. Now we must work and hope for the same.

In this we had the flow of events on our side. Though we would have scoffed in incredulity if someone had told us, the threat from German defences was on the wane. Shortages of manpower, steel and fuel were biting into German production, hampering both gunnery and fighter defences. The result was a real decline in bomber losses. In return for over 60,000 tonnes of explosive delivered in the last three months of 1944, Bomber Command sacrificed only one hundred and thirty-six aircraft. It was by no means the worst time to be flying to the Fatherland and a world apart from 75's darkest days between April and December 1943 when the losses cut deep and cut often.

On the morning of 25 October we were trucked out to B Flight dispersal to be welcomed by the groundcrew of NF980 F-Freddy.

They were quick to assure us that their charge was in prime condition and was the best aircraft on the squadron. In fact, I never met any groundcrew who were less than totally convinced of their own kite's supremacy. They all had the most terrific pride in their work.

We took off on a three-hour cross-country, culminating in a couple of runs over the bombing range. The flight didn't go badly and the landing was half-decent. It was as if we had not been away at all. We boarded the truck a rehabilitated crew prepared for inclusion on the Battle Order whenever Bob Rodgers thought fit. We did not have long to wait.

It was early morning on the following day, the 27th. I was being shaken with unreasonable determination by my batman. 'Sir, wake up, please. Flying breakfast at 0630 hrs, sir . . . sir, don't drop off again . . . Briefing at 0730.'

He achieved his purpose. The bell of lazy, warm sleep was shattered. Who the hell woke him up, I wanted to know. I threw off my bedclothes and looked out of the window. There was not a thing to see but fog. Oh, for the days when that would have been enough to keep our Oxford trainers safely at dispersal. Leaving Bill still half-dressed I cycled to the Officers' Mess. The Battle Order was posted. Only ten crews were listed, with our names against S-Sugar – the third trip we would fly in her.

The chatter from ten crews hardly compared to the usual uproar before Briefing. But the sudden silence and rising tension as the CO and his team entered the room was as arresting as ever. He sprang onto the platform. The curtain swept aside, revealing the map of Germany massively daubed in red around the Ruhr Valley. But this was not to be a third consecutive run to Essen. The CO said:

> 'Gentleman, your target for today is a large chemical complex on the east bank of the Rhine at Leverkusen. You will see that it lies about eight miles north of Cologne. It is of vital importance to the German war machine and to the industries of the Ruhr.
>
> 'The weather in the target area has been deteriorating for twenty-four hours and is not expected to improve in time for the attack. In other circumstances the operation might be scrubbed. But a Group decision has been reached and you are to be part of a force of exactly one hundred aircraft. You are to bomb through cloud using G-H radar.
>
> 'This will be the squadron's second operational use of G-H. It is vitally important that we can report a good concentration.'

G-H was the blind-bombing device employed nine days earlier over Bonn. It was developed from Oboe and used the same pulsed signal. It had better range and the great virtue of accommodating up to a hundred attacking aircraft. It was, therefore, much more than another Pathfinder aid. Its operational debut was on the Mannesman Steelworks in Dusseldorf during an area raid on that town on the night of 3 November 1943. Though adjudged a success, it was slow to be adopted by the main Groups and stayed firmly on the special equipment list. However, as the Allied armies pushed east mobile ground stations for Oboe were set up and advanced with them. Operating range was extended deep into Germany. The problem remained that there were not enough aircraft with the G-H sets. But then someone proposed formatting non-equipped aircraft behind an equipped leader, and the way was open to exploit G-H to the full. Bonn and the coming raid on Leverkusen were the test platform for this technique.

The Intelligence Officer showed us several very good close-ups of the chemical complex we were to go for. It was a monument to industrial brutalism built outside the town in otherwise unspoilt, wooded countryside. Its giant, slab-like, concrete buildings, joined by a web of steel pipes, tanks and gantries, made no concessions to the setting. Its wharfs violated the river. Black barges were visible alongside, loading or unloading the toxic stuff in which the place dealt. To me, it all looked ripe for demolition, a wholly worthwhile target and by no means a cover for more generalised bombing.

Opposition in the locality was expected to be slight. G-H was impervious to the weather but German fighters weren't. Our gravest danger would arise if we strayed south over the heavy AA batteries of Cologne, which remained as formidable as any.

Watches were synchronised on Gp/Cpt Campbell's count. 'I wish I was going with you', he said and we knew he meant it.

At 9.00 a.m. we boarded the crew trucks. As ours lumbered away I looked at the faces of my fellow passengers who included Bob Rodgers, Bill Osborne and their boys. They were as subdued as the weather was grey. Both crews were dropped off to shouts of 'Good Luck' from those remaining. Our turn came last.

'Anyone for S-Sugar?' the driver shouted, as she had on the occasion of our first raid together.

So it was beginning again.

We were first of the ten into the air. The murk at low level had thinned somewhat. One might have expected some weak sunshine and a suggestion of blue sky to develop. But we rose into greyness that still obtained at 8,000 ft over Woodbridge where we had been due to rendezvous with our nominated G-H leader, a Waterbeach kite. By the time the Dutch coastline appeared on Bill's H2S set conditions were deteriorating fast. We were being tossed around like the proverbial cork on the ocean, and formating was less of a concern than the fear of collision. Everyone but Bill and Mac was on watch, straining to make out the first, vague outline hardening to black and giving us perhaps two or three seconds in which to react.

'Only five minutes to the German border,' announced Bill over the intercom. But as he spoke we emerged into dazzling sunshine and a vivid blue sky. Huge anvils of cumulo-nimbus rose before us like sky gods mindful only of their own towering pride and importance and perfectly oblivious of our trespass. Then a Lancaster broke cloud ahead, her back, wings and tailplane shining with light, her props spinning faithfully. Another appeared, just as magnificent, and a third. These were not mere bombers, crude forms of steel and oil. They were guiding beacons of the spirit. With them flew our pride, our hope, our purpose.

Within two or three minutes the entire raiding force had appeared around us. I immediately began to search for the nearest available G-H aircraft. Up to this time, formation flying had meant little more to us than a tight and disciplined stream. As such, it had become almost second nature and was the subject of some sharp, inter-Group rivalry. The pilots of 3 Group were proud of their achievement in mastering this art. They were well aware of the condescension from certain quarters towards Main Force crews, and were not slow to point out when, for example, 5 Group were content with a gaggle.

But G-H was a harder taskmaster, requiring us to form up in a three- or five-aircraft vic. The moment for opening bomb doors and for release followed on from the vic leader's actions. It was a simple, visual mechanism that, effectively, placed all responsibility for the accuracy of the raid on the shoulders of the G-H navigator ahead.

I took up station, levelling out at 20,000 ft for the final, outbound leg. By the standards of Hamel (7,000 ft) or Le Havre (12,000 ft) this altitude may seem high for a single target. But the weight of AA fire over Germany made safety the prime consideration, particularly since vic-flying brought us much closer to other kites and multiplied the dangers if one blew up.

Our leader's bomb doors opened and we followed suit. We began our run above a sea of white cloud that looked both glacial and turbulent. Everything was set. Now that S-Sugar was riding steady in her vic, with no fighters and no real flak barrage to negotiate, this was turning out unexpectedly easy, a veritable milk run.

From behind his window Mac watched the bombs spill from the lead aircraft and pressed the tit.

'Bombs gone', he announced to the usual, thumping accompaniment and violent lift. It certainly didn't feel usual to drop on an unseen target in virtually clean air. Nor did it seem so to go through the motions with a photograph of solid cloud – but we did.

I pointed S-Sugar down into the claustrophobic gloom again and we turned onto our first homeward leg. Thus we remained, weary now but cocooned at least from fighters. We broke through the cloud base only a couple of miles seaward of the English coast. It had been like coming out of a long, dark tunnel. The boys even cheered.

So we were back. Number thirteen was lucky for us. In debriefing, the Intelligence Officer did his best to draw some useful information from us. But a blind drop above solid cloud with little opposition was hardly promising material.

Mac was mildly aggrieved at the limited role required for him by G-H bombing. 'Better with the bombsight', he stated flatly. But neither he nor anyone else could say for certain until the Photographic Reconnaissance Unit had overflown the target.

We waited through the following day for some word on the success of the raid. But none came. The ten-tenths cloud and deteriorating conditions in general forbade a reconnaissance flight. It also saw off an attack on Hanover for which twenty-three crews, including mine, were detailed.

The following morning, 28 October, we were again roused early from our beds. We had an hour to dress, grab breakfast and report to the briefing room. This time we were confronted with drab, cloudy skies and rain beyond the hut window. Visibility did not even extend to the airfield boundary.

Even so, two Battle Orders were posted on the mess notice board, a morning op for thirteen crews and an afternoon one for seven. It was the morning shift that concerned us. The word from dispersal was that we would have a light fuel load and the standard cargo of general-purpose five hundred and one thousand pounders. 'Army support', declared the mess sleuths.

We were allotted S-Sugar again. All the boys, not just me, were beginning to feel a certain propriety towards her. She obviously led a charmed life. On station now for nearly two months and a veteran of fifteen raids, she was yet to be grazed by a single bullet.

I was anxious that we should be allotted a regular aircraft again. Brought in to acknowledge merit and seniority, these informal arrangements gave a centre of gravity to crew operations. To bring one's own charge through a hard trip, to come to rely on her and take pride in her, to be familiar with her idiosyncracies, to polish her Perspex and talk Lancs with her ground crew . . . all this built on one's chances of survival. I decided that S-Sugar's luck must be ours. Other crews were after her. We could not afford to let her go. I *would* speak to Bob Rodgers about her. But for now that would have to wait.

For the third time that month Briefing was preoccupied by the huge naval guns of Walcheren Island. Access to Antwerp via the Scheldt Estuary had been a primary objective since the British captured the city on 4 September. War supplies essential to the crossing of the Rhine and the anticipated race to Berlin were stockpiled in southern English ports. But nothing could be shipped through Antwerp until the guns were silenced.

They had endured trial by water at West Kapelle Dyke on 3 October and by fire at Flushing on the 21st. But still they controlled the estuary. Now 3 Group was to return to the largest concentration at Flushing. The last visit was also the occasion of 75's last loss. It would be no easy ride.

We were shown recce photographs of Walcheren and the target area, the latter blown up to show a strip of God's earth barely two hundred yards across at the widest point. It ran east to west, connecting island to mainland. To the east the shore was lined by three docks and several groups of oil storage tanks clearly battered by a previous raid. We would be required to exhibit the same degree of precision from our bombing height of 10,000 ft. This was no easy matter if you subscribe to the official statistic, much bandied about after the war, of an overall bombing accuracy to within three miles.

At 0902 hrs I pointed S-Sugar's nose down the mile of runway and received my green from the caravan. At one hundred and ten mph on the clock I lifted her gently off the concrete.

We crossed the coast at Felixstowe already at our bombing height and in loose formation near the front of the stream. Over the sea East Anglia's cloud cover quickly broke up, then thinned to nothing. Visibility at ground level improved steadily. Now conditions for the attack were good.

Walcheren Island could be seen easily from a long way out, first as a grey-brown tongue of land jutting into the North Sea and then, gradually, as the image from the aerial photographs with Flushing and the gun emplacements brooding to the east.

Having fused the bombs and taken position in the nose, Mac began his instructions. As he did, the guns opened up, spitting their shells into our path. We flew straight down the isthmus, the sky around us already pockmarked with hanging, black puffs of smoke. The flak was not intense but it was accurate for both course and height. Walcheren's gun crews plainly knew their business and didn't believe in wasting a single shell.

Strings of bombs began to impact in the target area, some very accurate, some straddling the gun emplacements to splash harmlessly into the sea. Thankfully, this time Mac pronounced the desired words with some dispatch. The grips snapped back and the kite lurched and jumped as though bounding up a five-hundred-foot staircase. We hung on straight and level for twenty-seven seconds to get our shot. Then we were away.

In the midst of the shells S-Sugar's past run of luck had seemed a flimsy guarantee. But as I flew westward a few feet above the white caps and the boys belted out some dirty ditty with unfettered joy and vigour, a more positive interpretation recommended itself. She had pulled it off again. The sixteenth motif would be added below my port window. And still she was invulnerable. I really would *have* to talk to Bob Rodgers.

All of the squadron's thirteen participants returned safely. But several aircraft picked up some damage. The operation was a success with a large explosion, almost certainly an ammunition store going up, observed at the end of the raid. Even so, the planners at High Wycombe were taking no chances. Flushing's guns were to be neutralised come what may. On our return we learnt that another operation of equal size was readied for late afternoon. Fourteen Mepal crews were to fly the remaining, serviceable aircraft. But it never happened. In the short space of time between our landing and their take-off weather conditions went awry.

The second op of seven crews scheduled for the afternoon did fly, however. They were part of a force of seven hundred Lancasters and Halifaxes sent against the much-bombed city of Cologne (only Essen and Berlin received more main force attacks). The cloud was thin enough for them to bomb visually, to what effect at ground level did not bear thinking about. The attacking force met an AA barrage euphemistically described as moderate in squadron records. But the seven came safely home.

Two other developments came to pass at this point. The

175

Intelligence Section finally confirmed the destruction of the Leverkusen chemical complex. A belated message of congratulation arrived on the CO's desk from Exning and was posted on the mess notice board. Now we could expect a G-H assignment whenever conditions required.

The second development was personal and brought me sadness. My mother wrote to tell me that Bob, my collie, had been killed. She had been walking him in Old Wolverton when he took off down the street as if chasing a hare across Fifty-Two Acre Field. He died under the wheels of a car. That evening Dad recovered his body and carried it down to the river in his arms. He laid my old pal to rest in the bank, close to the spot where dog and boy used to swim in the Elysian summers of their youth.

October had been a damp, grey month and the 29th was no exception. Walcheren's naval guns came under the hammer once more, but not at Flushing. Fourteen of the squadron's crews went to West Kapelle and, according to records, bombed slightly wide of the aiming point. This was 75's last visit to the island. Nine days later the German garrison surrendered and the way was opened to equip the Allies for crossing into Germany.

We did not fly the West Kapelle raid. We were stood down that day. S-Sugar needed an air test, after which I took the opportunity to introduce her to Stony Stratford (though I still hadn't arranged the formalities with Bob Rodgers).

I flew first over the slow, olive-green Ouse, a gesture of parting, then turned in a wide arc around the town. Dropping low, we hedge-hopped in to target. We cleared the house at about one hundred and seventy-five mph and probably shook the foundations. I climbed away to 500 ft and heeled S-Sugar on to her port wing tip, giving her plenty of rudder to keep the nose up. As we came around for another pass my mother stood in the little rectangle of garden. Familiar with all this now, she watched and waved and felt whatever mothers of sons in the fighting services should on such occasions. Quite what the boys made of it all I'm not sure. I never thought to ask. There was no reason to since, of course, nothing was as good as low flying. Every airman knew that!

The 30th of October dawned fair but chilly, a fine autumn day in prospect. But there were two Battle Orders posted in the Flight Office and an early breakfast for six crews. They were woken to hear that the hydrogenisation plant at Wesseling was their target and take-off time 0900 hrs.

We, with twenty other crews, were granted a more leisurely start to the day. Bill and I cycled to dispersal to learn what we could. S-Sugar's bomb-bay had acquired a 4,000 lb cookie and three cans and clusters of incendiaries. A bowser crew told us the fuel load was to be 2,100 gallons. These bare facts were enough. This one would be a burn-out – area bombing in daylight, probably of a major city deep in the Third Reich.

It would be our first blitz since Bremen eight raids ago. All the targets we had hit before or since were either strategic (petrol dumps, refineries, etc.) or army support. All of us, especially the bomb aimers, infinitely preferred these to a big town blitz. Closely defined objectives and measurable degrees of success went hand in hand with a sense of achieving something tangible and worthwhile. By contrast, a road to victory measured in the number of German workers de-housed or the spreading of German public disaffection with their government was bound at times to be hard going.

I did not – we did not – have any of these thoughts in our heads as the map curtain was swept back at 1030 hrs. It was an afternoon attack and it was Cologne . . . Cologne which had suffered enormous damage from seven hundred bombers only two days earlier . . . Cologne with maybe a thousand heavy guns, and just to the south of them thousands of others in the most heavily defended corner of the world.

For me, though, not even Cologne seemed such a forbidding prospect by day. Sunlight leached away much fierceness from bomb impacts and flakbursts and substituted quantities of dust and smoke. Everything became greyer and less pulsatingly dramatic. In my head I knew it was all the same. But it did not seem that way. Moreover, if I could see the black kites dotting the sky around me, if I could gaze upward through the Perspex to the shining host at 30,000 ft and know that we were not alone, then I'd be all right. In daylight I would be all right.

So, I stared at the arrow and the line that delicately skirted the red daubs marking known flak, and thought exactly that. That and one other, banal and utterly selfish consideration: an ENSA show was scheduled in the station cinema that evening. We could still be back in time to make curtain-up.

An hour later Bill and I were in the mess picking over our flying meal. The tannoy crackled. The raid was postponed until further notice. We cycled to B Flight Office to learn that this was no permanent reprieve. We would still be going. But take-off time was put back to 1745 hrs. My hopes for a daylight op promptly crashed. Now, effectively, it would be a night raid. So much for ENSA.

We made our own entertainment, kicking a football about with more enthusiasm than skill (the NZ boys preferred an oval ball). The six crews who were dispatched to Wesseling in the morning came home with stories of intense flak and one damaged kite. It didn't do much for our peace of mind. But at 1600 hrs we were in the crew room, gathering up the accoutrements of a flying war. At 1755 we were beside the flight caravan, S-Sugar quivering and straining to be loosed down the flarepath. Number fifteen, the half-way marker, was beginning.

It was to be a big operation, typical for Cologne. Eight hundred Lancasters and Halifaxes from 3, 4 and 5 Groups were participating. The fighters that would have been our daylight escort were withdrawn. In their place diversionary and intruder raids were to be mounted by, respectively, 100 Group and the Mosquito Light Night Striking Force.

We crossed the coast at 8,000 ft. Cromer was barely visible in the deep, early-evening gloom. The jagged line of surf, just differentiated in the weak moonlight, marked the last of England we would see for four hours. My nerves were much worse this time. Always in the past, things had improved once we were in the air. But now my knees wouldn't stop shaking. I told myself that it didn't mean anything. I had been injured, after all. There were bound to be one or two mental scars. This was our first formidable target since the return to duty, and it was in darkness. It all seemed perfectly reasonable. But my knees didn't listen to a word of it. I could only try to keep my suffering a secret.

There were, of course, perfectly sound reasons for being nervous. Every command centre and flight office from Kiel to Munich was probably on alert. The deadly game of guesswork had begun. The flak ships along the Dutch coast were preparing for our arrival overhead. Inland, the Me 110 and Fw 190 pilots would, if they were to fly at all, be collecting their gear about now and wondering, like us, what the next hours held in store. Some of them might be in the air before the first marine salvo left the muzzle. Generally, though, they would be kept circling . . . circling . . . circling . . . eyes glued to their flashing beacons and on-board radar screens until our track was plotted and our purpose identified. Then, if they could, they would fall upon us.

No effort was spared by Bomber Command to subvert this eventuality. We cleared the flak ships at 19,000 ft and approached

Venlo veiled by the first bales of Window and some quite low but thickening cloud. Our course took us eastward, straight towards the Ruhr. Düsseldorf, Krefeld, Essen, Hamm, Duisburg, Gelsenkirchen, Dortmund . . . any one of them could have been the target. Already, the Mossies were pitching in. Up to a hundred miles away they were sowing confusion and uncertainty. The German command centres would be swamped with reports of raids that did not exist. How they reacted, and where they dispatched their fighters, could make the difference between life and death for some of us.

When the stream turned late and decisively to the south-east the die was cast. Cologne lay ahead of us, hidden by a thin but extensive layer of cloud and, maybe, also by mist up from the river. As yet we had not seen a single orange flare. But of searchlights there were perhaps a hundred. They lanced the cloud, transforming it into a lustrous and mobile, white sea. The heavy flak, which had been sporadic, developed into a sustained barrage. Perhaps hundreds of tons of AA shells were being thrown up. The barrels of those guns must have been glowing like hot coals. All this attention was directed at the Pathfinders, but it failed. The TIs went down and splashed red in the centre of the drop zone, well concentrated and distinguishable despite the cloud cover. Bombs from the first wave began to follow. But, apart from some bright, quickfire explosions, nothing else could be seen. It was certainly not as clear to the eye or as apocalyptic as Bremen or Kiel.

However, I did witness the end of two aircraft ahead of us. One of them carved a fiery trail down into the cloud. There seemed to be a reasonable chance that someone could get out. The other offered no lifeline. It took a direct hit in the bomb-bay and in the blink of an eye was a ball of shocking white and orange, expanding violently outwards across a large area of sky and then petering into a sickeningly slow drift to earth. I averted my eyes, not out of professionalism but in humility. Sometimes the cynical view was right: it *was* all a matter of luck. Every kite had its bomb doors open. One small splinter of flak hitting S-Sugar's cookie or incendiaries would bring the same end to us.

Mac had squeezed his long frame under my seat and down into the nose some time ago. Now he informed me that we were right on track. For the moment, I only had to keep her steady.

For his part, Tubby still had a stock of Window to feed down the chute. No sooner had he risen from the tip-up seat beside me than we entered a furious hailstorm of red-hot metal. An instant later there was an explosion beneath us, unseen but no distance away. The aircraft convulsed on the shockwave. Something very solid and fast-moving smashed upward, not into the bomb-bay but the cockpit. A Perspex panel above me blew out, spreading icy turbulence everywhere. A flood tide of fear surged over me. 'It' was happening to me again, and I was utterly helpless. But the seconds that followed were reassuringly normal. No crystal arrows filled my eyes. S-Sugar flew on in perfect equilibrium and I struggled to catch up.

Tubby reappeared all agog, asking if I was all right. Then he turned his attention to the floor less than an arm's reach to my right. It had been ripped open. Just above was his tip-up seat, upright now though he had not left it so. He pulled it down and ran his right hand around a raised and jagged hole, plumb centre and about five inches in diameter. He stared at it for a while, fascinated and horrified in equal measure.

'Oh, Shh . . . ugar', he said finally. It was as near to an obscenity as I ever heard fall from his lips.

No one was hurt, no vital equipment damaged. Mac got the bombs away. We executed the twenty-eight-second camera run though we knew the photograph would be a wash-out (without it the raid wouldn't count towards our tour). Before we parted from the fury of Cologne we saw other aircraft burning. We knew that many among the five and a half thousand young airmen who came to this turbulent place would never leave, and we knew how lucky we were not to be among them.

On the cold and draughty run to the Dutch border our only fighter of the night put in an appearance. Its silhouette was unfamiliar. It passed directly in front of us, climbing out of nowhere at an impossible speed and angle.

'Jet, skipper . . . jet!' yelled Geoff who had a clear look at it but no chance to react on the trigger.

However, this novelty provided only a secondary talking point. The boys came one by one to the cockpit to stand in the gale, which was quite moderate this time, and gape . . . first at the roof, then the floor and, finally, Tubby's seat. It didn't take long for curiosity to spiral down into scatology. 'F*** me,' said Bill, 'they're firing suppositories at us now.'

Someone thought that if ever our bombs hung up Tubby could drop a cookie of his own on the Hun, and another offered to remove the Elsan to the cockpit so all S-Sugar's future crews could sample her plumbing while over the Fatherland.

But it only got worse back at Mepal. For days S-Sugar's ground crew displayed the punctured article outside their hut. It was, after all, the trophy of a long-overdue blooding. Word spread and poor Tubby found himself, so to speak, the butt of jokes by people he hardly knew. These he accepted in good grace and by virtue of his native, self-deprecating humour.

S-Sugar's was the only damage sustained by any of 75's aircraft in the raid. But thirty-eight bitter losses were logged elsewhere, a high toll at this stage of the war.

Bomber Command was ever an unrelenting taskmaster, and the very next evening the skies over Cologne were filled with the sounds of Merlin and Hercules engines once again. We were rested but S-Sugar flew. Her metalwork had been patched and the tip-up seat and Perspex replaced in the one working day. Flying Officer Sadgrove and his crew took her up and bombed in the same ten-tenths cloud conditions. But the flak was slight this time and all eighteen of 75's kites returned safely. Possibly, Cologne's stock of heavy AA shells was depleted by the previous night's work. Certainly, the distribution of ordinance around Germany's cities was hampered by the sheer volume of rubble everywhere.

The city of Cologne had been bludgeoned with what must have seemed to its people unrelenting ferocity. Hundreds, perhaps thousands, of innocent lives were lost in the crashing masonry and conflagration. Yet, throughout, the *Luftwaffe* failed to fly to their defence. It responded neither in daylight nor in darkness. I believe that our jet sighting (confirmed at debriefing as an Me 262) was the only visual contact by any 75 crew in forty-six sorties flown during those four days.

The reason for the *Luftwaffe*'s absence was certainly a shortage of fuel rather than the counter-measures conducted by our Mosquitoes. That didn't render those measures any less necessary. But the series of attacks on synthetic oil plants begun by the Americans in May 1944 had yielded dramatic dividends. By autumn only about one-twentieth of the former volume of coal-derived aviation fuel was reaching German fighter stations.

November dawned dry but cloudy. Mepal was free of operations. I was left to ponder S-Sugar's future and ours. Did the holing over Cologne herald a change in her luck? More by accident than design I had not managed to buttonhole Bob Rodgers about her. Now I began to be glad of that, and still more so when my friend, Terry Winter, stepped in. S-Sugar was claimed and we were still looking for our talisman.

181

Chapter Twelve

Again the Jinx

If, before the night of 20 July 1944, someone had asked which was 75's unluckiest target, the answer might have been slow to come. But older hands on the ground staff would have thought back to the night two years earlier when six Wellingtons failed to return from Hamburg out of seventeen sent. Wellingtons, of course, carried only five crew members. But one of the FTRs had a 2nd pilot on board and that meant thirty-one empty beds in the sleeping quarters and thirty-one sparely phrased letters to be written by the station adjutant. One quarter of the squadron's fighting strength had been ripped away.

There were many subsequent raids on Germany's second city, notably in the nine nights of the Battle of Hamburg when firestorms raged and Window entered the air war. By the end of hostilities three-quarters of the city confines were destroyed, approximately the same area as in Berlin. But Hamburg exacted its toll, also. Ours would not have been the only squadron to evince a particular fear of the place. But, as it happens, another and quite small town in Germany came to earn this black distinction.

In the early evening of 20 July, when the boys and I had only just concluded our conversion to four-engine heavies and had yet even to fly a Lancaster, the briefing room at Mepal was alive with the noise of twenty-six crews.

Jack Leslie's address began with a name probably no one in the room would associate with a place of danger just west of the Rhine and on the approach to Happy Valley.

'Gentlemen, your target for tonight is a synthetic oil refinery at *Homberg*.'

Homberg. The groans from the floor would prove prophetic. It was to be 75's first contribution to the American-conceived Oil Plan. Ten weeks had passed since the Flying Fortresses of the 8th and 15th Air Forces had begun the offensive. It specified eighty giant synthetic oil refineries for destruction. To our unwavering C-in-C it was another panacea and a distraction from the task of razing German cities and towns. He had already been forced to put aside area attacks three times that year (first when his squadrons were pitched into the Transport Plan, bombing the French railway system in preparation for D-Day, then when tactical support was required for the Allied armies and, finally, against V1 and V2 flying bomb sites under Operation *Crossbow*). Now a fourth change swept the Target Indicator Board at High Wycombe HQ. The Germans, however, had observed the effects of the American campaign and well knew the need to protect their remaining oil assets.

Still, Homberg (or, to be exact, the Rhein-Preussen refinery in the Meerbreck district) was not an obviously high-risk target. It was no Krupp's or *Tirpitz*. It involved a very limited incursion over Germany, stopping short of the Ruhr. To the twenty-six crews from Mepal and those of all the one hundred and forty-seven Lancasters and eleven Mosquitoes taking part, it probably looked like a fairly simple night's work.

The enemy had other ideas. They mobilised a large number of fighters which caught the Lancs on the run-in. Twenty of the attacking force went down, nearly fourteen per cent. The others duly bombed, wrecking parts of the refinery. But it is doubtful whether the wreckage exceeded that done to 3 Group and, in particular, 75 Squadron. Seven aircraft never returned to Mepal.

It was a stunning blow to everyone on the station, most of all the crews who made it back to find so many familiar faces missing. Later it would be known that eight of these touched earth in Germany or Holland, buried their parachutes as best they could, and started walking. Just one, a mid-upper gunner, evaded capture.

As for Homberg, it achieved immediate status as the squadron's jinx target. Memories of the raid hung over the station like a dark and glowering raincloud. It seemed barely credible that this town with its inoffensive and unwarlike associations, millinery rather than military, should strike such fear into the heart of a heavy bomber squadron. But it did. At the time of our arrival two weeks after the raid no one was in a hurry to attack another oil target. Indeed, 75 Squadron was assigned no more until Kamen seven weeks later when, alas, all the woe fell upon F/O Topping and myself.

It was against this background that after breakfast on 2 November we trooped into the briefing room once more. The CO pronounced the name of the target slowly and evenly, with no attempt to ameliorate the impact of his words. There was a long hiatus while they sank in.

The CO himself and the C Flight Commander, S/Ldr Jack Bailey, were present at the Briefing of 20 July. Quite possibly, one or two of the crews being briefed now also flew then. There were perhaps five crews still on station who, like us, dated from that time or soon after. We knew . . . they knew . . . everyone knew the meaning of those two, damned syllables. *Homberg.*

The CO told us that 5 Group had bombed the target the previous day. Their efforts failed to satisfy High Wycombe HQ so the job had been handed to 3 Group. One hundred and eighty-four Lancasters drawn from the Group's ten 'line' squadrons were to bomb from 20,000 ft. Time on target was 1400 hrs. The weather forecast was good: scattered, light cloud, minimal ground haze.

The bombing leader told us that the Oboe stations would be transmitting but if clear air obtained markers would be laid, too. Well, of course, few bomb aimers worthy of the name would trade the exacting science of the Mk XIV bombsight for staring at the belly of the aircraft ahead. For them G-H was, effectively, a backup which they hoped not to employ.

The news that we were taking over from 5 Group caused something of a warm glow. Group rivalry was always present. We were only too aware of 5 Group's shining reputation. In particular, its élite 617 'Dambusters' Squadron had monopolised all the glamour targets. In the process they had developed a new and audacious technique of low-level marking and sent down Barnes Wallis's six-ton Tallboy bombs with astonishing accuracy. Of course, 617 was the stuff of legend. But the rest of 5 Group was more assailable and here, in Homberg, was a golden opportunity for an acknowledged 'chop' squadron to make its point.

Of more practical purport was the umbrella of two hundred beautiful Spitfires. If the *Luftwaffe* came up this time, they would not find things as they were on the night of 20 July.

Jack Leslie wound up by announcing, as we knew from the Battle Order, that he would fly on this one. Cheers went up from the floor. The quality of a Commanding Officer's leadership was a crucial factor in squadron morale. Obviously, the operational efficiency of aircrew was the main concern. But everybody, not just aircrew, appreciated the encouragement and interest of a good CO, and worked the better for it. It was typical of our man to choose a pressure raid like this. A few tales were told over a drink in the local of COs who gifted themselves the soft trips. But that wasn't Leslie's way. His crew was to be that of F/Lt Plummer for whom Operation *Hurricane*, the Duisberg raid of 14 October, had taken on such a literal and freezing meaning. Plummer was still recovering from frostbite. But his crew would have cause to curse his absence before this day was out.

We had been assigned HK600 K-King which I had not flown before. She had arrived, like us, on station in early August. Her first trip, like mine, was to Lucheux. Now she would bear us to the jinx target with just a massive 8,000 lb blockbuster and four 500 lb g.p.s hanging by the grips in her bomb-bay.

At 1140 hrs we received the green from the flight caravan. Fifteen minutes later East Anglia's airfield circuits emptied as the eastward stream took shape. We found our leader without difficulty but I was reluctant to formate too quickly. If the vic was to be more than three strong I liked to fly as one of the rear pair. That way I could control my own proximity to the kite in front and leave a safe distance if he blew up.

Over the Dutch coast the Spits arrived, weaving their contrails high above my canopy, wings glinting in the sunlight. I took off my flying jacket and rolled up my shirt sleeves. It was warm work wearing goggles and a flying mask tight across one's face. Below us the broad sweep of Dutch countryside was virtually free of haze. The main ground features and large constructions were perfectly visible. There seemed no case for bombing by G-H. Looking down through his window Mac knew what he wanted and it was to bomb visually.

North of Venlo we crossed into enemy skies. The target was somewhere on the veiled horizon. The flak began as a few clusters predicting our path. The fighters of July were absent but Homberg had another response. The puffs of black smoke ahead of us, so strangely static and anodyne by day, numbered scores, then hundreds, then thousands like some spreading, aerial pestilence. The sky became hideous with them. I needed all my resolve to reach for the bomb door lever on the left side of my seat and expose our 8,000-pounder to the muzzles of the guns.

Meerbreck and Rhein-Preussen lay before us. I waited for Mac's instructions. Already, smoke as black as carbon was billowing up from the first fires. Then, shockingly, the sky ahead was filled with smoke also. Two bombers had blown up together. One must have received a direct hit in the bomb-bay. The other had gone up with it. Debris showered out from the mushrooms. The larger remnants twirled gently down, trailing flames. There would be no survivors from 24,000 lb of exploding bombs and two thousand gallons of petrol. A few vestigial things – shoes, identity tags, some pathetic evidence of dissection – might be picked up by those scouring the ground below. Little else would remain from the fourteen lives, probably not enough to accord each an unmarked grave and the sacraments of burial spoken in a hated, foreign tongue.

It was as if I had been woken from a dream when Mac's steadfast voice sounded on the intercom, 'Left . . . left, skipper. Hold her there.'

'For Christ's sake let them go, Mac', I shouted, knowing that it was wasted breath but probably, somewhere in my perverse reason, not unproud of the fact. It was as well, though, that I did not have to aim the bombs. The man who did, issued one last, elongated, 'Steadyyy . . .', and the blockbuster banged out of the bomb-bay. Freed of her burden K-King wrestled several hundred feet higher, lifting our hearts as she went.

The camera run took 37 seconds, a long and tense passage in a hostile sky. Then I had the nose down and we were on our way without, it seemed, any damage. I checked that everyone was unharmed. Bill gave me a new course and we emerged into clean air.

So we survived the jinx target. K-King's wheels touched Mother Earth again at 1543 hrs, eighth down of the Mepal kites. Immediately behind us was F/L Andrew and his crew, home in F-Freddie on three engines. Their starboard outer received a hit over the target. The resultant fire brought them to the very brink of baling out. But they persevered and eventually it was extinguished. So instead of spending their first night on the hoof or incarcerated in Homberg's police station, they would be celebrating over a drink in the local.

All twenty made it home. But Homberg's gunners had their day. The news from dispersal was that no fewer than seventeen Lancs were damaged to some degree. Among them was Bob Rodgers's S-Sugar, holed for the second, consecutive time. K-King was in the lucky minority. But the luckiest was NE181 M-Mike flown by the CO with the Plummer crew. A solitary g.p. had hung up over the target – by no means an unusual occurrence. Normally, hang-ups were released manually when and where possible. Failing that, they could be defused and brought home. But neither option interested the leading spirit of a press-on squadron. With fires raging on the ground, the sky still full of flak and the stream beating it back home, Leslie announced that he was going round again. And he did, to no useful purpose since the bomb refused to budge for a second time. Commanding Officer or not, he acted without due care for his crew that day. Still, they lived to tell the tale.

M-Mike (dubbed The Captain's Fancy) went on to be 75's most famous kite, the only one to complete a hundred operations. She was retired on 17 February 1945 and finally struck off charge on 30 September 1947. The Plummer crew were to meet with a less kind fate.

As for Homberg, the bombing was reported to be concentrated and thus, in the immediate aftermath, presumed successful. But Rhein-Preussen was a sizeable target, quite able to soak up substantial damage. Furthermore, the Germans under the direction of Albert Speer had applied themselves with some genius to the task of keeping such bomb-damaged plants operable. Homberg would remain on the Target Indicator Board at High Wycombe and would be visited again by Bomber Command. For 75, the jinx had yet to be laid.

It was curious that up to this point in the war Bomber Command main forces had left the southern Ruhr town of Solingen in peace. The C-in-C's grand design of devastating the ninety or so main centres of German industrial activity did not include it. Yet Solingen was a German Sheffield and, furthermore, harboured a large aircraft factory where Junkers aircraft were assembled. Finally on 4 November, what had escaped the horrors of area bombing fell to strategic considerations. Number 3 Group was ordered to execute a precision raid.

In the precious few hours since the return from Homberg the ground crews had laboured to patch up and make ready every kite possible. They succeeded with twenty-one. But there was no place on the Battle Order for us. Instead, we stood by the caravan to wave away our friends and colleagues and the kites we all shared. Squadron Leader Bailey in M-Mike led them off at 1130 hrs. Behind him came the Aussie, McCartin, and his crew in K-King; Vic Andrew and his boys, airborne again after their last adventure; Jack Leslie, on the Order for consecutive ops but wisely electing to take up Nelson Bright's crew this time; Don Atkin and his boys, regulars now in R-Roger; Martin Kilpatrick in L-Lucy; and all the rest.

When the last of them had cleared the boundary we cycled off to Ely for lunch in The Lamb. This somehow developed into a mercifully brief, daylight raid on as many pubs as possible. But at four o'clock we were back beside the caravan to count in the homecomers. There were only twenty. Flying Officer J.H. Scott and his crew were missing, probably hit by flak. No one survived.

The raid itself was a failure, the bombing scattered. A return trip was inevitable. It was ordered for the very next morning,

5 November. This time, the Yates crew was listed in the eighteen on the Battle Order. Since Atkin and his crew had spurned the charms of Rio Rita for seven days' leave, we would be flying her.

The primary target was the Junkers factory. Conditions over Solingen were expected to be poor, with rain-bearing cloud obscuring the target. But that was no bar to G-H and we were instructed to formate behind nominated leaders. Our bomb load consisted once again of an 8,000 lb blockbuster and four 500 lb g.p.s. A one-hundred-strong guard would be mounted by Fighter Command.

The lead aircraft was airborne at 1010 hrs. Seven kites had got away at minute intervals when, at 1018 hrs, P/O Dare and his crew lined up in their usual machine, LM544 J. Some mechanical problem intervened and they were left blocking the strip. We were last of the ten behind them and waited, like the rest, in mounting anxiety as the minutes went by. Then the Watch Office gave the order to switch off. The earlybirds continued their climb in the circuit and the ground staff struggled with LM544. Finally, she was pulled to one side. Twenty-six minutes after the last 75 Lancaster had become unstuck F/O McIntosh lifted off M-Mike to recommence proceedings.

That aside, the journey to Solingen proceeded smoothly. We saw no fighters. But as on the previous day there was plenty of opposition from AA batteries. The target was partially obscured and we bombed in formation as ordered. By dint of the flak, though, it wasn't such a quiet and detached experience as our first G-H drop at Leverkusen.

After Mac's routine check for hang-ups I reached down to my left for the bomb door lever. Nothing happened. I tried again . . . still nothing. Again . . . but it was futile.

'Anyone feel a hit?' I asked.

Nobody had. But, obviously, our hydraulics were u/s. That meant four hundred miles of flying with reduced forward speed and impaired manoeuvrability in the event of a fighter attack. Fortunately, the fighters stayed on the ground.

Somewhere many miles to port and unbeknown to us we did pass one aircraft heading south-east, its crew intent on warfare. This was LM544 with P/O Dare at the controls. Three-quarters of an hour after we lifted off from Mepal as the last in the queue, LM544 rumbled down the runway. They must have been all alone over Solingen and bombed the fires left by the rest of us.

Only they knew why they decided to court trouble in this

way. They were an experienced crew with twenty or so ops under their belt. Naïve enthusiasm was not the explanation. Maybe one needed to look no further than the CO's gung-ho example over Homberg. This, after all, was 75 New Zealand Squadron – men who would stop at nothing to get the job done. Six of the seven on board LM544 were New Zealanders. Anyway, like Leslie, P/O Dare and his boys escaped unpunished, landing fifty-three minutes behind us.

Landing was the only vexing aspect of bringing R-Roger home with her bomb doors open. Since the stalling speed would be higher than normal I selected only partial flap and came over the boundary at 115 mph. That lovely little green light flicked on, telling me that the undercarriage was down and locked. R-Roger did not float far. She had been in the air for four hours and twenty minutes, quite enough for one day.

This time the raid was pronounced a success. The PRU pilot reported a good concentration of damage to the target area. Solingen and the Junkers factory had received its last call from a Bomber Command main force.

Guy Fawkes' Night passed, as did all Guy Fawkes' Nights during the war, in total blackout. Heavy rain drummed on the roof of our Nissen hut until dawn. In the morning the skies were clear. Air tests and fighter affiliation were ordered. We were assigned to R-Roger again. At her dispersal pan we talked with the ground crew. They had found no flak damage. The bomb door failure was mechanical.

After lunch the briefing room was taken over by sixteen restless crews. We sat in our seats at the back. For the eighteenth time I watched this ritual in which fear, humour (generally black) and professionalism all played their parts.

We were to take off in the dusk to attack the marshalling yards at Koblenz. Though an important crossing point of road, river and rail, Koblenz had, like Solingen, rarely if ever attracted the attentions of a main bomber force. Now, though, the Germans were pouring troops, tanks and supplies through the town, mostly by rail. Their objective was to halt the advance of Patton's tanks. Ours was to shut the door first.

To accomplish this, 3 Group was employing one hundred and seventy Lancasters carrying a variety of bomb and incendiary types, including 8,000- and 4,000-pounders. Our bombing height would be 18,500 ft, time on target 1930 hrs.

What followed four hours later was a text-book night attack. The

189

run-in was complicated only by one or two fighters engaging in the stream. But their efforts bore little resemblance to the running battles of even the recent past. The skies were dark but clear, and the marshalling yards were easy to identify visually. PFF Mosquitoes laid their flares on Oboe and the main force was called in. The area in and around the yards quickly became a contagion of orange-centred, concussive rings as the blockbusters hit and bright pins of light where the incendiaries landed. The town's AA batteries replied with all possible ferocity but we saw no one in trouble. As we turned away, the tormented ground was throwing up smoke and dust 10,000 ft into the air. It was impossible to believe that the yards remained open for the *Wehrmacht's* business.

This time R-Roger was a model of mechanical perfection and brought us safely away. At 2,000 ft over the English coast I engaged George and went back to stretch my legs and chat with each of the crew. As always, Tubby served up the coffee, sweet and thick as syrup, and handed each of us two biscuits. Spirits were high. We had survived to add one more op to our tally. We were, to quote Henry V, a band of brothers.

Furthermore, we were now due a spot of leave. Back at Mepal after five hours and ten minutes in the air, we debriefed, attacked our bacon and eggs in the mess and went to our beds content. The next day, 7 November, dawned fair. We left the station busy as always with aircraft coming and going on air tests, navigational cross-countrys and fighter affiliation. But of the next op there was as yet no sign.

I journeyed home with one minor doubt on my mind. Operationally, we had started all over again and added six more trips to our tally. In the process we had built up a good head of steam. I wouldn't have minded pushing on, say to number twenty-four. That would have brought us to within one leave of the tour's end. But the general rule was to grant leave at about six-op intervals. Our winning sequence was halted. I was left to wonder whether luck would smile on us so benignly in seven days' time.

The seven days were soon skittling past. There was less to do without old Bob and our walks down to the river. But the daily round of family life carried on determinedly unchanged. Though they were disappointed by our last meeting in the gardens of Littleport, my parents worked hard to conceal their anxieties. We avoided flying-talk. Instead, I lent myself to discussing the (for me, entirely irrelevant) goings-on along the street or in McCorquodale's print works or the church, the hostelries or any of the odd corners that blessed our town with its singular character and its sense of continuity.

Change was not something much prized there. Stony was one of those quiet, essentially rural towns that have a natural conservatism and an inbuilt suspicion of the new. The last great accommodation required of it was with the arrival of coachbuilding in neighbouring Wolverton during the High Victorian age of steam. The impact of war was tiny by comparison. Comforting though this was, it had its drawbacks. For one thing, in my log-book I could write of the Koblenz raid, 'Wizard night', quite unselfconsciously. In flying company I could liberally employ all the usual, slick airfield jargon. But this sort of language used around Stony would have produced a knowing smile if not a quick riposte – and quite right, too. The town measured itself in deep-rooted observances and social custom. Coming home to it was like taking a four-weekly, moral bath, and I was ever sorry when the moment came to leave.

On 14 November the boys and I returned to the station. Their appetite for the fray was undiminished. They wanted to press on. The level of activity during our absence had been fairly low. The squadron flew two more attacks on oil refineries and a mining op in Oslo Fjord. They were all pretty small affairs, totalling twenty-three sorties between them. But one of the oil targets was Rhein-Preussen. This time 3 Group dispatched one hundred and thirty-six aircraft. Mepal contributed twelve, all returning undamaged. The crews reported identifying the sprawling refinery through breaks in the cloud and seeing many explosions around it. Now we just had to hope that the job was done at last.

At this time the German Army was being rolled back remorselessly towards its own border. Under Operation *Queen*, the American 1st and 9th Armies were within a few miles of taking the fight onto German soil. However, intelligence reports showed the enemy massing troops at Heinsberg, due north of Aachen and just inside Germany. A counter-attack was in the making. Allied air support was requested and provided on a massive scale. While the 8th Air Force attacked gunnery positions, Bomber Command sent a large force to Jülich and also to Düren to disrupt enemy communications. Number 3 Group was sent against Heinsberg itself.

At 1530 hrs on 16 November the 9th Army troops dug in a few miles to the west would have watched the first of one hundred and twenty-five Lancasters sail into the flak barrage above the town, bombs spilling into the void. We were operating under the umbrella of a hundred Mustangs and Thunderbolts, so enemy fighters were of minimal concern. But our bombing height of 12,000 ft was ideal for the ground defences who had a real go at us.

My crew and I were flying S-Sugar again, one of twenty-five to take off from Mepal. We came in towards the rear of the stream. Huge, swirling clouds of smoke began to obscure the town well before Mac was ready to drop our 4,000 lb cookie and 9,000 lb of g.p.s. In the sky ahead hundreds of black smears marked the spent efforts of the AA gunners. But I saw not a single aircraft in trouble.

And so it turned out. We were the last to touch down at base. Two aircraft came home ahead of us with some damage, but nothing too serious. Everything had gone smoothly. Even the East Anglian weather afforded us a four-hour, afternoon break in an otherwise foggy day.

Generally, the weather that November was much less accommodating. Attacks were planned against Castrop Rauxel, Soest, Wanne Eickel, Sterkrade and Düren, amongst others. In the preceding hours each crew member girded himself inwardly, if not exactly conquering his nerves at least damming them up for a while. More often than not the crews were on board their kites and well into their checks before a voice on the r/t declared a wash-out. It was incredibly frustrating and anti-climactic, all the more since the crews would have to submit to the whole, wretched process again, perhaps in only a few hours time.

For three days after the Heinsberg trip no operational flying was possible. One day an obdurate fog hung across the country. The next, the airfield was swept by low cloud. A few hardy souls flew air tests and H2S navigation exercises. But for long periods Mepal was effectively closed down. An inactive airfield was a forlorn and depressing sight. Our Lancasters stood waiting, their noses pointed to the sky, Merlins inspected and made ready to go. But we did not venture out to them.

Then, early on the 20th, a Battle Order was posted again in the Officers' Mess. It was a maximum effort. The names of twenty-eight crews were neatly typed, ours against a Lancaster 3, ME321 N-Nan. We ate breakfast and speculated on the fuel load and the cookies, g.p.s or incendiaries already being lugged out of the bomb store. Obviously it was a daylight attack, probably in G-H formation. We peered at the overcast sky and the persistent drizzle and wondered whether this one would end like the others, before it began.

At 1030 hrs in the briefing room the name of Homberg came

rolling back towards us like a bad penny. A predictable chorus followed hard on the CO's words. What was this place? Some kind of indestructible monster? Aircrew sitting in the front seats turned to look about them, open-mouthed. Heads were shaken in disbelief.

The Intelligence Officer took over but struggled to add much to the sum of knowledge about Homberg. Then came the Met. Officer, well respected for his often individual and uncannily accurate forecasts. His gist was dirty weather all the way, ten-tenths cloud perhaps as much as three miles thick. Well, it was indeed another G-H attack so we didn't worry about it.

The section leaders followed. The Signals man, F/L W. Naismith, was quite a character on station, having flown three tours already. He had taken to filling in for one particular crew, captained by F/O H. Rees, and was at the w/t for each of their last three ops. This did not please the CO who expressly banned him from any more. But Leslie was in a weak position here. He himself had flown to Saarbrücken on the night of 5/6 October as Terry Ford's rear gunner, of all things. Leslie's motive was to further 75's serviceability status with a record offer of aircraft. But Homberg was a vital cause for 75, too, and Naismith could argue a powerful case for his participation. If so, he won and his name was typed on the Battle Order.

When all was said we migrated to the mess for our flying meal. The speculation now was more introspective. The jinx again! How will it go with us today? What will they throw at us this time? One or two blithe souls risked a joke to lighten the atmosphere. But the laughter in response was too thin and too febrile to carry much conviction. We lit cigarettes and, as we talked, made a show of them to prove to one another and to ourselves that hands were steady, nerves under control. Waiting was always like this. In the end and even though it would bring us irrevocably closer to the time of fear, we yearned to be in our kites, to be running up the engines and taking heart from their wonderful, throaty roar, to be getting on with things.

Our kite, ME321 N-Nan, was still new. There were just three white-painted bomb symbols below the pilot's window. She'd been to Castrop Rauxel nine days earlier, then Dortmund and Heinsberg, each time with different crews. Each time she returned them unscathed. We had not even air tested her. But now the boys were busy at their stations, Tubby standing beside me as usual.

Don Atkin received his green from the caravan and loosed R-Roger down the mile of shining-wet runway. It was our turn. I swung N-Nan around, too preoccupied with final checks to watch R-Roger unstick herself and rise away. Then we were ready, the Packard Merlin 38s (which delineated N-Nan as a Mk 3) running at a raucous 3,000 rpm, the whole kite shaking and straining at the bit. The green glowed in the dismal afternoon light. I let her go with a wave to the dozen or so onlookers devoted enough to cycle out in the rain and stand up to their ankles in mud. Giant raindrops migrated up the windscreen as our speed passed 80 mph. Beyond the point of no return now, N-Nan was going light and wanting to fly. I was busy with the rudder to stop her swinging and was just about to lift off when some bright spark in the Watch Office switched on the flarepath lights. Heaven knows why he thought the nineteenth aircraft in the order should need his assistance at this critical stage. But we got away despite it and the undercarriage was scarcely raised when we entered dark cloud.

One kite unseen a minute ahead of us, another a minute behind . . . few flying conditions demanded greater concentration or caused greater anxiety than these. A pilot had but the vaguest inkling of his position. I relied wholly on Bill to keep us on track, and he on me to watch my instruments and follow his instructions faithfully. But that was what all our hours of training had been for.

We climbed upwards, at intervals easing into a turn to port. There was no sign that we might top the murk. We were confined in an overcast and private place from which only the bluish emission from the exhaust stubs and the fabulously transparent, white-tipped circles of the props offered any visual relief.

Despite the trying conditions, by the time we set course for the first leg I was beginning to sit up and pay attention to N-Nan. There was something about her, something in the weight and smooth responsiveness of her controls, that I had encountered in no other Lancaster. She imparted a sense of assurance in every manoeuvre. I made up my mind that if she and we came safely through this op, I must talk to Bob Rodgers about her. We had waited long enough for a kite of our own and I would find nothing better than this one.

Over Holland at our bombing height of 20,000 ft we were still immersed in cloud, still flying in fear of collision. Somewhere out there was an attacking force of one hundred and eighty-two Lancasters of 3 Group with the impossible orders to bomb in formation. Soon the Oboe pulses would line up on the narrow channel of sky above Meerbreck and the refinery. But far from running-in in formation we hadn't seen another aircraft since Mepal. We had not felt many slipstreams, either. There was a disquieting possibility that whilst we laboured through the gloom, the rest were luxuriating in a sunlit formation above us.

I told Mac that I was taking us up. I called for climbing power which was 2,650 rpm and +4 boost. N-Nan strained for height. Tubby deserted his Window duty to search the bleak greyness above, likewise Archie in the astrodome and, behind him, Geoff. These were grievously tense moments. A growing shadow seen too late . . . and it would be all over.

Slowly, we nosed upwards through the cloud. But our wingtips remained cloaked and no ray of sunlight penetrated the Perspex above my head. N-Nan struggled on to 25,000 ft, definitely her ceiling. The buffeting increased so someone was out there. But it was still impossible to see who.

I called up Mac, 'Sorry, chum, we're not going to get above this stuff. You'll have to do the drop some other way.'

A brief pause and then he replied, 'Bomb aimer to pilot. Request to bomb by H2S.'

'Agreed,' I said, 'Bill, any problems?'

'No problem', came the reply.

Mac fused his seventeen babies and prepared for Bill's command. He, meanwhile, was deep in concentration over the H2S screen. The run-in was curiously disconcerting in that the smoky residues of flak were quite lost in the cloud. They must have been there – this was Homberg! But their invisibility generated a profound unease rather than the customary, cold fear.

'One minute,' Bill rasped, then, 'Five-four-three-two-one . . . release!'

'Bombs going', Mac replied, and the solid thump of the cookie and the lighter percussions of the 500-pounders confirmed it. With no camera run to concern us Bill was on the intercom almost immediately with our course change. He was superb throughout and in the most demanding circumstances. He just never seemed to make a mistake. As one who knew his limitations and could never follow suit, I could only defer to his mental acuity and powers of concentration.

I turned N-Nan away as we left the target area. The cloud persisted every mile of the long way home. It was a wearying journey. By now, though, I was so enamoured with the aircraft that I spent much of the time anticipating my request to Bob Rodgers and the joys thereafter of calling N-Nan our own.

We broke through the cloud base at 800 ft to find the same grey, cold and wet conditions prevailing. But back home N-Nan gave me a gentle three-pointer. We were dog-tired but in great spirits. They did not last long. The mood at debriefing was grim. This damned place, Homberg, had reached out and mauled the squadron again.

To begin with, only twenty-two of our aircraft were known to have bombed. Pilot Officer Dare brought LM544 J home early with de-icing difficulties. Two others missed Homberg altogether and bombed the last-resort targets of Hamborn and Duisburg. On the return, Don Atkin and crew in R-Roger went one better and missed Mepal. They put her down at the fighter airfield of Tangmere, near Arundel. It was a mystery to us why they were so far off track but no mean feat to land safely on a very short strip.

The terrible news, though, was that three others were logged missing. All three were fine and experienced crews, close to the end of their tours. Ron Gordon and his five English crewmates were on number twenty-eight. They all died, together with a pool w/op who had just married and moved to the village. The w/op whose place he had taken was a New Zealander, F/S Bill Otway. A throat infection had saved his life. Despite pleading with the MO to let him stay, he had been dispatched to Ely Hospital for two days. Now he must come to terms with the severance of six friendships and ask himself a thousand times the unanswerable question, 'Why them and not me?'

Flying Officer P.L. McCartin and crew also failed to return. McCartin had been a pupil of mine in February at South Cerney. He and his w/op were Australian, the rest English. They had arrived on station in mid-August, ten days after us. This trip was their twenty-second. Only the rear gunner extricated himself from the aircraft, and he was captured.

Probably the most experienced crew on the squadron at this time was that of Hubert Rees. The crew included Naismith, the Signals Leader. According to Mepal records this raid was Rees's thirty-fourth trip. Over the target he found himself minus a tailplane and fighting to keep some degree of control. He succeeded and all seven managed to bale out. They would finish the war as prisoners and Rees would be awarded the DFC.

That evening in the mess we knew only that the damned jinx had claimed twenty-one more victims. There was intense speculation about collisions and strikes by falling bombs, and some pained protests over the height of the cloud tops and the impossibility of fulfilling our orders. None of it made any difference now. The day had brought pandemonium and the waste of some fine crews. It seemed hardly credible that a concentrated and effective raid had developed. But if not, the enemy would be stood to their guns in readiness for a further attack. And someone, probably us, would be ordered to oblige them and return.

I had one last thing to do before leaving the mess for bed.

'Yes, Harry?' said Bob Rodgers when I walked over.

'The kite the boys and I flew today, Bob . . . I'd like to fly her regularly. Could you see to it?'

'Which kite was that?'

'ME321 N', I replied, trying not to reveal the total infatuation that I had developed for this machine.

He smiled and nodded his head.

'She's yours', he said.

The following morning she was listed beside our names on a fresh Battle Order. The word from dispersal was that bomb and fuel loads were identical to the previous day's. The jinx target still held us in thrall and I did not doubt that we were going back. A few jokers poured scorn on the idea. There might be some justification, the argument ran, to send us four times like this to a major city. But to *that* nondescript rat hole? Not a chance. To my ears they didn't sound as if they quite believed that themselves. Bill put them to the test. He had a keen, statistical interest in bookmaking – though he didn't believe in taking chances, operational or otherwise, himself. Even at odds of five-to-one against any other target he couldn't find a single taker.

At Briefing, the CO's twelve opening words, 'Gentlemen, your target for today is the Rhein-Preussen refinery at Homberg,' met with a stark silence. By now nobody cared about the strategic importance of the target. Nobody cared about oil or diesel or aviation spirit. Had even one of the briefing officers said what was all too plain to us – that we were locked in a battle to the death with this terrible place and we *had* to finish it for once and for all – it would have been different. But, instead, we heard all the same justifications, the same figures and forecasts. We heard but we did not much care.

The exception, of course, was the CO who was as focused as ever on pressing home the attack. As befitted his pugnacity and leadership, he put himself down on the Battle Order with a scratch crew in M-Mike.

Bob Rodgers and his crew were also among the squadron's twenty-one participants. And it was they who lead off at 1226 hrs, with Nan, myself and the boys immediately behind. As I swung around to line up on the runway I could glance across to the queue of Lancs, ungainly in their progress, and wonder. Bill Osborne behind us in L-Lucy, then Terry Winter, Terry Ford, Martin Kilpatrick and the rest . . . surely they all felt, as I did, that this was the most grindingly hard moment in our time at Mepal. The ruthlessness of the planners came through loud and clear. I could imagine the middle-aged staff officers at Group, grand in their ribbonry and not an op between them, poring over recce photographs of the previous raid and saying, 'Where shall we send them today, chaps? Why not back to their jinx target? Let them have another crack at *Homberg.*'

The green flashed and I let Nan go. At least the weather was better now, the air calm and clear, though this was forecast to deteriorate. A G-H attack had been ordered but, again, flares would be laid if conditions allowed.

We flew the outbound doglegs unharassed beneath our fighter umbrella. Only in the approach to target at our bombing height of 20,000 ft did the nature of the enterprise reassert itself. The familiar shell-bursts began to hang in the sky, multiplying every few seconds. An aircraft about a mile in front of us was hit, and then a second. Both began to trail smoke and flame. Their noses turned slowly, irrevocably downwards and their fate was sealed. A third aircraft, again about a mile ahead, took a direct hit, obviously in the bomb-bay. The prodigious explosion distributed hundreds of burning fragments across the sky. There could be no parachutes but, sickened, I searched for them all the same. The thought came to me that this was 75's jinx target. It was 75's aircraft that suffered such a fate here. What little chance was there that none of these were ours? I began to long for debriefing and confirmation that all our crews were safely home.

At this point I became aware of someone, not Tubby, standing at my shoulder. It was Archie. How long he had been there I do not know. He was curiously still, like a statue, and said and did nothing except stare into the distance towards the carnage. In itself, there was nothing wrong with him coming forward. I might have preferred him to be a few feet further back, on watch from the astrodome. But that was of no importance.

'Archie?' I enquired. He gave me no reply. After a few more seconds he lowered his eyes and returned to his station.

It was a small event but not necessarily an irrelevant one, and not one that a skipper should ignore.

In the distance the industrial haze of the Ruhr obscured the horizon. But the Rhine divided Homberg from that fearful place, and the town, the suburb of Meerbreck and the refinery were easy to identify visually. The latter was taking heavy punishment as we ran in. Amidst the general tumult were some impressive, yellow-white flashes followed by smoke that was too black and thick to issue from mere ground explosions. Mac unloaded his bombs into this chaos, hoping like the rest of us that he would never have to do so here again. I pushed Nan's nose down, the airspeed rose and Homberg slipped behind us.

Nan touched down at Mepal at 1652 hrs. Four minutes later the CO brought M-Mike home last of the twenty-one. 75 had weathered the jinx with all crews intact.

Faces were flushed with excitement and relief in the mess that evening. The refinery was seen to take a beating. Nothing could be certain ahead of the PRU flight but there were real hopes that we would not have to go back again. The drinking was dedicated and the singing full-hearted.

Living so precariously as these young men did, one couldn't begrudge them the occasional or even frequent liquid indulgence. Generally, though, I tried to walk the line between sobriety and hanging on to my trousers. In this, I found the stock-in-trade of every flying instructor – calm authority and a friendly disposition – an absolutely indispensable aid.

However, singing was not to be avoided, even by the tone-deaf like me. Not all renditions were unsuitable for mixed company. The lovely Maori song, *Now Is The Hour,* was almost an anthem of the squadron. But the spirit and unselfconscious pathos of the times is altogether more evident in *The Lancs of Mepal.* Who penned it or whether it was once *The Wimpeys of Feltwell* (or *Stirlings of Mildenhall*) or, indeed, whether it was simply adapted from some other squadron, I cannot say. But I reproduce it here and ask the reader to picture it sung by one hundred young men for whom every word was meaningful.

The Lancs Of Mepal
(sung to the tune of 'Lily of Marlene')

The Lancs of Mepal, they're on their way,
Off to bomb the Jerries, they bomb them every day,
And when they wish to show their might,
They bomb the sods by day and night,
The Lancasters of Mepal, the Lancs of 75.

Off we go from Briefing and leap into our kite,
Open up the throttles and roar into the night,
We've left the flarepath far behind,
It's bloody dark but we don't mind,
The Lancasters of Mepal, the Lancs of 75.

There's the bloody searchlights waving round the sky,
Not much ruddy power and not too bloody high,
I hope they don't start shooting till we're through,
They may get me and they may get you,
The Lancasters of Mepal, the Lancs of 75.

Now we're through the target setting course for home,
Soon we'll see the Sandra's waving o'er the 'drome,
That's if we don't go off the track,
And stop a crafty burst of flak,
The Lancasters of Mepal, the Lancs of 75.

Junkers off to starboard, Focke-Wulf off to port,
Gunner calls to skipper, range is getting short,
Prepare to corkscrew starboard, go,
We know our stuff and we're not slow,
The Lancasters of Mepal, the Lancs of 75.

Now we're in the circuit with a turn to land,
No intruders round us, ain't it bloody grand,
We fooled the Hun once more tonight,
Dropped a load right on the Reich,
The Lancasters of Mepal, the Lancs of 75.

When the war is over and there's no more ops to do,
We'll think of all our pals,
The one's who did not get through,
The pals who were with us through thick and thin,
That we one day the War would win,
The Lancasters of Mepal, the Lancs of 75.

I drew Bill away from the piano and the choruses – bawdy and
otherwise – the pint-balancing and worse, considerably worse, to
talk about Archie's appearance in the cockpit. Did he not think it
curious?

Bill pondered for a moment, then said, 'Well, twenty-first trip on
the 21st November, twenty-one kites, jinx target and all. You know
what a superstitious so-and-so he is.'

I knew, of course, but I hadn't rationalised it in quite these terms. But Bill wasn't finished yet.

'It needn't mean anything. Maybe he just wanted a good look at Homberg and saw some Lancs go down for his trouble. Except . . . have you stopped to work out how many trips he's done?'

He had a point. We did our arithmetic and found that including his original stint, Archie had flown at least thirty-four. He was operating well beyond the usual quota. He had just seen the Rees crew go down on their thirty-fourth with his own section leader on board. Archie would not be Archie without inviting some such consideration within, and drawing all manner of dark conclusions. But that did not detract from the reality of his situation, in fact the twin realities. On the one hand, he had done enough by any measure and couldn't reasonably be expected to go on for a further nine ops. On the other, he would be anguished by letting down his mates. We would have understood, of course. But, most probably, Archie's natural inclination was to keep silent and bottle it up.

For now, I decided to respect Archie's loyalty to us, in effect to do nothing. I did not want to change a winning team. Besides, a w/op (or, come to that, an engineer) was less crucial to a crew's *fighting* capacity, though not its safety, than the bomb aimer, navigator or gunners. Archie could fly on while he wanted to. But I would watch over him as well.

Earlier that day, when we were around half-way home, three crews left Mepal to mine Oslo Fjord. One could not envy them. The flight duration was long, some eight hours in the air. They were vulnerable to flak and fighters. The ice-cold, northern waters offered no prospect of rescue for anyone unlucky enough to ditch.

Two of the kites came home within three minutes of each other. The third, skippered by F/Lt L. Martyn, was never heard from again. Its cosmopolitan crew of two New Zealanders, an Australian, three Britons and a Canadian were popular around the station and only four ops short of their finish.

Sorrow had given 75 only the briefest respite. Nothing much had changed at all.

CHAPTER THIRTEEN

ALL OVER BY CHRISTMAS?

Refineries and coking plants, marshalling yards and entire towns . . . together with the hardy perennial of mining sea areas, the duties placed upon 75 Squadron over the next three weeks satisfied every official analysis and theory about the bomber offensive. Not that we gave much consideration to the respective merits of the Oil Plan favoured by General Spaatz, USAAF Commander in Europe, the Transport Plan of Lord Tedder, Eisenhower's deputy, or our own C-in-C's private obsession with area bombing. Grand strategy was something of which aircrew were sublimely and properly ignorant. We went out to do what we were told must be done for victory, and did so in the hope that each trip would bring the day nearer.

Only a month or two earlier it had seemed possible, even likely, that the German surrender would come by Christmas. But now, with Arnhem lost and the *Wehrmacht* fighting valiantly with its back to the Rhine, a winter stalemate was clearly in prospect . . . though not the winter offensive which Hitler was about to unleash. The Ardennes was the quietest part of the front. All the action was in the north and south where the Allies, under Montgomery and Patton respectively, were still trying to press home their initiative.

Whenever the war in Europe might finally end, I was quite determined that our little part in it *would* be completed by Christmas. We had settled into a trouble-free run. We had seen off the jinx target. We had our own beautiful kite. Everything was set fair for the last nine ops when, after breakfast on 23 November, the tannoy crackled into life. Crews listed on a new Battle Order were to attend Briefing at 1030 hrs.

There were twenty-five crews present in the briefing room. A daylight G-H attack on an oil target was announced: the Nordstern refinery at Gelsenkirchen, a few miles north of Essen. Like all ten refineries in the Ruhr, the Gelsenkirchen plants were long recognised for their strategic importance. From the earliest days of the bomber offensive they were the object of regular (and supposedly) precision attacks. But use of the term 'precision' was highly inadvisable in 1940 as, in time, the Air Staff would be forced to concede.

Number 75 Squadron's Wellingtons did not set course for Gelsenkirchen until the hours of darkness on St Valentine's Day, 1941. It is doubtful whether that raid, like those before it, had more than a marginal effect. These were the days when, with only dead reckoning and moonlight by which to navigate to a map reference deep inside Germany, three-quarters of the crews never found their targets. Those that did dropped small bombs of minimal destructive power. The RAF was still using Amatol, a low-grade explosive developed in the First World War. There was not much of it inside the casings, either. A 250 lb bomb would contain a meagre 60 lb of Amatol (at a time when the Germans were packing in a far superior explosive to the tune of fifty per cent of bomb weight).

All this served to render the night precision offensive utterly futile. Crews were dying for no useful purpose. One month after 75's visit to Gelsenkirchen the Air Ministry agreed. The Battle of the Atlantic was forcing itself to the fore of Whitehall thinking. Oil gave way to naval targets, chiefly U-boat pens. It was just as well. The night attacks on oil had been so inaccurate, the damage so limited, that the Germans never even realised a systematic offensive was underway.

Gelsenkirchen received later visits from 75: once in daylight in June, 1943 when one Stirling of eleven was lost, and once at night in June, 1944 when fifteen Lancs survived the trip. And then it was to be our turn, with G-H to guide us and, for the first time in my experience, skymarkers to back it up.

Skymarking by the Wanganui method was the blind-bombing alternative to the familiar business of grouping TIs at ground level. The latter was done either visually, the cipher for which was Newhaven, or by H2S, cipher Paramatta. Wanganui involved PFF aircraft dropping a sequence of parachute flares above the cloud. These drifted slowly to earth. Bomb aimers in the approaching stream then released as the flares traversed the graticule.

The Wanganui method had its supporters and detractors. By the end of the war it was said to produce very accurate and concentrated bombing. But it was rarely used by us because 3 Group had become so totally committed to G-H. Indeed, G-H lent 3 Group operations a mantle of expertise and specialisation the lack of which had been sorely felt down the years of heavy losses and second-rate equipment (the other groups that regularly employed it were 5 Group and 8 Group, very much the prestige elements of Bomber Command).

In the briefing room, mention of Gelsenkirchen provoked a fine outcry. The spiritual connotation of the name was completely at odds with the profane nature of the enterprise. There was something strange about the word itself, something cold and hostile, something uncompromising that did not rest easily on the Anglo-Saxon ear. And then, of course, there were the inevitable associations with the Ruhr and the long and inglorious past sequence of attempts to flatten the place. Whether for these reasons or some other that I cannot divine, Gelsenkirchen had a moving effect on those of limited digestive prowess. In this it was not alone amongst regular German targets (for some of us, a little too regular). As soon as the curtain swept back on a red-arrowed Dortmund or Bremen or Cologne, one could sense a subtle shift towards the briefing room door, followed at the earliest opportunity by a brisk walk to the latrines behind the ops room. Irritable Bowel Syndrome may have acquired its name in modern times but it was alive and kicking in 1944.

The poor devils need not have worried. Doug Sadgrove lifted his kite off the runway, first up at 1238 hrs. We followed in Nan one minute later, with Don Atkin behind us in R-Roger, these days his usual charge. As good a G-H attack as any of us were ever likely to fly was getting off the ground.

With the Allied armies so close to German soil the riskier aspects of meteorological forecasting were eliminated. The Met. Officer could predict cloud conditions with reasonable certainty. On this day he predicted ten-tenths cloud cover over the target. Hence the use of skymarkers. He was spot on. We came in under our fighter umbrella above solid cloud massing to 8,000 ft. The defenders responded with a predictable barrage of heavy flak but I only saw one Lancaster go down (out of one hundred and sixty-eight, all 3 Group). The waves of vics were well concentrated and the release disciplined. For those who had come adrift the skymarkers formed a neat and precisely-laid circle. All the bombs, whether aimed or released in formation, deluged the markers with virtually no spread or creep-back.

Only a large black stain in the cloud tops provided any clue as to events on the ground. But Bill's Gee fix confirmed that the release point was accurate. Everything suggested an exemplary attack. I pushed Nan's nose down towards the blanket of cloud and rode its fleecy surface all the way back into the Mepal lanes.

All twenty-five aircraft were undamaged and home in time for tea. There were no dissenters in the mess: the Ruhr had lost a little of its power to intimidate (it still retained plenty, of course).

A second blessing was that Archie had operated throughout with not the slightest suggestion of any failing. Bill thought he was completely at ease with himself and saw no problem with him continuing. That was good enough for me.

For three days the squadron flew no operations, though one was scrubbed on the tarmac. The weather at Mepal was wet and misty at times but tolerable for flying. The usual air tests and H2S cross-countrys were flown but, on 26 November, six crews took part in an exercise to practise defence against jet fighters. This was the first time that jets had figured in the thinking of the Group training officers.

On the same day, Bill and I ferried the CO down to Hendon in the station's Airspeed Oxford, thence to Waterbeach. What vital questions of Group activity he discussed on these visits I cannot say. He never shared them with us. But on the return journey he suddenly asked me how old I was. 'Twenty-two, sir', I replied.

'Damn! You make me feel quite old', he replied from the distant perspective of twenty-five, 'By the way, Harry, you're due some congratulations. I called my office from Hendon and they told me your promotion to Flight Lieutenant has been confirmed. Now you can sew on that second ring.'

Promotion from Flying Officer was automatic after a certain period so the news, whilst welcome, was not exactly surprising. Still it was a good excuse for a round of drinks in the pub that evening.

It was not long before 'F/L' appeared in front of my name on the mess notice board. The order of things dictated that after oil would come marshalling yards – and a daylight return to the devastated city of Cologne.

The story in the briefing room was becoming a familiar one. Again, cloud cover was forecast over the target. Again, the attack would be solely by 3 Group Lancasters and it would employ G-H.

This time, though, the success of the raid turned out to be less than certain. Cologne remained a daunting foe. There were still four or five AA guns for every aircraft in the sky. Their fire was both heavy and accurate. I saw smoke and flames from several aircraft ahead. I well knew what those crews were experiencing and feared that they must be lost.

We came over the centre of the city in a stream which was not as compact as it should have been. Somehow, despite this, the drop was well concentrated. The cloud cover gave us no real possibility of checking visually but the explosions all seemed to be in one area, the sign of a good attack. However, Bill's Gee fix indicated an overshoot of a few hundred yards to the north of the yards, by the river.

All of 75's aircraft survived the flak. Flying Officer D. Leadley and crew in HK593 were probably among those I saw in trouble. They overcame it and limped away on two engines to put down on the emergency landing strip at Manston.

Four other crews came home to report the strange story of the G-H aircraft which led their formation. Whilst much of the lead-in to the Cologne yards was poor, the effort by this crew was simply inexplicable. On the long, curving approach to target they eschewed the safety of the stream and wandered blindly away and back again at least once before departing for München-Gladbach. All four of our crews followed dutifully for a time and reported being taken fifteen miles off track. After the drop the others beat it home by the designated route but the G-H leader wandered back towards Gladbach, as though hypnotised by the place. The aircraft was hit by concentrated fire from the AA batteries and spiralled down almost immediately.

In fact, the only aircraft lost that day was a Witchford kite, HK624 skippered by F/O E. Ingram. Its IL lettering may indicate that it had been very recently transferred from 195 Squadron (itself formed from Witchford's C Flight only on 1 October 1944 and re-mustered at Wratting Common a few days before the Cologne op). The mystery of the erratic course, particularly after the drop, will never be resolved. The usual catch-all of 'special equipment failure' does not suffice. But there is a second peculiarity that is no less puzzling. The crew numbered *nine*, including a second pilot and a mid-lower gunner. The latter was highly unusual and hardly a worthwhile precaution on an escorted, daylight raid late in 1944. None of the nine survived what appears to have been an act of needless self-destruction.

Nearly a month after this raid Bomber Command went back to attack a rail target in Cologne. It was part of the effort to counter Hitler's offensive in the Ardennes. Only twenty-seven Lancs participated but, of these, six never returned. Among them was a PFF kite of 582 Squadron captained by Sq/Ldr R.A.M. Palmer. He was awarded a posthumous VC for 'conspicuous bravery whilst acting as Oboe-leader for the attack'.

To we who live, success bought at the cost of self-sacrifice is an unutterably poignant and virtuous thing. We accord it the highest

206

honours. Sometimes we remember it for generations. Ultimately, however, military virtue is a matter of usefulness. Palmer and Ingram stand at opposite ends of the scale. In death, of course, they are equal and none of these things has any meaning. Another and greater question rises with the sun.

After the marshalling yards – a gesture in the direction of the Transport Plan – the pendulum swung again. Harris' personal initiative came to the fore. We were returned to night operations over Germany and the area offensive.

The Battle Order was posted at lunchtime. There were our names alongside Nan, in a list of twenty-one. This would be our sixth successive trip in her, all of them to the Reich, and our twenty-fourth overall.

The CO had placed himself on the Order with a scratch crew, flying K-King. The word from dispersal was that a rare 12,000 lb, three-can bomb had been wheeled out of the dump and was on its way to K-King's pan. Furthermore, it was the *only* three-canner to be dropped that night.

This massive piece of ordnance seemed to hold a fascination for the CO. When the first one was deployed by the squadron three weeks earlier he went along to offer the bomb aimer his advice (I believe he actually dropped the thing). The second he let pass. But this one, the third, proved irresistible. The rest of us would have to make do with paltry one- and two-can specimens.

It was not a policy with which Mac or, I imagine, any of the senior Air Bombers on the Squadron, would have agreed. These chaps were pretty much of one mind on the value of pilots. Whether Commanding Officers or complete rookies, we were all basically aerial lorry drivers. The brains of the operation were always to be found, respectively, working over a map and a bombsight. This was a valid opinion, and the holders of it were entitled to some consideration in the placement of a 12,000 lb bomb.

The other news was the quantity of petrol being pumped into each kite: two thousand gallons. Back to the Valley, said the station wiseacres. And they weren't wrong.

'Gentlemen, your target for tonight', said the CO emphatically, 'is the industrial town of Neuss in the south-west of Düsseldorf.'

It was not difficult to read the underlying message. No mention of anything more specific than industry – this was to be a blitz. That meant, in effect, targeting the working-class population in their homes. Just another job, we would say to ourselves and think no more about it, if possible.

The attacking force would constitute one hundred and ninety-three Lancasters of 3 and 8 Groups. Though modest in number, it was well fitted to the size and significance of the task. Long gone were the days when numbers were everything. Qualitative factors had come into play. The average survival time of crews had lengthened. Consequently, techniques were better honed. Their aircraft, of course, were immeasureably superior to the twin-engined Hampdens, Whitleys and Wimpeys of pre-history. With 12,500 lb of bombs on board each Lanc, the total lift would be not far short of half that of any of the great thousand-bomber raids of 1942. And whereas then the new RDX explosive had finally replaced Amatol, now a preponderance of bombs were HE grade. One can well imagine the cataclysmic consequences for a quite small town such as Neuss.

It was our first night operation for a fortnight, and the latest I ever took off for Germany. Loaded with Benzedrine we lifted off into fine skies at 0252 hrs, second in the order behind Bill Osborne in L-Lucy. That meant arriving over Neuss at the indecently early hour of 0500 when, with any luck, most sensible crews would have concluded that their night's watch had passed uneventfully and a warm bed awaited.

It was also the first full Wanganui attack we had ever flown. The method employed single flares dropped twice *en route* by Oboe to guide the stream into the bombing run. Then green flares were sent down to mark the aiming point. Our Pathfinders managed to deposit two clusters. Mac, and every bomb aimer early in the stream, was left with nothing visible through the ghostly green cloud and no clue as to which markers to bomb. Bill took the fastest Gee fix of his life. One cluster, he thought, might be too far south. That was enough for Mac who duly unleashed his blockbuster and the 1,000 and 500 lb g.p.s on the other one.

By the time we left the target area behind, something of Neuss was already apparent. The cloud began to be suffused by a widening, dull red light in and around which were stabs of intense whiteness as the cookies and blockbusters exploded. Down there the town was ablaze, but little of it was visible to us. Down there was terror, for were we not the *terrorfliegern?*

During all this time there was barely a flakburst in the sky. The defenders were either sleepily unprepared for our arrival or had assumed that all the action tonight was occurring elsewhere in the Ruhr, courtesy of another Group. Of night-fighters there was not a sign. Of course, Geoff and Norrie still searched the night for a sudden, black-on-black smear at the corner of their vision or an unexplained movement by another kite close by. They still shielded their eyes from the brightness of fire and guarded inwardly against the encroachment of tiredness or inattention. But this was a night very different to those of even two months earlier. Then, enemy skies were a giant spider's web, and bombers black insects that teetered over it. At the first tremor, not one but dozens of spiders were tensed to lunge from the darkness with nightmarish speed, spitting venom of fire into their helpless prey. We knew when we were lucky.

The luck did not quite extend to the CO, his scratch crew and their three-canner. They did not reach   Neuss . They were all right . . . no harm befell them. But either the navigator miscalculated or Leslie refused to heed his course changes, for they found themselves locked into an Essen-bound stream of Lancs and Hallies. The air in the cockpit must have turned blue when the mistake was discovered. Leslie decided that it was too risky to cross streams and reintegrate with his 3 Group colleagues. Instead, the three-canner was piled on top of the Krupp family's misfortunes and K-King turned for home with the skipper furiously pondering his excuse to the debriefing officer. He touched down at 0738 hrs, behind everybody. But he hadn't thought of a way to curtail our mirth once the news got out.   Neuss

Finally, in writing of this mirthless business of area bombing one has to acknowledge the moral dimension. After the war the full effects of Allied bombing were visible to all. The general devastation and the lowness to which a defeated people had been brought stung the emotions and beggared the intellect. Nothing softens the hatred for one's enemy more than the sight of his humanity.

It was not like that in wartime, of course. Thirty thousand British civilians had died under the *Lufwaffe*'s bombs before our area offensive even began. Popular sentiment was right behind us, as all aircrew knew. Save for a few difficult priests and politicians, nobody mentioned the moral conduct of the war.

Particularly in the early years of the offensive, nothing mattered, not crusading clerics, not moral certainties, nothing besides winning the war. Defeat to the despotic power that was Nazi Germany would have meant, at best, vile repression. More probably, it would have meant national dissolution and slavery. This we knew. We did not yet know that, for some, defeat would have meant the vast, genocidal machine, the concentration camps, the poison gas, the mass graves . . . very possibly on British soil. But even without this most terrible knowledge the case for doing everything in our power seemed irrefutable.

Naturally, had the public been asked if they wished their sons to murder and maim women and children, the answer would have been very clear. But they were not asked. Opinion was united on the supreme need for victory. Aircrew went out to pulverise the beast by any means they were told would advance it.

That said, these two words, 'area bombing', do not sit well with a quiet conscience even today. Originally, the area policy was postulated on the grounds of fatally wounding Germany's war-will and spreading public dissatisfaction with her government. 'Morale bombing' was its other, regularly-used title. But death by blast, death by incineration, death by suffocation are the real meanings of the term.

I suppose every man must seek his own accommodation with his conscience. Neuss was the third and final town blitz in which we participated. I am grateful that there were so few. But it must be said that if every Briefing had required us, in the official euphemism of the time, to de-house the civilian population, it would have made no difference. We would have gone out and done our duty just the same.

As it was, our duty on the last day of November was reconnected with oil. Shortly after breakfast we took our seats in the briefing room. The attack was to be on a coking plant at Osterfeld, not far from Essen. Only sixty aircraft, all 3 Group, were scheduled for the trip. Number 75 Squadron was to send eighteen of these. At about the same time sixty more Lancasters from other 3 Group squadrons would attack the nearby plant at Bottrop.

Since Nan had gone to Maintenance for service we were allocated a veteran Lancaster 1, ME751 M-Mother. She had entered service with 115 Squadron back in April 1944 and had a lot of flying hours behind her. But she also had four Merlin 24 engines that each produced two hundred and thirty more horsepower than Nan's American 38s. Both the S-Sugars I had flown were fitted with the same engines. I knew that we could expect to get off the deck and climb a lot quicker, and there was no danger of being short of airspeed while in formation, as could and did occur from time to time.

Trouble there would be amidst the vics over Osterfeld, but nothing as trifling as lack of speed.

We lifted off at 1050 hrs for a rendezvous over Woodbridge forty minutes later. Cloud conditions were unremitting for the entire journey out, as forecast. We crossed into enemy skies above ten-tenths cloud with the tops at 10,000 ft. Under all this somewhere ahead of us was the vast industrial complex that we must now destroy. We came in well compacted, probably too well, and passed very close to a great, black island of smoke spread out over the cloud tops. That was Bottrop on fire. The batteries began to spit up their 88 mm shells. The sky became dirty. We rocked and bored through it with just Mac uncaring and at his window, watching for the G-H leader to open bomb doors.

'Two minutes to target', announced Bill, although his function was purely advisory at this stage.

The flak showed no sign of slackening.

'Open bomb doors, skip', Mac said, seeing our leader do so.

'Bomb doors open.' I replied, pulling the lever down to my left. And now we would wait again.

Suddenly, ahead of us in the stream, a vic of three kites was consumed in a prodigious burst of flame which immediately erupted outwards under the force of a secondary explosion. The leader had been hit in the bomb-bay, the others were too close. No one could have survived, I knew. There was no point in looking for parachutes. I flew on straight and level, Tubby standing beside me, both of us dumbstruck by the appallingly unfair swiftness and violence of it all. But there was still that deeply-drawn breath of relief that somebody else, and not oneself, had run out of luck. And hard on the heels of *that* was a pang of guilt. One grieved for whoever was in the kites and wondered if friends might not be coming home. If so, there was nothing to be done for them now. We stared more fixedly than ever at our own leader's bomb-bay. His bombs fell away and Mac was quick on the button.

Both Mac and Norrie – who had a particularly good view of the release point – thought the bombing was concentrated. The attack was probably successful, though it was impossible to tell with any certainty. Some black smoke curled into the cloud but there was nothing else to indicate the effect on the coking plant.

I flew M-Mother home with my thoughts still of the poor devils in that doomed vic. After we landed at Mepal and debriefed, I wrote in my logbook, 'Heavy enemy opposition. 3 Lancs seen going down. Bombing concentrated.' It turned out that only the first of these statements was true.

The vic I saw go up in flames claimed the lives of two, not three, crews. They were F/O J. McIntosh and crew in NF980 F-Freddie and seven boys in a 115 Squadron kite, PD367. Mepal and

Witchford, whose fates were so often intertwined, had shared their suffering yet again. The third kite in the vic was one of ours, skippered by F/O J. McDonald. It was heavily damaged and incredibly fortunate to be just far enough away to escape the worst of the blast. The fact that I had 'seen' it go down demonstrates just *how* lucky McDonald and crew had been. They landed back at Mepal without injury at 1459 hrs.

Everyone else came through safely, though Bill Osborne was bedevilled by some gremlins in L-Lucy. The starboard outer went u/s shortly after take off. Returning to base would have been wise. But in such circumstances few crews did (I'm sure because they worried more about their peers' opinion of them than they did about their own survival). Bill cut some corners and, though without fighter cover and unable to climb above 14,000 ft, bombed successfully ten minutes behind us.

November closed at Mepal with a tally of two hundred and eighty-six sorties for the loss of six aircraft. It might have been worse, given the high prevalence of Ruhr targets. Probably, the loss rate of a little over two per cent was quite general at this point in the war. The day before the Osterfeld raid, Bomber Command had dispatched two hundred and ninety-four Lancasters to the regular target of Dortmund, on the eastern edge of the Ruhr. The defenders clawed six of them out of the sky. This, again, was a loss rate of just over two per cent – half what it used to be, but quite enough for us. So it was without much enthusiasm that, on the morning of 2 December in a chill briefing room, we heard the CO pronounce the name of this much-feared city.

No doubt the people of Dortmund would have been even more perturbed at the prospect of our arrival. By the war's end, their city had absorbed over eighteen thousand tons of RAF main force bombing. More than half the built-up area was a wasteland for 'the women of the rubble' to load stone-by-stone into handcarts and push away.

But today we would not lay waste to houses and factories generally. The target was a major oil coking plant on the northern outskirts. It would be another step in 3 Group's transformation from a force attacking area targets at night to one blind-bombing strategic targets in daylight. Mepal would contribute seventeen of the ninety-three aircraft, and we would be back on board our Nan.

Successful G-H bombing required a good lead into target, a tight stream and a concentrated drop. Naturally, this unholy trinity presupposed that the Oboe stations were transmitting accurately, but that was out of our control. Over Dortmund it appeared that the pulses were up to a mile out of alignment. On top of that, the stream was perhaps half-a-mile wide and more extenuated than usual. We dropped amidst only a moderate and unexpectedly erratic flak bombardment, and saw no one in trouble. We also saw nothing of our results on the ground other than a few thin spirals of smoke. An overshoot was the obvious conclusion.

Most times, aircrew felt peculiarly detached from the mayhem they had created so many thousands of feet below. But some connection, if only the sight of smoke and dust from the impact, was necessary to the preservation of a warlike spirit. Repeatedly bombing on navigational aids above ten-tenths cloud with tops at 12,000 ft did not do for crew morale what our inspirational visit to St Trond had done, or even the 'wizard prangs' to Montvilliers and Koblenz. True, all this heavy cloud had the advantage of shielding us visually from the AA gunners. But their radar still functioned well enough. No, there was something about the G-H method that was dangerously akin to being just a job. The thought stuck in my mind. I began to wonder if it could blunt our appetite or make us stale, because that might prove costly.

On the fine, cold morning of 4 December the CO briefed twenty crews to attack an oil target at Oberhausen, north-east of Duisburg. The Paper Doll was being loaded with a 12,000-pounder but this time Leslie wasn't able to drop it. While his boys were climbing to their bombing height over the North Sea, Bill and I flew him down to Hendon in the Squadron Oxford. In his meeting, Leslie was informed that his tour of command at 75 was at an end. It was a bitter pill made sweeter by the award of a DSO. As soon as he came on board the Oxford for the flight back he started to talk about it.

'That must be the one that stands for Daylight Sorties Only', I said.

'You must be kidding, Harry', he replied. And it was true. He had assumed command in May, led the Squadron through the drama of D-Day and flown on practically all the most daunting ops since. The DSO tended to be given out to retiring squadron COs almost as a matter of course. But nothing could devalue the award to Leslie. He had earnt it. Bill and I shook his hand and wished him well.

We landed at Mepal not long before the Oberhausen crews began arriving in the circuit. All twenty came home, though the trip had been markedly unpleasant and the results inconclusive.

A little later I was cornered by Archie, 'Skipper, I've got to talk to you. Is it all right now?' Naturally, I concurred.

'I'd like to make the next trip my last', he said, not to my great surprise, 'You know I've done a fair few ops and there doesn't seem much point in flogging on for ever.'

Well, that was certainly true. I told him I understood and asked whether he would like me to talk to Bob Rodgers.

'That'd be fine, skipper,' he said, already looking happier for it, 'Can I tell the boys?'

They were as relieved as was Archie that a decision had been made. His predicament had been crew gossip for the last fortnight. Now we could look forward to a really good send-off for him once the next target had been safely plastered.

The next target represented a departure from oil and a return to transport. And a well-defended place it was, to the north of Dortmund and the Ruhr Valley. During the misnamed and misguided precision offensive of the early years, it was the principal rail target, and it gave rise to the hoariest entry in the RAF's joke book. When the squadron COs of 1941 surveyed a roomful of eager, young faces and proclaimed, 'Your target for tonight is the marshalling yards at Hamm', the cry would unfailingly come back, 'Not Hamm again!' The chance to send up operational duty *and* rationing was too good to let pass.

This little piece of theatre never played at Feltwell, where 75 was then stationed. For some reason Hamm did not appear on the menu until our time.

At 0600 hrs on the fine but very dark morning of 5 December, my batman shook me with his customary, unreasonable determination. No special pleading ever called off the dogs . . . no suggestion that he should resign and let the WAAFs have a try . . . no advice to transfer to *Stalag Luft 3* where he could persecute as many RAF officers as he wished. He was a nice chap and a damned nuisance.

Resigned to consciousness and an early trip to Germany, I left my bed for the hostile cold of winter. The winter of 1944–45 was gathering its icy forces. I felt sorry for the armourers and ground crews who were already starting work out there, though I suppose they felt sorrier for us.

In the mess the Battle Order was posted: twenty one crews with ourselves flying Nan. A quick flying breakfast and off we went to hear Jack Leslie conduct his penultimate Briefing. Twenty-one of Mepal's Lancasters, out of a 3 Group force of ninety-four, would bomb on G-H with sky markers as backup. An escort of Spitfires would keep us safe from the *Luftwaffe*. Solid cloud was anticipated all the way, with tops at 14,000 ft. But we were bombing from 20,000 ft. Take-off time was 0900 hrs, time on target 1130 hrs. If it all went to plan, we would bring Archie back to Mepal and an op-free life at about 1400 hrs.

Archie's progress to dispersal was an eye-opener for me. I had no idea that he was so well known and liked. Several aircrew wrung his hand in the locker room and again in the crew truck. Then the ground crew repeated the exercise. I, for one, found myself thinking forward to our own last ride out to dispersal in three ops' time. But Lady Luck had a way of disappointing those who dwelt on such things and I put it out of my mind quickly.

We took off at number four in the order and, I am pleased to say, gave Archie a restful last trip. Hamm, which had a long-established reputation for fierce resistance, put up only a perfunctory display of flak. I could never fathom why a target fought like hell one day and, the next, failed to register our existence until too late. But that was the way things were and one just had to be grateful for days like this one.

The bombing was probably scattered – some of the leading was, frankly, poor. Bill took a Gee fix on our drop and pronounced it accurate. But we were at the head of the stream. Flying Officer Harry Tweed, in PB418 C-Charlie, came in at the back and saw the ground through a gap in the clouds. He reported bombs falling not on the marshalling yards but a harmless wood some four to five miles further on. As ever, there was no single interpretation of events under the bombing.

The only difficulty over Hamm experienced by a 75 crew was again Bill Osborne's in L-Lucy. Just as before, he lost an engine and could not formate with his designated leader, a Waterbeach kite. He bombed the skymarkers and made it safely home.

So Archie Bain finished his tour and left our number. He got himself rolling drunk in the Sergeants' Mess that night, and why not? There was no precious ribbon for Archie to sew on but, by God, he deserved it.

It was impossible not to like and admire Archie. He was good company and, by common consent, the most popular member of the crew. His character was highly individual but it was also a wel-ter of contradictions. Wickedly funny and outgoing when the mood took him, he was also often secretive, sometimes intensely so. He had a generous heart and would do anything to help his crewmates. Yet he would accept no such help himself. Furthermore, he had a maddeningly self-destructive streak. Perhaps, like many brave men in operational life, he had concluded that he wasn't going to survive the war. Fate already owned him. When he did not die on board our P-Peter he was genuinely surprised and, for a while, he plainly felt a sense of release. But now I think he was never fully free. Little by little his particular fears, whatever they were, crept up on him again. He began to look out for the Reaper not as before but in some new and unexpected guise. I am grateful that we confounded that and delivered him safely to the end of his long and arduous tour.

The fact is that I did not really know him. None of us did, which is a pity because there was more to Archie Bain, both good and bad, than to most men I have met.

The last time I saw him was twenty-four years later, at a reunion of the squadron in Mepal. At one o'clock in the morning, as my wife and I drove back to our hotel in Ely, we came upon him. He was walking in the deserted street and, although a diabetic by that time like me, was obviously the worse for drink. I don't know where he thought he was going or if he cared. I pressed him to come with us to the hotel but he wouldn't have it. He looked at me with his shining eyes and that impish expression, smiled and went on his way. Archie always had his own way to travel and it was not profitable to engage him in any discussion to the contrary.

His place in the crew was taken by F/S Bill Otway, the New Zealander who was grounded by the MO immediately before his crew were lost over Homberg on 20 November. Bill had flown twenty-five trips with them. He had been out of action since. But I knew his old crew were well regarded on station. There was no doubt in my mind that he was the man we wanted. The only drawback was that we would have two Bills on board. That would mean dropping the unprofessional familiarities we habitually employed over the intercom. From now on it would be 'Skipper to Navigator . . .' and, 'Navigator to Bomb Aimer . . .'.

For the next few days Bob Rodgers quietly dropped us from the Battle Orders. Bill Otway had not flown operationally for almost three weeks. But now the opportunity would arise for an air test or two or, maybe, a cross-country so the new man could acquaint himself with the rest of us, and vice-versa.

The first Battle Order from which we were stood down was an attack on the Meuseberg-Leuna oil refinery, a formidable target deep in the east of the Reich. It was the night of 6 December. The raid was a big one and was met by intense, heavy flak. Several aircraft went down including, eventually, my old friend HK574, the indomitable R-Roger.

I have seen the story in print elsewhere. But I believe the boys and I were in an unparalleled position to determine all relevant details. For we were dispatched the next day to bring home the crew and conducted the first full and frank debriefing.

R-Roger's tribulations began after she, Don Atkin and his by now experienced crew had bombed the refinery successfully. The flak got them on their way out of the target area and at 2133 hrs the starboard outer engine burst into flames. The Graviner did its job but sparks continued to glow, to the consternation of all on board. Worse was to come. The starboard inner went u/s and had to be feathered. R-Roger began to lose height – only slowly but at one hundred feet per minute from an altitude of 14,000 ft, making landfall was by no means certain. Then an electrical short-circuit knocked out the Gee set and Atkin and his boys were pitched into a terrifying guessing game. In desperation, they began to throw out everything possible to lighten the load. It wasn't enough. Still over water, they had to concede that there was nowhere to go but down into the cold maw of the North Sea.

The Lancaster was by no means renowned for its ditching characteristics. While Atkin strove to keep the kite straight, trimmed and nose-up, the rest must have thought that this was definitely journey's end. It came soon enough but in the form of a noisy and magnificent ditching. The kite was in one piece and riding high. Atkin had pulled it off.

All seven reported uninjured and scrambled out onto the starboard wing. A thick fog cloaked the night. The sea was eerily calm, indeed, almost devoid of swell. They inflated the little, circular dinghy and evacuated in good order. But, seeing that R-Roger refused to sink like any sensible aircraft, they did not cut the painter (the rope that attached dinghy to aircraft). Without a Gee fix, their w/op, F/S Curtis, had not been able to send a position with his SOS. The painter was their umbilical cord connecting them to a good chance of being spotted by Air-Sea Rescue once the sun came up and the mist cleared.

Hunched against the damp, December air, they waited for the dawn while the dinghy rocked gently to and fro. There were rations for all on board and a small radio that could broadcast on an ASR frequency. The w/op got busy with that while the others discussed who would fire the Very flares and how close a passing aircraft should be when the opportunity arose to do so.

They wondered at their miraculously aquatic Lancaster still drifting alongside. They knew that, eventually, the sea must claim her. But they tried to shut out thoughts of the awful death should it yet claim them, too.

Five hours later the first light of day suffused the mist to the east. Then, from across the water a plaintiff voice cried – not, it must be said, a human voice.

'A bloody cow!' someone in the dinghy cried. Nobody else heard it and the poor chap was silenced by derisory remarks about his mental stability. Then the bovine call floated towards them again.

All eyes strained in the direction of the sound, for that was salvation. That was England. They began paddling and a few feet later England reclaimed them from the sea.

Not waiting for dawn they set off in motley fashion across the wide foreshore. They negotiated some rather tricky barbed wire, then a few hundred yards of cowpats. A second fence loomed out of the mist and on the other side, a road. As they were walking, a USAAF truck rumbled into view. A few minutes later they tumbled off the tailgate to report to the duty officer at USAAF Martishall Heath.

Their tale impressed him but not for the obvious reasons.

'Don't you know', he asked incredulously, 'that you walked through a goddammed *minefield* back there?'

And so it was that the nation's defences, which Hitler's crack commandoes never dared to test, were penetrated in complete ignorance but with impunity by one of 75's intrepid crews. Technically, R-Roger had reached landfall. But her crew had flown her up the course of the benign River Orwell, ditching in the shallows by the bank.

At Mepal that morning, the incident was viewed initially as crew error – a 'black'. Atkin and his boys had already earned a reputation for a certain, wayward brilliance.

Jack Leslie called me into his office and said, perhaps somewhat uncharitably, 'Harry, fly down there and bring these idiots back.'

Nan was fuelled up and the boys and I made the twenty-minute hop to Martishall Heath. I parked her close to the Control Tower where our heroes were waiting. We found them each clutching a bottle of Southern Comfort and well on the way to hazy contentment.

The Yanks found the whole affair entertaining. It confirmed all their preconceptions about the eccentricity of Englishmen (obviously, New Zealanders were Englishmen). English engineering, however, was another matter. The Lancaster's reputation had

218

preceded us, and a steady stream of ground and aircrew came over for a close study of Nan.

The general drift was complimentary but jingoistic, 'Yeah ... but it ain't got nuttin' on the Fortress.'

Tubby tried to court favour by pointing out that her Merlins were 38s made by Packard in America, and they punched out 110 hp more than the usual Rolls-Royce 22s. However, Americans tend to be wise to the patronising line. 'Jeez,' came the reply in a mock-horrified tone, 'you guys shouldn't oughta take that. You gotta get yourselves some Cyclones.'

Back at Mepal, Don Atkin's feat in ditching R-Roger safely on two port engines began to overide the comic aspects of the event. Conditions on board prior to the ditching came to be better understood. Within forty-eight hours a rumour was circulating that Atkin had received a letter personally signed by the C-in-C, commending him on his airmanship and confirming an immediate DFC. On its heels followed another rumour to the effect that this was a hoax. To this day I don't know which was true. But I can find no record of the award.

As for R-Roger, even in her death throes she had treated her crew with kindness. She sank into the Orwell silt only with the greatest reluctance. There was time for a salvage team to take off some of the equipment not previously disposed of by her crew. But there was no attempt to salvage her complete. She was left to her watery fate. Her colourful career had reached its end, as all good things must.

Another good thing came to an end a day or so later. Jack Leslie left the station, his command over.

He had transferred from the RNZAF to the RAF on 10 April 1940. From the beginning, he appears to have been a dynamic character. Danger followed unerringly. During his first tour of duty he was twice mentioned in dispatches yet was decorated with the Air Force Cross, a non-operational recognition. But this was the man who, at Mepal, announced his arrival by diving on the airfield on two engines. He dropped the squadron's first 12,000 lb bomb personally and the third one he put on Essen in error. He squeezed himself into a rear turret to fly the Saarbrücken raid, 75's record offer, as a gunner. On the squadron's dreaded return to Homberg he went around again simply to shift one recalcitrant 1,000-pounder. His press-on spirit was renowned, sometimes feared. But he infused every Briefing with it and never left anyone in doubt about his opinions of the enemy and of the job we were there to do. He was, in short, utterly courageous and irrepressible, a chancer and just plain wrong at times, undoubtedly, but a true leader for all that. He left with his DSO and a reputation that would be hard indeed to follow.

The job fell to W/Cdr R.J. Newton, DFC, who arrived early on 11 December, just in time to see sixteen kites sweep down the runway and lift off for Osterfeld.

The attack of twelve days earlier had, apparently, resulted in little lasting damage to the coking plant. No doubt, what torn and buckled pipework could be cut out and replaced, what walls and roofs could be rebuilt, what stores and silos could be repaired and replenished, were all attended to. Oil was Germany's jugular vein. The salvage crews laboured with heroic energy and ingenuity to build up what Allied bombers had just knocked down.

Nan needed some repair work of her own. The radar mechs were dissatisfied with her H2S, and she was not passed fit for operations. For the trip to Osterfeld we were allocated another Lancaster B3, PB761 Y-Yorker.

It was one of a number of unfamiliarities with which we found ourselves. One was most welcome. Bill Otway, our new w/op, was flying with us for this, his twenty-sixth and our twenty-eighth trip. However, we would be without our esteemed flight engineer. Lately, Tubby had been experiencing a mild recurrence of his air sickness. It was really no more than a nuisance and there was not much that could be done about it. But it played on his mind so I told him to see the MO. To my surprise, he was grounded for forty-eight hours. In his place the engineering section leader, F/L S. Cowan, came on board. Notwithstanding his seniority and obvious expertise, I would not have wished it that way. Tubby and I understood one another and worked well as a team. I did not relish testing the Ruhr defences alongside a stranger, even if he was the top engineer on the station.

As luck would have it, we also had a second dickey with us. Flying Officer T.D. Blewitt was a tall but slight, quiet-mannered New Zealander. He had waited five days for this. Now, at last, he was getting started. But there was little sign of the pounding heart and sweating palms that I was sure Messrs Aitken & Co. would have devined in me back on 8 August. My strongest impression of Tim, for that was his name, was how self-assured he was. I could only wish him thirty trips that did nothing to alter that, the least remarkable of them Osterfeld today.

A second dickey was assigned no real duties, other than to absorb everything he saw. Tim would occupy the tip-up seat for most of the flight, complicating F/L Cowan's engagement with me accordingly.

So it was that I lifted off Y-Yorker from the main runway and headed for the Ruhr with seven crew of whom only four were operationally acquainted. A skipper had to ensure that a change of personnel did not lead to weakened crew procedure. If it did, and the enemy intervened at the vital moment, there might be no reprieve. But over Osterfeld, intervention by the enemy was minimal. No *Luftwaffe* fighters came up to challenge our escort. And for some extraordinary reason, the guns that brought destruction on 30 November did not even achieve half the rate of fire.

As usual with these daylight G-H ops over ten-tenths cloud, the lead-in was anything but uniform. Three of the Mepal crews reported an undershoot by between one and seven miles. One crew reckoned they were led twenty miles off track. Another bombed Essen. Bill thought his Gee fix showed the release point to be accurate. But it was all a puzzle, really. Unless one demanded a transfer to PRU, it was likely to stay that way.

There were no losses among the one hundred and fifty Lancasters that flew to the Ruhr that day. Tim Blewitt had his easy introduction. Tubby was mighty relieved to see us back. He had been feeling sheepish about his grounding and, ever since, had agonised over the possibility that today of all days Lady Luck would desert us.

I thanked F/L Cowan over a pint in the mess.

'Try and get me a seat if we have to do it all again tomorrow', he said.

The next day, though, he and we stayed behind while sixteen crews took off to attack the Ruhrstahl works at Witten. The *Luftwaffe* had obviously been applying some serious thought to these blind-bombing raids. Over Witten they struck at the first wave of vics, downing six kites. Then they raced for the cloud cover and safety as the Spits came in. Two other Lancasters collided right before the eyes of F/O Alex Simpson, a 75 pilot and friend of mine. In the resultant explosion one of the Merlins was detached. Still fully-cowled and with the prop milling, it came straight for Simpson's cockpit. He plunged his kite downward and, somehow, the thing passed clean over.

The eight losses from one hundred and forty aircraft on the raid could have been higher. Another 75 pilot, F/L L. Hannon, collided M-Mike with an unknown Lanc but both stayed airborne. At debriefing the verdict was that this had been a scattered raid. Tim Blewitt's crew, on their first trip together, found nothing to report.

One other crew, captained by F/S V. Zinzan, did likewise. Sometimes, though, nothing could mean a lot. Zinzan had the dubious honour of flying L-Lucy. He brought her home very late and rather heavily, crashing her on the tarmac and breaking his bomb aimer's left leg.

All in all it was a good trip to miss.

Up to this time I was quite confident that we would finish our tour by Christmas, indeed comfortably so. We had but two trips to do and twelve days in which to do them. But during the morning of 13 December the winter turned against us. Visibility deteriorated from two thousand yards to less than eighty. The fog that would hamstring air operations across East Anglia for two weeks or more had arrived.

The next day, a mining op to the Kattegat was cancelled and, the next, a raid on Hanover. Four aircraft did finally manage to get away for the Kattegat but, on their return, they could land no closer to home than Lossiemouth. On the 15th, a Siegen op was recalled after take off because fighters based across the Channel couldn't get airborne, either.

The Siegen op did go, though without us. To my intense displeasure, an experienced crew who shall be nameless took up Nan and collided with another kite. The only damage was to her starboard rudder. But I wondered whether 16 December might be the day on which her luck began to change. That date, though, is remembered for an altogether more dangerous development.

It was three months earlier, deep in the pine swamps of Gorlitz in eastern Germany, that the events which would shape this day were set in motion. The story goes that at Hitler's *Wolfschanze*, the Wolf's Lair, the Chancellor himself and his coterie of senior generals were in conference. Jodl provided a sober analysis of the situation in the West. The clear conclusion was that a forthright defence of the Westwall, the Reich's western fortifications, was now the only prospect.

As Jodl commenced his remarks about the position in the Ardennes, the Chancellor cut him short. There was a long silence while Hitler cogitated over the map. Then, with a firmness and clarity those in the room had not heard for many months, he said, 'I have reached a momentous decision.'

They waited while he looked at each of them in turn.

'I will go on the offensive', he announced, '*here* . . . out of the Ardennes', and he slapped his hand down upon the map. 'And the objective, Antwerp.'

Thus history is made.

The generals were sent away to consider how it might be done. With the greatest secrecy, commanders were appointed under the ageing but respected and loyal von Runstedt. Crack units of the *Waffen SS* were quietly withdrawn from the front. A conscript army, the *Panzergrenadiers*, was raised and imbued with fervour for their great and sacred task. Thousands of tanks, self-propelled guns and artillery pieces were secreted in dense forest, ready for the day. Fuel and ammunition was drained away from other, already stretched demands. Plans were laid for a thousand *Luftwaffe* fighters to launch massive strikes at 2nd TAF airfields.

Finally, by the second week of December, the impossible had been done – for that is how the Allies would see it. On the 16th, high on the snow-covered Schnee Eifel, the first American forward post came under attack. The Ardennes Offensive that would dominate Allied strategy for the next month, including the tactical employment of heavy bombers, was launched.

At first the scale of what was taking place in the Ardennes was not clear to Allied commanders. The interpretation that held sway was that this was a local, diversionary raid to drag forces out of Patton's attack on the Roer River Dams in the south. For Bomber Command it was business as usual. Large raids were mounted on the 17th and 18th on Ulm, Munich and Gdynia. Number 3 Group was not employed, though ironically the East Anglian weather was fine on both days.

It was the 19th before a small attack was ordered against the railway yards at Trier. By this time the fog was back at Mepal. But seventeen crews, including us, were briefed to fly.

Trier was founded by the Romans as an outpost to ward off the bellicose and untamable Germanic tribes. A couple of millennia later, ownership of the town had changed hands but its purpose was still hostile. In preparation for the 1914–18 war the Germans had built rail lines from marshalling yards at Cologne and Koblenz, and spur lines to Bitburg and elsewhere. Trier was the key, therefore. If supply trains could not reach the spurs, the spurs could not feed road centres like Prum and Germund, both only a few miles from the Ardennes frontier.

Together with a second dickey, we rode out to Nan and waited at her freezing cold dispersal while the CO debated with the Met. Officer and with Group. It wasn't long before the inevitable message from Control. The pattern was set.

The *Wehrmacht*, meanwhile, found its progress slowed by

unaccountably stubborn American resistance and many a blown bridge. Americans were meant to have no stomach for the fight, to be racially divided and inferior. The shocking massacre of prisoners at the Baugnez junction, and elsewhere, occurred. Some German commanders had encouraged their men to this end, telling them to remember their bombed-out homes and their dead.

Both the *Luftwaffe* and the 2nd TAF were experiencing the same problem as us. The Ardennes that December was a cold and harsh wilderness. Mist hung in the air all day or low cloud swirled about the hills. It was no place to fly fighters.

On the 20th, we awoke to a thick fog across the airfield yet again. Visibility was down to forty yards. But still we trooped into the briefing room to hear Ray Newton tell us we were to attack Trier. It did not happen, and later that day the boys and I knew that for us, at least, it was unlikely to do so.

Bob Rodgers called me into his office to say we had been given seven days' leave. I refused pointblank. Here we were on number twenty-eight – why prolong it so close to the end?

'Face it, Harry', he said, 'you won't have time to get your last two done *and* get home by Christmas. It only gives you three days and it's a sure bet every one of them will be foggy. Enjoy your leave and come back in a week. We'll still be here.'

I broke the news to the others. The three English lads were disappointed, but not that disappointed. Christmas at home was a lot better than Christmas on the squadron. For the NZ boys, of course, home was a long way away and feelings were different.

The next morning, the 21st, it looked as though Bob Rodgers was right about the fog. Visibility was fifty yards. We left the station early. But the fog lifted and at 1214 hrs Bob himself led twenty aircraft away for the attack on Trier. It was fairly unremarkable apart from an electrical failure on board one of our G-H-equipped aircraft which wrecked the afternoon for four other Mepal crews, and L-Lucy who refused to part with her bombs over the target.

Then, for one day only on the 23rd, the skies were clear. The attack was repeated, except that this time TIs were dropped dead centre in the yards. The sight of bomb bursts and a great pillar of white smoke seemed to galvanise everybody. The raid was a huge success. Trier was never visited again by Bomber Command.

Had we known about the two ops, we might have felt somewhat aggrieved. We could have flown both. It could have been all over by Christmas, as I so wished.

Instead, the English crewmembers had arranged for each of the

NZ boys to spend the White Christmas of 1944 in one or other of our family homes. Bill Birnie came back to Stony with me. We visited The Case a few times with Dad, inevitably. On Christmas morning we went up to the allotments and cut sprouts like ice crystals on the stem. On Boxing Day we walked the towpath of the frozen Grand Union Canal all the way to Deanshanger and back – a good six miles – and watched the kids as they skated by, whooping with delight. Back home, we thawed ourselves feet first at the little fireside. We talked till late in the evening about everything but flying, and tried to forget about marshalling yards and AA batteries for one more day, at least.

CHAPTER FOURTEEN

N–NAN

On 28 December the fog lifted. Bill and I journeyed back to Mepal through a landscape so ice-encrusted and devoid of life, it looked like the Russian Steppes in deepest midwinter. A few snow-capped onion domes would not have gone amiss. As it was, the less exotic but still fantastical form of Ely Cathedral proclaimed the spirit of the place. From miles to the south we saw it and knew that the airfield and two last operational flights were drawing near.

It had still been springtime when I journeyed as now to an airfield – Westcott it was – to find myself a crew and to fly Wimpeys. In my wallet had been a scrap of paper containing the sum of my knowledge of bombers. Gleaned over hours of mess-talk and compiled one rainy afternoon on leave, it logged all the ways to get the chop . . . and some of the ways to avoid it. Well, I suppose one had to start somewhere.

Now, from the high ground of our twenty-eight raids, I could look a little deeper into this bombing business. I could discern not only the manifold dangers in which luck played a central role, but others from which it was entirely absent. These were the subtle dangers, the conditions of mind and spirit which, though hard to divine from without, were every bit as deadly as a well-aimed shell.

A tour was a construct of three aspects, each distinct, each characterised by a potentially lethal weakness. In the beginning, of course, was naïvety. A few hours flying together at OTU and Finishing School barely qualified as preparation for the real thing. From the moment a sprog crew arrived on station it had to learn – before the lesson was driven home by the enemy. There was plenty of help at hand. The path to survival was well-trodden even though not everyone reached its end.

The dozen or so ops in the middle of a tour tended to coincide with the assumption that this learning period was over. The logbook was filling up. The enemy and Lady Luck had done their worst. One was not blasé about being shot at but had reached a certain, internal accommodation with it. Instead of operating at maximum vigilance throughout, there might . . . perhaps . . . occasionally be a tendency to cut corners or relax a little. But *might* and *occasionally* were enough. Even that was complacency and it invited the Reaper along for the ride.

Towards journey's end aircrew had survived and surmounted these hazards. They were secure in the knowledge of their own expertise. But then came the still more insidious danger of staleness. It was all too easy to weary of the sheer repetition in operational life. The months of Battle Orders and Briefings were bound to pall, along with the pills to keep you wide-eyed or to knock you out; the ops scrubbed on the tarmac and others re-ordered because of scattered bombing; and, always, the losses, the pals known but briefly and who, in the relentless drive to mount the next op, somehow went unmourned.

Naïvety, complacency, staleness: these were killers in their own right. The cruellest was naïvety, but the most undeserved was this business of going stale, like old bread.

As Bill and I trudged past the picket post on arrival at Mepal, I asked him tongue-in-cheek whether the boys would like me to volunteer them for Pathfinders. I refrain from communicating the full force and colour of his reply with which, anyway, I was in total agreement. One tour would be quite enough for me. I had no wish to be the shining hero, coolly intent upon a second tour and then a third. I took my hat off to the chaps who were, particularly those who put their names forward for the forty-five-op tour of PFF duty. But to me it seemed reckless to spurn the gift of survival offered by Lady Luck, like the gambler who, not content with a big win, has to stake everything on one last roll of the dice.

In any case, aircrew were hardly in short supply at this juncture. The Air Ministry had set the ball rolling with ambitious objectives for aircraft production and crew training back in the dark days of 1941–2. The area bombing directive issued by the Ministry on 14 February 1942 (St Valentine's Day again), sanctioned the destruction of thirteen German urban centres. Dozens more would join them as the offensive gathered momentum. The flow of men and machines to operational squadrons, and the *number* of squadrons, increased dramatically even though losses were escalating also. But by late 1944 losses began to subside as the defenders thirsted for oil. Bomber Command could, if it chose, bring to bear a force hundreds of aircraft stronger than the great thousand-bomber raids on Cologne, Essen and Bremen. Tour-expired crew who had flown the Wimpeys and Stirlings in those armadas could quite expect, after six months' grace and a spell as OTU instructors, to be called to bomb Germany thirty times more. Whatever the RAF had in store for us individually, we could be confident that it was not that.

Operationally, the enemy offensive in the Ardennes was still calling the shots. On the previous day, the 27th, two hundred Lancasters attacked the railway yards at Gladbach-Rheydt, south-west of the Ruhr. (Rheydt was infamous as the target from which W/Cdr Guy Gibson went FTR on 19 September. He made himself master bomber for the raid which, in the event, was somewhat chaotic. He drove his Mosquito into the ground on the run home but, with no radio message, the cause was never explained.)

To return to the raid of the 27th, Mepal dispatched twenty aircraft. They found opposition over the target was slight. But many of them had to take violent evasive action as bombs cascaded from other aircraft high overhead. Captained by P/O H.S. Miles, NN710 Q-Queenie was unlucky. Bombs were seen to smash through her and she spiralled to earth. There was only one parachute. Pilot Officer Miles had arrived on station on 15 December and was due to fly as my second dickey on one of the postponed Trier ops. Instead, he flew to Trier on the 21st as second dickey to Bob Rodgers and returned on the 23rd with his own crew. That was all Fate allowed him.

In the afternoon of the 28th, as the boys and I checked in from leave, twenty-one Mepal kites participated in an attack on the huge marshalling yards of Gremberg, in Cologne. Again, heavy flak opposition was slight but the greater danger was bombs from aircraft flying between 500 ft and 2,000 ft above. Several of the Squadron's kites had to take evasive action but this time everyone escaped harm.

Brighter but bitterly cold weather extended into the 29th and so did the operational effort. A Battle Order went up after breakfast, listing just nine crews including us. Meanwhile, the kites were bombed up with a 4,000 HC and 1,000, 500 and 250 lb g.p.s. This was the loading for Trier and the clear imputation was that we were going back, or to another yard like it.

It was to another like it.

'Right, gentlemen', announced Ray Newton in his easy way, 'the target for today will be marshalling yards at Koblenz.'

Hitler's desperate last gamble was now in its thirteenth day.

Except in his presence, not even von Runstedt, Model and von Manteuffel, his own commanders, entertained the prospect of capturing Antwerp. But there was a possibility of seizing the land and towns west of the Meuse, of putting off the day when the war in the West would be waged on German soil.

However, even this modest objective reckoned without the unsuspected fighting qualities of the American soldier. Outnumbered, unprepared and lightly armed, the Americans faced the Panzer and Tiger columns, the youthful but still idealistic *Panzergrenadier*s and the seasoned *Waffen SS* – all of them, men on a sacred mission to save the homeland – with extraordinary tenacity and skill. The greatest American battlefield victory in Europe was in the making.

Not Antwerp, not even Liège came under threat from enemy tanks. General von Lüttwitz did lay seige to Bastogne. But his premature demand for capitulation was answered in inimitable, demotic style by the local American commander who said, simply, 'Nuts!' The worst efforts of the beseigers wrought no change, and at 1650 hrs on 26 December the main American Infantry relief column entered the town.

The nearest the Germans came to the Meuse was three miles. Then the dense December fog lifted sufficiently to allow 2nd TAF fighters into the air. Typhoons of the RAF launched a rocket attack that devastated the 2nd Panzer Division. The remnants were left to fend for themselves and, on the night of the 26th, von Manteuffel authorised them to break out on foot. What, the Germans must have asked, had become of the easy victory that was promised them over this unmotivated and racially divided foe?

Heaven knows what they would have made of the racially divided foe that boarded Nan at 1145 hrs on 29 December. It would have taken a particularly fanatical or foolhardy Nazi to explain it to Mac. I am sure he could have crushed the average coal-skuttle helmet with one good blow. As it was, he merely intended, in his beguiling and friendly way, to drop eleven thousand pounds of bombs on any of the said helmets populating the yards at Koblenz.

We had bombed Koblenz before, on the night of 6/7 November in aid of Patton's forces. Now it was funnelling supplies to the distended new front in the Ardennes. Posited on rapid advance by tanks, Hitler's offensive was always bound to pose logistical problems. Our job was to compound these, to deny the passage of fuel and ammunition through Koblenz and thereby help shrink the famous bulge.

At 1200 hrs Bob Rodgers swung his kite onto the runway. A

minute later as he lifted off, F/O Egglestone, a rookie skipper on his second trip, let L-Lucy go. We followed at number three. In all, one hundred and seven Lancs of 3 Group flew out over the North Sea, forming up on their leaders in readiness for a G-H drop. That number rapidly reduced to one hundred and six. Flying Officer Egglestone had one of L-Lucy's engines cut out – again – and could not hold station.

We flew against a strong headwind, dropping L-Lucy behind. Her crew would have been perfectly entitled to head for home. No one would have thought any the less of them. But they were young and keen and, inevitably, they were naïve. They discussed the situation and took their decision. They would go on.

The escort of Spitfires and Mustangs swept our path of fighters. But nothing could be done to discourage some distinctly active AA batteries. They peppered the sky on our run in but the formations around us cruised on straight and level. The strings of bombs began to fall, the differential between the leaders and the aircraft behind them only the blink of an eye. A trail of explosions hit the sinuous, tightly compacted rails, and foul black smoke billowed up through the five-tenths cloud.

This time there were no highflyers, no need to fear falling bombs. From Nan's station it looked like a professional job delivering the required standard of bombing. But when we joined other crews in the truck at B Flight dispersal we heard a different story. Some formations had been led less than well, bombing as much as seven miles short. There were reports of considerable scatter – and some scorn that conventional marking had not been employed. One 75 kite was clobbered the second after she released. She came away safely. Two others, including L-Lucy and the Egglestone crew, were late.

They both came home. L-Lucy had bombed the fires of Koblenz all alone and from a hazardously low altitude. The AA gunners did their worst but could not bring her down. They put ninety-two holes in her, though, and gave her crew a sound education.

For us, I have to say, the raid was only significant for bringing us within one trip of our goal. We spent the evening at The Three Pickerels in mellow mood.

'One more like that', we said, and reached across the table to touch glasses. I hoped it wasn't too much to ask.

At this time I was finding it harder to sleep at night, not particularly because of operational fears – though they played their part – but because it was so damned cold. The coal stove was centred in

230

the room, far from my bed. I took to laying my fur-lined, American jacket over the bed clothes, but it didn't do much for freezing feet. Wakefulness, of course, soon brought thoughts of how vulnerable we were even after twenty-nine trips and, perhaps, how stale.

Had we still been flying regular night ops, sleep would have come through the ingestion of a blockbuster. But these were unnecessary now, along with the benzedrine which kept us going till dawn. Somnolently-speaking, it was every man for himself with a hut-full of snorers and whistlers to plague the hindmost.

The 30th of December dawned grey and frosty but still fog-free. Snow was falling gently. By the time we finished breakfast the airfield was covered. There were no bombing operations planned but the squadron was not stood down. Snow-clearing parties were dispatched to the runways. At 1635 hrs Bill Osborne and his crew lifted Y-Yoke off the deck. She was the first of four G-H-equipped aircraft setting off to sow mines in the Heligoland Bight. They all returned four hours later, though not without incident. Flight Sergeant R. Pearson and his crew saw an enemy fighter only half a mile away. It dropped flares which Pearson's gunners shot out. Pearson then corkscrewed into the safety of the cloud cover. The Osborne crew also saw a fighter, a Ju 88 at a range of one thousand yards. But it did not attack. Flying Officer E.G. Parsons and his crew had a combat with another fighter, claiming it damaged. Mining remained a dangerous business and the squadron was fortunate not to have suffered losses. For Parsons and his boys the luck would run out over Heinrich-Hutte the following March. There they would lose a port wing and spiral down with not a man among them able to escape.

We awoke to the last day of the old year to find activity burgeoning across the airfield and a Battle Order pinned to the board. We were so close to completing the task set before us all those weeks ago in early August. Now the final hurdle was in sight. We came to the door of the Briefing Room as seven men with one dominant, thoroughly predictable idea. Just this op and we've made it . . . just this last bloody one!

The last bloody one was to be complicated by the addition to our number of a second dickey. He was P/O R.J. Aitchison, a keen young New Zealander with a pleasant face, thinning blond hair and a ready smile. He was waiting for us at the door. Introducing himself as Rob, he shook each of us by the hand energetically. He had arrived on station with his all-English crew – an unusual combination – four days earlier. Now he looked to us to set him on his

231

way. No doubt, in his innocence he thought it a fine thing to get a push from the hoary hand of experience. The hoary hand, however, was more preoccupied with its own survival and was not best pleased by an additional responsibility.

It occurred to me, though, that this responsibility might have been given to us with a wider intention. Bob Rodgers's term in command of B Flight had been marked by a thoughtful approach towards his aircrews. He did not narrowly pursue absolute operational standards, as had Garth Gunn. Nor did he did forge his command in the fiery spirit of 75, as had Leslie in his more senior role. Rather, he was a quietly supportive figure, at times almost brotherly. He understood and cared about his crews. Seeing that they operated under the accretion of tension and loss, he turned a particularly Nelsonian eye to all excesses in the mess. Seeing that they were susceptible at different times to the likes of naïvety, complacency or staleness, he did what he could to open their eyes to these dangers.

Now I thought I saw his artful hand in the arrival of a second dickey amongst us. We would have to strive for professionalism in the air one last time and would abet our own safety in the process. This interpretation made us as much the beneficiary of Rob's arrival amongst us as he himself.

'The target today', the CO announced, a certain, routine note in his voice, 'is marshalling yards at Vohwinkel in, er . . .' He straightened the curtain pull while seventeen crews shifted uneasily in their seats. Nobody was too sure of the exact location of Vohwinkel. It was not a name we had heard before. When the curtain swept back a ghastly groan went up. '. . . the Ruhr. This is a 3 Group effort. One hundred and eighty aircraft will attack at 1400 hours from a bombing height of 19,000 ft.'

For the thirtieth and last time I watched for the hour it took Briefing to unfold. The manifold aspects of bomb load, take-off time, intelligence, weather, call signs . . . every blessed detail, was provided and dutifully digested. The choice of target – marshalling yards deep in the German supply system – was almost certainly linked to events in the Ardennes. The rationale was the same as that for the recent attacks on Trier, Rheydt, Gremburg and Koblenz.

All Briefings for a Ruhr op required a close study of the 88 mm gun concentrations around the valley. The map was scarred with red, so much of it I wondered why we continued with the delusion that quiet skies were waiting for us somewhere out there. They weren't. It was impossible to reach any Ruhr target without running a gauntlet of shellfire. One could never say so publicly, of course.

That would have brought an instantaneous reprimand from the Station Commander for lack of patriotism or for damaging morale. Sitting motionless in his seat beside me, Rob still had a touching faith in the quiet sky theory. But if he was lucky he would live to learn like the rest of us.

'N-Nan', shouted the WAAF driver.

'That's us', I replied.

A chorus of 'Good luck' rang out from the other crews as we jumped down from the tailgate.

'And to you', replied the boys.

Tim Blewitt was in the truck with his crew, on his way out to The Paper Doll.

'You lucky devils,' he said, 'We've still got two dozen to go.' Then, recognising that a second dickey was starting his account with us today as he himself had done three weeks earlier, he acknowledged Rob with a wave and said, 'See you in the smoke.'

'Good idea. I'm gonna pinch one off these blokes now', cut in Geoff, waving a thumb over his shoulder in the direction of the waiting ground crew. He hadn't changed. He was still quite incapable of passing over a quip in silence, still performing his self-imposed duty of cheering everybody up.

The truck grunted into gear and rumbled away. We walked across to Nan. The erks looked mighty cold, hunched up in their overalls and leather jerkins. They gathered by the ladder and blew on their hands and stamped their feet to get the circulation going. Most of them had been on station for years rather than months. Their effort and devotion had been lavished on many a kite, and many an aircrew had come to know and rely upon them, however briefly. We knew that each time Nan took to the air someone would be waiting for us at dispersal whatever hour of the day or night we returned.

'She's A1 today, sir', said the NCO, who loved Nan at least as much as we did.

'Good luck', he said and shook my hand. Then he moved on to each of the boys. His crew did the same. I climbed on board no longer worrying about staleness, but proud of who we were and what we were doing.

Checks were accomplished well within the fifteen minutes I generally allowed. Everyone was set. I waved to the boys on the chocks and swung Nan round to the perimeter track. Good practice recommended the cautious skipper to tarry at dispersal until the rest had rolled by on their way to the caravan. But there were only seventeen in the queue and someone had to get the show on the road. It was 1130 hrs exactly when, first in the order and with Nan's Merlins singing and every rivet and panel raring to go, the Aldis flashed green beside us.

'Let's go, boys', I said, as I had from the very beginning. Whatever was to happen in the coming hours, those words would never fall from my lips again.

Halfway down the long, main runway Tubby had the throttles locked. Nan bore on, tail up and going light. At 110 mph on the airspeed indicator I lifted her off. The undercart was all but fully retracted as we cleared the airfield boundary and, in a wide, climbing circuit, cut our way into dense and turbulent cloud at 1,200 ft.

Back over an unseen airfield Bill gave me a course to cross East Anglia and leave England behind. It was not an emotional parting. Visibility was zero, the ride rough. Everyone except the two Bills went on watch for converging aircraft. I called them upon the intercom at regular intervals but they were all as sharp as pins. Standing in the cockpit beside me, Rob was on watch, too. He must have been wondering what on earth the enemy was for if our friends could put paid to us so easily.

Almost at the rendezvous point we emerged from darkness into sunlit cloud. All around us great, anvil-headed cumulonimbus billowed to a stupendous altitude. Back in my instructing days I had been told a story about these vast storm clouds by a senior officer who had come up for retraining. During the monsoon in Burma, he said, a squadron of Spitfires was patrolling in formation. They blithely flew into a particularly muscular cumulonimbus but never emerged on the other side. The vicious updrafts within the cloud had torn the wings from every one, or so he claimed. There may have been a grain of truth in his story, there may have been none. But it had a salutary effect on me. Whenever a cumulonimbus lay across my track I gave it a wide berth. At night, of course, it was different. They were invisible. I must have flown unawares through many of them and, thus far, come to no harm.

Our G-H leader was nowhere to be found but we took up station on another towards the front of the stream. A powerful, north-westerly wind had come to bear and the cloud mass was breaking up rapidly. Still in good order we cleared the Dutch coast, passing Rotterdam on our port side. Our fighter umbrella wheeled in, looking down now upon a tight stream of one hundred Lancasters formed up in their vics and far removed from the extended gaggles flown over France in August.

So it proceeded over the border until Krefeld when the Ruhr defences burst into life, as we knew they must. A barrage of heavy flak crashed about us. The weight of fire was moderate by Ruhr standards but sustained and accurate, and quite sufficient to disrupt our run in. We rocked through the dirty air, anxious like everybody about our proximity to other kites. Inevitably, the vics opened up. The stream began to lose its coherence and a few high flyers appeared. G-H bombing was a matter of discipline in the air or it was nothing. But that discipline was slipping away. Within their sand-bagged encirclements 20,000 ft below, the gun crews were savouring a rare victory.

The wind did the rest. The bombs, when they fell, exploded beyond the sweep of interconnected railway lines, indeed beyond the town itself. It was a clear overshoot and would surely contribute nothing to the overall military objective.

But I can't say that these frustrations counted for much on board N-Nan. We came away with joy and relief bubbling up as irresistibly as champagne from a shaken bottle. There were no thoughts now of staleness, actual or otherwise, and no words wasted on the bombing we had just witnessed. The time had come to celebrate the fact of being alive. A party atmosphere swept through the aircraft. We crossed Holland at 5,000 ft while the boys bawled a gloriously crass ditty into the intercom.

'Take over for a while', I said to Rob, and went back to be greeted by unforgettable smiles and happiness. Tubby passed out the coffee as always. To judge by the hullabaloo it might have been hooch.

'A toast . . .,' Bill announced, 'to us.'

'To our future', I said, realising as I pronounced the word that I had not allowed myself much unqualified optimism for the past twenty weeks. It would have been unwise to tempt fate so. But now that consideration was superfluous and it was to our future that we enjoined our cups.

Over the English coast and still at 5,000 ft I relieved Rob at the controls. Bill Otway contacted base to be told that we should break cloud at 1,500 ft over Chatteris and wait our turn to land. We came out of the cloud over the town. It was raining steadily and visibility was poor. The wet streets glistened below. Bill received the all clear to enter the circuit. As we crossed the Old Bedford River the flarepath shone ahead of us.

'N-Nan you are clear to land', came a WAAF voice from Control.

Her words brought a lump to my throat and I knew I would be struggling with my feelings all the way to dispersal. I brought Nan down to 1,000 ft and onto the downwind leg. The undercart down and locked, I turned her with half-flap down to make our *final*, final approach. We picked up the green of the glide path indicator and, a moment later, crossed the airfield boundary. I levelled off and nodded to Tubby to hold the throttles closed. Nan resisted until she was well down the flarepath. Then she gave up the struggle gracefully and settled onto the tarmac to wild, triumphant cheering from all the boys, and Rob, too, who couldn't resist joining in.

We were first down of the seventeen. The time was 1622 hrs and it was over. At dispersal I sat in my seat in valedictory mood while the others gathered their gear. It was an emotional moment, for I knew I would never fly Nan nor any Lancaster again. I had been drawn to the RAF by the glamour and adventure of a fighter pilot's war, only to discover that flying itself was the thrilling, the wonderful thing. I had done everything possible to avoid the dreaded posting to Bomber Command, only to find that for me the Lancaster – and one Lancaster in particular – was the heart and soul of flying.

I reached the hatch on the point of tears. But Nan's ground crew had clamoured around the ladder, smiling and shaking the boys' hands. We organised ourselves into a group. In the poor, winter's light someone took a photograph. I have it still, so many beaming, young faces with such good reason to be happy, though it must have been a bitter-sweet moment for Bill Otway who had been only a few trips away from this with his old crew. And, who can say what emotions it stirred in the figure to our left, the second dickey who had it all to do.

We jumped down from the crew truck still singing and entered the briefing room. Ray Newton and Bob Rodgers congratulated each of us warmly. In the Ops Room, the WAAF who recorded the landing times on the blackboard smiled on us indulgently. For us, at least, she would never have to chalk the doleful letters, FTR.

After debriefing, I telephoned the landlord of The Case to ask if he could relay my news when Dad popped in that evening. But the good man didn't wait and went straight round to our house with bottled beer and a flask of gin to celebrate.

On a professional note, the raid we had just completed was confirmed unsuccessful, except in that everyone came home safely. The consensus of opinion was that the bombs had impacted in fields to the south and south-east of the yards. Probably, Vohwinkel would appear on the Battle Order again. But that was for another day. First, there was the New Year to see in.

The party in the Officers' Mess was well underway when Ray Newton arrived. Had it been Jack Leslie still, we might have been treated to the sight of our CO climbing on a table and belting out some rousing, but profoundly anti-German, little number. Newton was less extrovert but also, perhaps, more at peace with himself. Even so, a new CO had to make a strong impression and, that night, he did so with some unconventional views on this bombing business. He had been one of the two Flight Commanders at 75 back in the spring and summer of 1942 when the squadron was flying Wimpeys from Feltwell. In those days, apparently, men were men.

'If you want to do a good bombing run,' Newton said, recalling the Feltwell spirit, 'you don't look out. You put your head in the cockpit. And if you want a photograph you count to 20 . . . and then go round and take some more!'

The assembled throng cheered to the rafters, and Newton topped it off by shouting, 'And that was in the days when flak defences were comparatively good!'

Cries of 'Line! Line!' rang out. The squadron kept a Line Book for just such occasions. Recorded there were the best examples of Mess wit brought into being by a liberal flow of alcohol and the companionship of like-minded souls. The CO's contribution was entered with due ceremony and timed at 22.50 hrs.

Close to midnight Bill and I slipped across to the Sergeants' Mess party. Mac, Bill, Geoff and Norrie were already well-oiled. Even Tubby, moderate in all things, looked distinctly flushed.

A nineteen-year-old under the influence of alcohol is not a pretty sight, even less so when the influence renders him far from speechless. However, it was obvious that Norrie had something to say which could not wait.

'Shhkip,' he said, looking deeply uncomfortable, 'I've got a confession. Couldn't tell you before. Thought you might kick us out't crew.'

He paused to chew his bottom lip.

'Go on', I said, wondering what he could possibly mean.

'Well . . . remember the Kiel trip?'.

'How could I forget', I replied, 'I reckon we did three targets.'

'Yeah, well . . . it were my fault.'

We had our problems that night, it was true. But I couldn't for the life of me see how a rear gunner was to blame. The answer came before I could demur.

'It was the blinkin' tail light, you see. Forgot to switch the shiny little bugger off', he said, waving the guilty finger under my nose. 'That's why Jerry had a go at us. I'm . . . sorry, skipper.'

Actually, Jerry had a damned good go at us. And why not? There we were, on our own, inviting just that as we cruised above the defences of northern Germany and Sylt.

The tail light was indeed the rear gunner's responsibility. He was required to switch it off once airborne, letting the kite behind know that we were clear. But it was impossible to be angry with poor Norrie on the day our ops were completed. Even if it *was* fuelled by alcohol, his confession took humility and guts. He knew that I regarded him both personally and as a rear gunner as utterly dependable. He just couldn't live with the knowledge of having let us down, even that once. And who but quiet, truthful Norrie would have resisted the temptation to keep his secret, and confessed now, on New Year's Eve?

Still, the thought of him wrestling with his conscience for four months – and losing – had a certain, wicked justice about it. No official punishment could have fitted the crime quite so exquisitely. It tickled my sense of humour. I tried to suppress my amusement but it was no good. The others snorted beerily. Poor Norrie was left looking on, wondering what he'd said that was so funny.

It was two in the morning when we slunk away to our beds. But I slept badly and by six-thirty had showered and dressed again. The New Year had dawned bright and fair. The airfield was still. There were no preparations for a mid-morning raid today. I eschewed my bicycle and, alone with my thoughts, walked out into the cold, morning air. At B Flight dispersal Nan awaited the arrival of her ground crew. Quietly, I walked my last inspection exactly as I had for each of the nine occasions on which she had taken us to Germany. This time, though, I did not clamber aboard to join Tubby in the cockpit. This time I wished her well and walked slowly away to the mess. After breakfast I delivered my log-book to the CO's office where it would be retained until my return from a fourteen-day leave.

As this day wore on, it became apparent from the quickening activity around the airfield that operations were planned for nightfall. Ray Newton boarded Nan and landed thirty minutes later, after a satisfactory air test. The Battle Order was posted and Briefing was announced for 1830 hrs. Nan would be flown by the CO with Rob Aitchison and his crew on their first op. As a non-combatant I couldn't be told the target. But the Vohwinkel photographs had been pinned on the Flight notice board. The yards were largely untouched, most of the bombs having carried south of the aiming point. Our final raid had failed and it was reasonable to assume that the squadron would be sent back tonight.

The boys had arranged a farewell drink at The Three Pickerels with some of Nan's ground crew. Though I would remain on station an extra day to do my packing, the others were going on leave in the morning. But notwithstanding that, I wanted to see my Lancaster take off one last time. I excused myself and was in the flight caravan when the first of the twenty-one kites lined up on the runway.

At 2130 hrs Nan roared down the flarepath and was quickly gone into the night sky. She never came back. At two in the morning I returned to the caravan and, a few minutes later, the first kite touched down. Nineteen more quickly followed. Then the awful waiting began. After a barren half-an-hour without radio contact or news from another airfield we knew the worst.

Wing Commander R.J. Newton DFC, Rob Aitchison and the entire crew were killed. Later it would be known that they had drifted about twenty miles ahead of the main force. Perhaps the navigator missed a dog-leg in the route. In any event, a night-fighter found Nan over Holland and sent her down. Poor Rob did not even make it to the German border.

Ray Newton was the tenth in the line of 75's Commanding Officers since operations began, and the third to lose his life. It was only the second operational flight of his second tour with the squadron. His tenure was too brief. As a reminder of it he left only his remarks of the previous evening, entered in the Line Book for those who would come after to read, and wonder about the man.

For me, life was already changing irrevocably. The comradeship of my crew was no more, of course. We were seven tour-expired aircrew going out to meet our futures. We said goodbye with promises to get together again and write regularly. Only Mac, I think, found it difficult.

The same feelings came upon me two days later, and not only in respect of the separation from my crew. I left Mepal with a keen sense of loss for many things. The noisy babble as crews waited in the briefing room, the comic request to be excused when the target was announced, the Merlins discharging that familiar puff of blue smoke on start-up, the throbbing line of Lancs snaking slowly towards the take-off runway, the roar of engines and the rush of air as Nan took to the skies and, when we came home, the feminine voice in Control saying, 'N-Nan, you are clear to land.' . . . These were already totems of a past life. But it had been a life of such dazzling intensity and emotional power, it would live with me forever.

I sat in a draughty corner of a railway compartment. The other occupants, all civilians, were in robust, good humour, talking and joking animatedly. But they paid no heed to me, nor I to them. I stared fixedly through my watery reflection in the window, not really taking in the flat, bare, winter landscape outside. I was going home and should have felt buoyant and without a care in the world. But I left Mepal behind me with a heavy heart, and my thoughts now were with my Nan and her gallant crew lying at peace in a cold, Dutch field.

Finis

EPILOGUE

I finally flew a Beaufighter, though not against the enemy as I had promised myself and not in British nor even European skies. Early on the morning of 7 July 1945 I lifted her off the runway at Baigachi, the home base of Burma Communication Squadron. Ostensibly, it was a pleasure trip, an escape from routine. But it meant much more to me. I had conceived this ambition six years earlier, and given up on it with the posting to Bomber Command. I could hardly believe my luck that it should be realised two months after VE Day, and in such an unlikely place.

The aircraft was wonderfully agile and, of course, faster than a Lanc – faster than anything I had flown before. I did what I loved best: flying low. I remember stirring up the valley-mist, rising with a turbulent, olive-green river past peasant villages and neatly cultivated fields, high into the steep-sided hills which only months before had swarmed with Japanese. It was a far, far cry from the gently bucolic Cotswolds or the fields east of Stony Stratford. But it made the wait worthwhile.

The squadron was equipped with an odd assortment of aircraft, mostly American transports. Our workhorses were the twin-engine Dakota and Beechcraft Expediter and the single-engine Argus. Quite how a Beaufighter came to be attached to the squadron no one seemed to know. The same could be said of an American Vengeance dive-bomber which, likewise, was a recreational machine.

Our real purpose in life was to ferry military personnel, food and medical supplies across the vast tracts of uncharted and densely-forested hill country. The flights were frequently seven or eight hours' duration and extremely tedious. Several of our ports of call were quite sizeable towns including, of course, Rangoon (via its airfield, Mingladon) and Mandalay, Meiktila, Moulmein, Mergui and Akyab. Others such as Comilla, Bhamo, Tavoy, Prome, Alipore and Manipur Road were less so. Landing facilities here tended to be just clearings cut once and continuously defended against the sleepless jungle. But even these could seem a luxury. Occasionally, I was required to set down not on a strip at all but the golden, tropical beach of Charchapli, only to find it writhing before my eyes and scuttling away at an alarming speed . . . giant sandcrabs.

In March 1946 the Squadron moved south to Rangoon. A month later I took off for my last trip, flying an Expediter to Myitkyina and returning after eight hours in the air to Mingladon. My passenger was the Station Commander, G/Cpt Ward, who came along for the ride.

Two weeks later again, I shook his hand and headed for a berth on a troopship. I left behind the Beaufighter and flights over the jungle canopy, the drenching heat, the mosquitoes and the dignified, distant Burmese of whom I had come to know very little. I was on my way home to my family and Eileen and to a life outside the RAF. My love affair with the aeroplane was over.

In the years of austerity which followed and through the flowering of the sixties, the war slowly receded from my thoughts. Family and business life occupied me fully. The times were good and we prospered.

Letters arrived occasionally from New Zealand. There the 75 spirit remained strong, underpinned by a Squadron Association which actively promoted contacts and events. We English, on the other hand, seemed more disposed to let things lie. The bonds forged on ops were lifelong. But they required us to share little in civilian life.

One late-summer's day in the early 1960s – I can't be sure of the year – I was driving home to Surrey from a business meeting in Spalding. The sensible route south would take me through Peterborough and down the A1 trunk road. Mepal was some distance to the east. But I had time on my hands and a sudden impulse to look over the old place. Well, why not?

The moment I drove into the village of Sutton feelings came upon me like uninvited guests: curiosity, puzzlement, surprise and something disconcerting but as yet unclear. I found St Andrew's Church with its octagonal double-crown and black-faced clock, a landmark familiar to all Mepal aircrew. But looking up to it from ground level, seventeen or eighteen years after last seeing it from the air, I was unsure from which direction we used to overfly it. I tried to recall how it all was *then*. But the images would not come freely. They had been locked away too well and for too long.

Leaving the church behind me I drove to the northern edge of the village. The road to Witchford and Ely led me to a disused entrance on the left. It was blocked off by a patchy hedge and a woven wire fence. Seeing the land beyond expansive and empty, I left the car and stepped through. I walked for eighty yards in complete wonderment until the soft, springy grass beneath my feet gave way to tarmac. Though overgrown, and humped and fissured by years of neglect, this was without question the perimeter track of the old Mepal airfield.

I followed it anti-clockwise, the direction that we used to roll our kites towards the control caravan. Quite what remnants of the past I had expected to see – whether, indeed, I had formed any such expectation – I cannot say. Not Lancasters nor any physical trace of them, that was certain. But the totality of the change was something for which I was not prepared. Only the rooks soared and circled in the wind and, save for a few stubborn, sad buildings, all that greeted me on the ground was pasture. These fifteen hundred acres once witnessed vigour and dedication on a scale that would confound any modern enterprise. Now they gave sustenance to a hundred or two peaceful, black and white cows.

I halted on the No. 2 runway. It was quite overtaken by nature but I tried to recall how it had once been. How I longed for the ghosts of this place to speak to me. I listened for the noise of hard, physical work to resound from distant dispersals, for shouts to hang on the wind and snatches of flying talk to surprise me at my shoulder and fade again as aircrew cycled past. I tried to recapture the picture as a Bedford breezed by with seven young faces peering out vacantly at a world they were leaving behind. Most of all I yearned to hear, to experience, the ground-shaking roar engulfing everything as another matt black kite heaved her crew and her bombs into the air. But there was none of this. There was no resonance for me at all.

I walked on, passing wooden buildings in utter disarray and beyond naming. Their utilitarian nature and cheap construction were never meant to endure. The fire tenders' shed was still in good repair and in use, though only for the storage of some blunted farm implements and long-redundant machinery. A hundred yards further on I reached a pair of long, interconnected huts, their grey corrugations mottled with age and the spores of lichen. The knowledge that this was our old locker room arrived together with a lump in my throat.

The door had dropped on its hinges. I leant heavily against it and stepped inside. The room was dank and dirty. Even the cobwebs were blackened. Obviously, it hadn't seen a visitor in years. But this is where the boys and I had donned our gear and girded ourselves within for another op. We knew it as a vital place, full of tense and noisy chatter. But in the silence and stillness there was not a single echo from our past lives.

Past lives. Too many lives, over a hundred and not a few of these friends, were lost just during my brief time at Mepal. We knew the risks, of course. We were all volunteers. But death, when it comes, is an intolerable affront. I found it possible to envy soldiering types who, fighting their war across the ditches, woods, fields and towns of occupied territory, at least had the chance to administer to their fallen comrades. So often, this was not the case with aircrew. They did not die in our arms. We did not close up their eyes. We did not bury them. They simply went missing.

Under the spell of this shadowy place the feeling which was unclear to me in Sutton intensified. It was a sense that my years of careless forgetting were a kind of betrayal. I had been lucky enough to survive and to watch my children grow. I was given time to comprehend the incredible bounty of living. But these other lives – no different to my own – had proved too slight and transient or too unlucky to navigate the tide of wartime devotion, courage and fire. They had gone from this world at once and without equivocation. The service police had come to the huts to remove their meagre stores of letters, family photographs, keepsakes. And that was the last of them, save for the few vestiges that inhabited memory. As for the rest, I do not apologise for quoting the incomparable words on the headstone of John Gillespie Magee, the Canadian Pilot Officer and poet killed at the age of nineteen. They are from his poem, *High Flight*.

> I have slipped the surly bonds of earth
> (and danced the skies on silver-laughtered wings),
> Put out my hand and touched the face of God.

The disfigured walls, the cracked, concrete floor and blackened panes of the old locker room called to mind none of this glory. The air was heavy with damp and earthy decay. It did not commend me to stay.

Outside in the sunlight the cows contemplated the meaning of my existence. On the horizon Ely Cathedral floated above the sea of the fens. It dominated the view to the east, a great, grey ship with wildly eccentric, castellated funnels. Eternal and unchanging, it could not have been in greater contrast to the old airfield.

I could still picture the Cathedral as we saw it from the cockpit, angled beyond the black bars of the windscreen . . . the curvature of the control column, the crowd of levers, switches and white-needled dials all before me. If it is not too ungodly to say so, the Cathedral and the Lancaster were equally wonders of their kind.

Several of the Lancs I flew survived their operational days, including S-Sugar whose luck I considered to have run out in November 1944, U-Uncle in which I was second dickey to John Aitken and the perpetually unlucky L-Lucy whom Norrie illuminated over Kiel. By late 1947 the last of these had been struck off charge. Though inevitable with the coming of peace, the breaking of Lancs by the hundred seems almost criminal now. Across the world only fifteen are preserved (two being airworthy) with one more in painstaking reconstruction at Ohakea in New Zealand.

One to escape this holocaust for some years – a remarkable irony given its one-op history – was our very own P-Peter which bore us on the fiery trip to Bremen on 18 August 1944. Number 5 Maintenance Unit carted her scorched and punctured carcass away from dispersal and rebuilt her. But she never returned and never flew operationally again. Instead, she was sold to Flight Refuelling Ltd and converted into a test bed for the probe-and-drogue refuelling connection.

I should also mention that other great survivor, HK574 R-Roger, Rio Rita. After she ditched in the Orwell River, the Maintenance boys stripped what useful equipment they could and left her to sink slowly into the mud. There she remained undisturbed for nearly fifty years. Then a group of aviation historians organised a dig, exposed the hulk and recovered a number of artifacts. Doubtless, some of these were retained by the diggers but many went on sale in a local shop. The waters of the Orwell River closed again over R-Roger and there, I suppose, she will stay forever.

The seven men whom I am honoured to call my friends as well as my crew all fared pretty well. But only Geoff Fallowfield and Bill Otway are alive as I write. First Norrie, then Archie, passed away in the 1980s. Dear Mac, whom we all loved like a brother, had suffered from heart problems for many years and died in his garden in Napier, New Zealand in 1996. A few months later Denys passed away. He was the oldest of us all and had lived to a venerable age. My ever-reliable friend and fellow-officer, Bill Birnie, died in 1994. At his funeral a picture of the crew was laid upon the coffin.

My old B Flight Commander, Bob Rodgers, survives to this day, living in Christchurch, New Zealand. But not all the other characters in my story, particularly the senior officers, lived so long. Jack Leslie, a beacon of energy and determination at Mepal, lived a quieter life at home in Auckland. One day in the late 1950s he jacked-up his car in the drive of his home and was discovered sometime later by his two sons, crushed to death. Ray Newton's life ended, of course, on that fateful New Year's Day in 1945. His successor was another fine officer, W/Cdr C.H. Baigent, DFC, known universally as Mac. To my regret I met him only fleetingly. He commanded for a second term after the squadron repatriated to New Zealand and surely had a distinguished career ahead of him. But quite suddenly in 1953 cancer claimed him. He was thirty years old. A still greater tragedy befell Jack Wright, who had been the respected commander of A Flight. By what inner path he came to this I cannot even imagine, but one day in the late fifties he loaded his shotgun and killed first his wife, then himself.

Of the three second dickeys whom we initiated only the first, Bill Osborne, survived a tour. He became quite a character on the station. He had a great knack of capturing anyone's essential features with a few, affectionate strokes of the pen. At most times an Osborne caricature was to be found on the mess notice board.

On the day of my de-mob I bumped into Bill in the corridor of a railway carriage. I was dressed in the regulation civvy suit; he, a career pilot flying jets, in uniform. Time was moving on and the great days of the Lancaster were already gone.

Tim Blewitt, the middle of our initiates, died in the early hours of 17 January 1945. The previous evening Tim and his crew had boarded PB761 Y-Yoke, the kite in which the boys and I had taken him to Osterfeld. The target this time was a benzol plant at Wanne-Eickel. They bombed successfully but came down on the journey home at Wood-Ditton in Suffolk. Tim and his bomb aimer were killed on impact. Y-Yoke quickly became an inferno. The surviving crew members dragged the navigator clear but he was beyond help and succumbed in hospital two days later.

The cause of the crash was pilot error. In the official accident report Tim's relative unfamiliarity with night flying was cited as a contributory factor. This seemed a harsh and convenient judgement to me. Immediately prior to the Wanne-Eickel raid Tim and his crew had twice experienced the tensions of briefing, gearing-up and the long wait at dispersal only for Control to call them back. One can only guess at their feelings as they climbed aboard for a third time in twenty-one hours.

A few days after this event I returned from leave to collect my remaining possessions and be signed-off by Mac Baigent. I found that my treasured American flying jacket was missing. Tim had 'borrowed' it that night. I couldn't resent the fact, of course. I just wished it had brought him some luck.

Through the remaining months of war 75 fought on with declining losses as the German war effort collapsed. One more disaster lay in wait, however. On 21 March, 3 Group dispatched one hundred and sixty Lancasters to the Münster Viaduct. Something went badly wrong and the 75 formation found itself over the target but below another stream of bombers, with flak coming up thick and fast. Three aircraft went down, including that of Jack Plummer, DFC on his twenty-ninth op. There were four survivors from his crew and five from the crew of F/O A.E. Brown's Lancaster. Both pilots were killed. But nobody got out of the third doomed aircraft. This was the Lancaster of F/O D.S. Barr. It was the last in the long list of 75 Squadron's losses and its letter was P-Peter.

I walked slowly and solemnly away from the old locker room, leaving unexplored the foursquare, red brick Watch Office. Its steel-railed balcony still looked expectantly towards the grassy triangle of runways. But my expectation was dampened somewhat by the sight of a car in its shadow, wheel-less and supported on bricks. Of all the airfield buildings this one might have made an appropriate and durable monument to 75. Evidently, it served as an amateur workshop instead, and I no longer cared to see how modern times intruded into my dreams of the past.

Back at my car at last, the burden of what I had seen and felt fell fully upon me. I did not bother to hold back the tears. I would not have been the first man in or approaching his middle years to give way to emotion in this place. My Mepal days were something for which I was still profoundly grateful. In many ways they were a tremendous adventure. But I drove away mindful only of the sacrifices I'd seen here and hoping to God, as many have before me and since, that each and every one of them was somehow necessary, somehow worthwhile.

Site Plan of Mepal Airfield

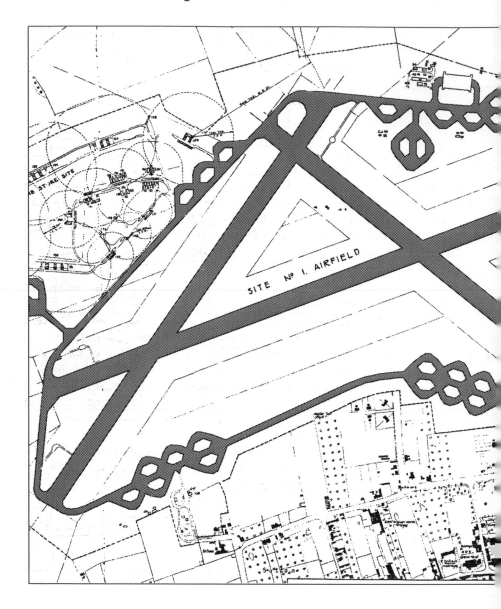

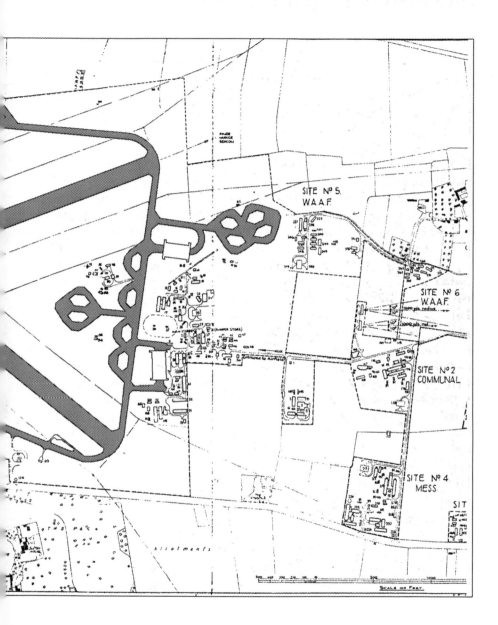

INDEX

Aitchison, P/O Rob J. 231–2, 238,
    239
Aitken, F/O John 82–4, 87, 160,
    168
Alvis 141
Andrew, F/Lt Vic 161, 186, 187
Ardennes Offensive 222–4
area bombing 135, 143, 209–10,
    227
Armstrong, P/O 117
Army: 1st Bucks Battalion 61
Atkin, Don 187, 188, 193, 196,
    204, 217, 219
automatic pilot 98

B-17 Flying Fortress 76, 90, 219
Baigachi 241
Baigent, W/Cdr C.H. (Mac) 246
Bailey, P/O Rob 64, 73, 77
Bailey, S/Ldr Jack 184, 187
Bain, W/O Archie 118–19, 129,
    156, 167, 205
  and the automatic pilot 98
  completes tour 213–14, 215–16
  Homberg raid 198, 200–1
  Nuremburg raid 81–2
  postwar 245
  P-Peter 9–10, 12, 103, 105, 106,
    112, 113
Bakewell, P/O 56
Barker, P/O Snow 118, 123
Barr, F/O D.S. 247
Barraclough, Group Captain 50
Battle of Britain Sunday 161

BBC 144–6
Beaufighter 31, 241–2
Birnie, P/O Bill 76–7, 104,
    129–31, 167, 197
  leave 225
  navigating 116, 195
  postwar 245
  training 63–4, 68–9, 72–3
Blenheim 31
Blewitt, F/O Tim D. 220–1, 233,
    246–7
Bomber Command
  3 Group 76, 78
  75 Squadron 49–50, 57, 76,
    78–81, 117
  115 Squadron 96–7, 211
  149 Squadron 139
  617 Squadron 143
  92 Training Group, Westcott 59,
    62–72
  No.1653 Heavy Conversion
    Unit, Chedburgh 72–5
  No.3 Lancaster Finishing
    School, Feltwell 75–6
Bonn 165
Boulogne 161
Bournemouth 45, 46
Box, Sgt Alan 80
Bremen 104–13
Bright, Nelson 187
Bristol Channel 58
Brown, F/O A.E. 247
Brunswick 91
Brunton, F/O 82

Bunn, F/Sgt 67
Burma Communication Squadron
   241–2

Cagny 160
Campbell, Gp/Cpt Patrick 150,
   171
Cardington 15–16
Chedburgh 72–5
cine-camera gun (CCG) 67
Close, Sgt Norrie 98, 103, 109–10,
   121–2, 167
  first operation 88–9
  Kiel raid 237–8
  postwar 245
  training 65–6, 67, 73
Coastal Command: 42 Squadron
   15
Cologne 175, 177–81, 205–6, 229
Comet 24
Connor, F/Lt 20–1
Cooper, F/Sgt 99
corkscrew 67, 109–10, 121–2,
   128–9
Courtman-Stock,F/O 56
Cowan, F/Lt S. 220
Curtis, F/Sgt 217

Dale, S/Ldr 34, 37, 41
Danzig, Gulf of 133
Dare, P/O 188–9, 196
de Havilland, Geoffrey 24
de Havilland School of Flying 17
Dinant 78
ditching 217–19
Dortmund 117, 164, 212
Doudeneville 137–9
Downing, F/Sgt Cyril 15, 66
Drummond, S/Ldr Lin 96
Duisberg 164–5, 184–5
Duren 191
Dusseldorf 171

Eastwood, P/O 18, 19–23, 25, 26
Edgerton, F/Sgt Leslie 117

Egglestone, F/O 230
Eindhoven 133
Emmerich 161
Empire Air Training Scheme 31
Essen 167, 169, 209

Falaise 91, 92–4
Fallersleben raid 57
Fallowfield, Sgt Geoff 103, 122,
   167, 233
  postwar 145, 245
  training 65, 67, 69, 73
Feltwell 75–6, 78
Fighter Command 14
fire 110–11
Flemming, F/O Alan 123
Flushing 165, 175
Ford, Terry 198
Forêt d'Engles (Fort d'Anglos)
   86–9
Franks, Norman 117
Frayne, Geoffrey 55

Galletly, F/O Alan 164
Gee-box 66–7, 116
Gelsenkirchen 202–4
G-H
  bombing 165, 188, 193, 203–4,
    212, 213, 235
  radar 170–2, 173
Gibson, W/Cdr Guy 228
Gironde Estuary 91
Gladbach-Rheydt 228
Gordon, Ron 196
Green, Charlie 13–14, 16
Gremberg 228
Gunn, S/Ldr Garth 81, 85, 100,
   148, 161–2, 232

Hadley, F/O 161
Halifax, Nova Scotia 31, 45
Hamburg 78, 182
Hamel 92, 172
Hamm 214–15
Hampden 31

Hannon, F/Lt L. 221
Harding, F/Lt 51–2
Harquebec 137
Harris, Sir Arthur 50
Hatfield 17–30
Heinrich-Hutte 231
Heinsberg 191
Heligoland Bight 231
Hendon 205
Henn, F/Sgt 34–5, 37, 41
Hockwold 76
Homberg 81, 182–7, 192–6, 197–9, 219
Home Guard 13–14, 16
H2S airborne radar 116, 139

Iceland 31–2
Ingram, F/O E. 206–7
Ireland, P/O 56

Johnson, John 165
Joy, F/Sgt 67
Julich 191

Kamen 149–57, 160–1
Kane, Cobber 26
Kiel 124–31, 237–8
Kilpatrick, Martin 187, 198
King, F/Sgt 82, 133
Kitson, Maurice 38
Koblenz 189–90, 228–30

Lancaster 46, 75–6
  HK593 206
  HK624 206
  HK600 K-King 160, 185–6, 187, 207
  HK562 L-Lucy 123–4, 126–31, 160–1, 187, 198, 212, 215, 222, 224, 230, 245
  HK596 O-Oboe 134, 165
  HK557 P-Peter 100–114, 245
  HK574 R-Roger (Rio Rita) 92–4, 95–8, 118, 148–57,
  160, 187, 188, 190, 193, 204, 217–19, 245
  LL866 S-Sugar 85–9, 116, 117, 123
  LM594 133
  LM544 J 188–9, 196
  LM276 S-Sugar 137, 138–9, 140, 170–5, 177–81, 186, 192, 245
  ME751 M-Mother 210–11
  ME321 N-Nan 123, 192, 193–6, 197–9, 204, 220, 229–30, 233–6, 238, 239
  ND768 F-Freddie 117
  NE181 M-Mike (The Captain's Fancy) 186, 187, 188, 199, 221
  NF980 F-Freddie 169–70, 186, 211
  NN710 Q-Queenie 228
  PB418 C-Charlie 215
  PB761 Y-Yoke 231, 246
  PB761 Y-Yorker 220–1
  PD367 211
  P-Peter 9, 11–12, 91, 162, 247
    see also Lancaster HK557 P-Peter
  R5674 76
  R5846 76
  U-Uncle 82–4, 90–1, 245
  W-Willie (The Paper Doll) 116, 233
Lawrence, Lawrie 38–9, 46
Lawton, Sgt L.A. 80
Le Havre 134–46, 172
Leadley, F/O D. 206
leave 60, 131–3, 190–1, 224–5
Lens 89–91
Leslie, W/Cdr Jack 81, 119, 140, 187, 213, 219–20, 232, 237
  briefing 86, 89–90, 124
  Homberg raid 184–5, 186, 193, 199
  Neuss raid 207, 209
  postwar 245

Leverkusen 170–3, 176
Liberator 90
Lille 86–9
Lind, W/Cdr 64, 72
Little Rissington 46–7, 48–50
Littleport Hospital 157–66
Lossiemouth 15
Lucheux 82–4
Luftwaffe 94, 181
Lulsgate Bottom 57

Maaka, F/Sgt Inia (Mac) 118, 128,
   142, 149, 153, 179
  first operation 88
  G-H bombing 173
  as pilot 98, 104–5
  postwar 245
  training 64–5, 73
  when Yates injured 155, 167
Magee, John Gillespie 244
Manchester 31
Mare de Magne 82
Marham 78
Martyn, F/O (later F/Lt) L. 131,
   201
Mayhill, Ron 160
McCartin, F/O P.L. 187, 196
McCurry, S/Ldr 157, 158, 159,
   160, 162, 165
McDonald, F/O J. 212
McIntosh, F/O J. 188, 211
medical examination 15–16
Mepal 11, 76, 115, 199–200,
   242–5, 247
Meurer, Captain Manfred 96
Meuseberg-Leuna oil refinery
   216–17
Miles, P/O H.S. 228
Miles Magister 51
mine-laying 147–8
Mitchell, W/Cdr Vic 57
Montrose 51–4
Moody, S/Ldr 54, 55, 59
morale bombing 210
Moriarty, F/Sgt D.J. 160

Mosquito prototype 24
Mulcahy, P/O 91, 118
Munster Viaduct 247
Murrell, Texas 48–9
Mustang P51B 94

Naismith, F/Lt W. 193, 196
navigation system 66–7, 116
Neuss raid 207, 209, 210
Newbury, F/Lt 56
Newton, W/Cdr Ray J. 220, 224,
   237, 239, 246
Nickel raid 71, 75, 78, 135
Nordstern refinery 202–3
Normandy 74, 81, 160
Nuremberg 9–10, 81–2

Oakley 66–71
Oberhausen 213
Oboe blind bombing aid 92, 171,
   194, 212–13
O'Callaghan, F/Sgt Eldrid 123,
   165, 168
Oil Plan 182, 202
O-Oboe 135–6
Operation *Hurricane* 164–5, 184–5
Operation *Millennium* 49–50
Operation *Queen* 191
Osborne, F/Sgt Bill 171, 198, 208,
   212, 215, 231
  postwar 246
  as second dickey 140, 141,
   142–3
Oslo Fjord 191, 201
Osterfeld 210, 220
Otway, F/Sgt Bill 196, 216, 220,
   236, 245
Oxford, Airspeed 34–43, 46–50,
   52, 139–40, 205

Palmer, S/Ldr R.A.M. 206–7
Paris 75
Parsons, F/O E.G. 231
Pearson, F/Sgt R. 231

Pedley, S/Ldr 17, 21, 22–3, 25–6, 30
Penhold, Alberta 34–43
Plummer, F/Lt Jack 165, 184–5, 186, 247

radar 94–5, 116, 139
  see also G-H
RAF
  Bournemouth 45, 46
  Cardington 15–16
  Marham 78
  No.6 Advanced Flying School, Little Rissington 46
  No.3 Advanced Flying Unit, South Cerney 54–60
  No.1 Elementary Flying Training School, Hatfield 17–19
  No.2 Flying Instructors' School, Montrose 51
  No.10 Initial Training Wing, Scarborough 16–17
  No.36 Service Flying Training School, Penhold 34–43
  Stratford-on-Avon 16
  see also Bomber Command; Coastal Command; Fighter Command
Rangoon 242
Red Deer 35, 37–8
Rees, F/O Hubert 193, 196
Reykjavik 31
Rhein-Preussen 191
Robson, Rob 38, 46
Rodgers, S/Ldr J.R. (Bob) 168, 171, 186, 197, 224, 228, 229, 232
  postwar 245–6
Rollins, Bob 132
Royal New Zealand Air Force 76, 78–81
Royan 146
Ruhr 149–57, 164–5, 169, 170–3

Ruhrstahl works 221
Russelsheim 91, 118–23

Saarbrucken 164, 219
Sadgrove, F/O Doug 181, 204
Sawrey-Cookson, W/Cdr Reginald 48
Scarborough 16–17
Schnauffer, Major Heinz-Wolgang 95
Scott, F/O J.H. 187
Sewell, Wing Commander 51, 53
Siegen 222
Simpson, F/O Alex 221
skymarking 203
Smith, F/Lt Graham 56
Solingen 187–9
South Cerney 54–60
Southward, F/O 164
spearheading 149–50
SS California 32–3
St Trond 95–8
Steer, Miss 38
Stettin 82, 99, 133
Stirling 73, 74, 75, 139
Stony Stratford 13–14, 16
  leave 60–1, 72, 131–3, 190–1
  overflying 11, 23–4, 48–9, 102, 176
Stratford-on-Avon 16
Streib, Colonel Werner 96
Stuttgart 81
Sylt 131, 238
Symondson, S/Ldr 54

Tallboy 143, 184
Tiger Moth N6848 18
Tomlin, P/O 56
Topping, Bill 160–1
training 16–30, 31–43, 46–50, 51–4
Transport Plan 207
Trier 223, 224
Tweed, F/O Harry 215

Upwood 47–8
USAAF Martishall Heath 218–19

Villeneuve-St-Georges 117
Vincent, F/Sgt 123
Vohwinkel 232, 233–6

Walcheren Island 164, 165, 174–5, 176
Walker, P/O 66, 67
Wanganui method 203, 208
Wanne-Eikel 246
Ward, G/Cpt 242
Ward, John 35–41
Ward, Sgt Jimmy A. 79–81
Waterbeach 139, 140, 205
Wellington 31, 45, 66–72, 79–80, 203
Wesseling 176, 178
West Kapelle 176
Westcott 59, 62–72
Westell, F/Sgt Denys 'Tubby' 121–2, 161, 219, 220, 221
  Cologne raid 179–81
  fire on board 110
  postwar 245
  training 73–4, 76
  when Yates injured 155, 167

Whitley 31
Widdowson, S/Ldr R.P. 79–80
Williams, P/O Eric 57
Williamson, S/Ldr 96
Window 107–8, 152
Winter, F/O Terry 167, 181, 198
Witchford 91, 96–7, 206, 211, 212
Witten 221
Wolsfeld 164
Woodbridge 70–1
Wright, Jack 246

Yates, Harry
  childhood 12, 132
  dog 14, 60, 176
  family 11, 13, 60, 72, 101–2, 131–3, 163, 176, 190
  gets commission 58
  gets wings 42
  girlfriend (Eileen) 101–2, 132, 163
  injury 154–66
  as instructor 54–60
  mumps 46
  promotion 205
  volunteers 15

Zinzan, F/Sgt V. 222